ROMEO AND JULIET

WILLIAM SHAKESPEARE

ROMEO AND JULIET

With Contemporary Criticism

Edited by JOSEPH PEARCE

IGNATIUS PRESS   SAN FRANCISCO

Cover art:
Jean Auguste Dominique Ingres
Paolo and Francesca. Oil on wood, 35 × 28 cm.

Photo Credit: Harry Bréjat.
Location: Musée Condé, Chantilly France

Photo Credit: Réunion des Musées Nationaux / Art Resource, N.Y.

Cover design by John Herreid

Tradition is the extension of Democracy through time; it is the proxy of the dead and the enfranchisement of the unborn.

Tradition may be defined as the extension of the franchise. Tradition means giving votes to the most obscure of all classes, our ancestors. It is the democracy of the dead. Tradition refuses to submit to the small and arrogant oligarchy of those who merely happen to be walking about. All democrats object to men being disqualified by the accident of birth; tradition objects to their being disqualified by the accident of death. Democracy tells us not to neglect a good man's opinion, even if he is our groom; tradition asks us not to neglect a good man's opinion, even if he is our father. I, at any rate, cannot separate the two ideas of democracy and tradition.

—G. K. Chesterton

Ignatius Critical Editions—Tradition-Oriented Criticism for a new generation

CONTENTS

INTRODUCTION

Joseph Pearce
Ave Maria University

As with so many of Shakespeare's plays, the exact date of *Romeo and Juliet's* composition is shrouded in mystery and is the cause of much scholarly argument and disagreement. When it appeared in print for the first time, in 1597, the title page referred to its being performed "with great applause" by Lord Hunsdon's Men. Since Shakespeare's acting troupe was known as Lord Hunsdon's Men only between July 1596 and March 1597, it is assumed, logically enough, that the play must have been written in 1595 or 1596. Some scholars believe, however, that it was written as early as 1591, arguing that the Nurse's remark " 'Tis since the earthquake now eleven years" (1.3.24),[1] constitutes a clear allusion to the London earthquake of 1580. Countering such a suggestion, advocates of the later date refer to William Covell's *Polimanteia*, a work with which they presume Shakespeare was aware, that alludes to an earthquake of 1584.

Much less controversial than the dating of the play is the principal source upon which it is based. All critics seem to agree that the main wellspring of Shakespeare's inspiration for *Romeo and Juliet* was Arthur Brooke's long poem *The Tragicall Historye of Romeus and Juliet*, published in 1562. Although Brooke was himself indebted to a tradition of romantic tragedies emanating from the Italian Renaissance, it seems that the essential ingredients of Shakespeare's play are taken from Brooke's poem. Since Shakespeare's modus operandi often

---

[1] All quotations from *Romeo and Juliet* are from the edition published by Ignatius Press: *Romeo and Juliet*, ed. Joseph Pearce, Ignatius Critical Editions (San Francisco: Ignatius Press, 2011).

involved the confuting of his sources, correcting their biases and using modes of expression more conducive to his own beliefs, it is worth looking at Brooke's poem in order to see what it is that Shakespeare does to it. Before doing so, we should remind ourselves that this "correcting" of his sources is something with which Shakespeare would remain preoccupied.

Shortly before embarking upon the writing of *Romeo and Juliet*, Shakespeare had written his play *King John* as a reaction against the anti-Catholic bias of an earlier play entitled *The Trouble-some Reign of King John*. A few years later, Shakespeare wrote *Hamlet* in response to an earlier play that scholars now call the *Ur-Hamlet*, which was probably written by Thomas Kyd. Although Kyd's play has been lost to posterity, the fact that Kyd had been tried and imprisoned for atheism in 1593 suggests that Shakespeare had sought to "baptize" the story of Hamlet with his own profoundly Christian imagination. This revisiting of older works to correct their defects was employed once again in the writing of *King Lear*, in which Shakespeare clearly intends to counter the anti-Catholic bias of an earlier play, *The True Chronicle History of King Leir and His Three Daughters*, which was probably written by George Peele, and also in Shakespeare's writing of *Macbeth* to comment upon an earlier play on a similar theme, *The Tragedy of Gowrie*, which had been banned, presumably by direct order of the king himself. Since this process of creative revisionism (to give it a name) seems part of Shakespeare's inspirational motivation in selecting a theme upon which to write, it would be a sin of critical omission to fail to examine how Shakespeare's play confutes the bias of its source.

The bias of Arthur Brooke's *Tragicall Historye of Romeus and Juliet* is scarcely difficult to detect. On the contrary, the poem wears its author's anti-Catholicism on its sleeve and emblazons it across its proud and prejudiced chest:

> To this ende (good Reader) is this tragicall matter written, to describe unto thee a coople of unfortunate lovers, thralling themselves to unhonest desire, neglecting the authoritie and advise of parents and frendes, conferring their principall counsels

with dronken gossyppes, and superstitious friers (the naturally fitte instruments of unchastitie) attemptyng all adventures of peryll, for thattaynyng of their wished lust, using auriculer confession (the kay of whoredome, and treason) for furtheraunce of theyre purpose, abusying the honorable name of lawefull marriage, the cloke the shame of stolne contractes, finallye, by all means of unhonest lyfe, hastyng to most unhappy deathe.[2]

Having discussed the original source and motivation for Shakespeare's writing of *Romeo and Juliet*, let us proceed to a discussion of the play itself. Broadly speaking, it seems that there are three ways of reading it. The first is the fatalistic reading, in which fate or fortune is perceived as an omnipotent but blind and impersonal force that crush the "star-crossed lovers"—and everyone else—with mechanical indifference. In such a reading, free will, if it exists at all, is utterly powerless to resist intractable fate. If the fatalistic reading is accepted, nobody is to blame for the events that unfold throughout the play because there is nothing anyone can do to alter them.

The second way of reading the play is what may be termed the feudal[3] or romantic reading, in which the feuding parties are held to blame for the tragic fate of the doom-struck and love-struck lovers. In such a reading, the hatred and bigotry of the Capulets and Montagues are the primary cause of all the woes, and the lovers are hapless victims of their parents' bloodlust who are nonetheless redeemed and purified by the passion and purity of their love for each other. In our day and age, this is perhaps the most widely accepted interpretation of the play's overarching morality or deepest meaning, harmonizing as it does with the ingrained Romanticism and narcissism of

---

[2] From the original preface of Arthur Brooke's *Tragicall Historye of Romeus and Juliet* (1562).

[3] I am taking linguistic liberties, creating a neologism based etymologically upon the Old English *fæhthu* (enmity), from which "feud" is derived, as distinct from the common usage of "feudal", which has its roots in the Latin *feodum* (or *feudum*), from which "feudal", "fee", and "fief" are derived, possibly from the original Frankish *fehod* (cattle property). See the *Concise Oxford Dictionary of Current English*, 5th ed. (Oxford: Oxford University Press, 1964).

the zeitgeist. Such a reading allows our contemporary epoch to moralize about "love" and "hate" without the imposition of conventional moral norms. It is the morality of John Lennon's "All You Need Is Love", a "love" that is rooted in the gratification of desire and that has its antecedents in the Romanticism of Byronic self-indulgence.

The third way of reading the play is the cautionary or moral reading, in which the freely chosen actions of each of the characters are seen to have far-ranging and far-reaching consequences. In such a reading, the animosity of the feuding parties and its consequences are weighed alongside the actions of the lovers and of other significant characters, such as Friar Lawrence, Benvolio, Mercutio, the Prince, and the Nurse. Each is perceived and judged according to his actions and the consequences of those actions on others, and each is integrated into the whole picture so that the overriding and overarching moral may emerge. It is surely significant, for instance, that *Romeo and Juliet* was written at around the same time as *The Merchant of Venice*, a play that is preoccupied with the whole question of freedom of choice and its consequences.[4] Clearly such questions were at the forefront of the playwright's mind as he grappled with the hateful or besotted choices of his Veronese protagonists in *Romeo and Juliet*, as they had been when he grappled with the choices facing his Venetian heroes and villains in *The Merchant of Venice*.

In spite of the willful blindness of many modern critics, it is clear from *Romeo and Juliet* itself, and from its place within the wider Shakespearean canon, that the only correct way of reading the play is the third way. It is, however, not the present writer who affirms this as an opinion but the play itself that insists upon it as a fact.

---

[4] *The Merchant of Venice* was probably written in late 1594 or, more likely, in 1595. As already discussed, the most likely date for the writing of *Romeo and Juliet* is 1595 or possibly 1596. For a full discussion of the role of choice and its consequences in *The Merchant of Venice*, see Joseph Pearce, *Through Shakespeare's Eyes: Seeing the Catholic Presence in the Plays* (San Francisco: Ignatius Press, 2010), chapters 6 and 7.

The play's opening scene shows us, in no uncertain terms, the ugliness of the world in which Romeo and Juliet are living. Sampson and Gregory, two servants of the house of Capulet, revel in the rivalry between the Capulets and their Montague enemies and indulge in salacious and uncouth reveries in which they fantasize about the rape of the Montague women. Thus the vicious vindictiveness of the "ancient grudge" between the two noble households is exposed in the vile vernacular of the servants. The presence of such hatred is, however, merely the backdrop to the play's depiction of "love"—or that which purports to be love but which is, in fact, a false and fallacious parody of it.

This false and fallacious love is first brought to our attention by Montague, Romeo's father, in his description of his son's odd behavior, in which the play's prevailing metaphor of light-shunning darkness is introduced for the first time. Self-obsessed and obsessive "love" is an enemy of the light, making of itself "an artificial night" (1.1.138), locking itself into the introspective and private chambers of the self and shutting up the windows of true perception. The consequences of such self-centered love are potentially self-destructive, a fact to which Shakespeare draws our attention in Montague's ominous words:

Black and portentous must this humour [mood] prove,
Unless good counsel may the cause remove. (1.1.139–40)

This couplet contains not only the "black and portentous" prophecy of the play's tragic end but a crucial clue that "good counsel" is the necessary component in removing the causes of the portended tragedy. In the end, it is the almost total absence of "good counsel" that leaves Romeo and Juliet at the mercy of their own woeful passions.

Also embedded in these two lines is a significant clue that the feudal, or romantic, reading of the play is awry. If, as romantic readers of the play maintain, Romeo's love for Rosaline is false whereas his love for Juliet is true, there is nothing "black and portentous" about his "humour" because it will dissipate like the insubstantial thing that it is as soon as Romeo sets eyes on Juliet. Nor is "good counsel" necessary, because Romeo's true love for Juliet will exorcise his false love for Rosaline without the need for counsel, good or bad. Montague's lines are, therefore, worthless from the perspective of a feudal or romantic reading; and yet we must surely see these "black and portentous" words as potentially pregnant with meaning. Since their deepest and most portentous meaning refers to the whole panoramic scope of the play, telescoping us from the opening scene of Act 1 to a dark vision of the catastrophic and cataclysmic climax of the final scene of Act 5, are we not forced at least to consider the possibility that Shakespeare is being censorious about the nature of Romeo's love throughout the whole play, not only about its moping extravagance in the opening scenes? Such a conclusion is reinforced by the fact that the light-shunning metaphor, introduced in relation to Romeo's obsessive love for Rosaline, is maintained throughout the length of the play, especially in relation to Romeo and Juliet's tragic love for each other.

Prior to any further discussion of this tragic love story— perhaps the most famous love story ever written—we should take a step back in order to look at love itself. What is love? And, equally important, what is love not? Romeo, with the naïve certainty of youth, is confident that he has the answer:

> Love is a smoke rais'd with the fume of sighs;
> Being purg'd, a fire sparkling in lovers' eyes;
> Being vex'd, a sea nourish'd with loving tears.
> What is it else? A madness most discreet,
> A choking gall, and a preserving sweet. (1.1.188–92)

Love, for Romeo, is a blinding force; it is smoke that gets into the lover's eyes, a bitterness on which he chokes, and a vexatious sea in which he flounders. It is, to put the matter in a nutshell, mere "madness". It is, therefore, no surprise that Romeo confesses that, afflicted with such blindness and madness, he is utterly lost and does not know who he is:

I have lost myself; I am not here:
This is not Romeo, he's some other where. (1.1.195–96)

In this adolescent discourse on the nature of love, Romeo
will win no prizes for originality. To say that "love is blind" is,
after all, one of the most hackneyed clichés that one can find.
And this appears to be Shakespeare's point. Romeo's love for
Rosaline is not the real thing. It is nothing but a shallow and
trite cliché. What Romeo calls "love" is not really love at all—at
least it is not love in the deeper and deepest sense of the word.
Illustrating this, several critics have shown how Romeo's words
parody the famous love sonnets of Petrarch, thereby reducing
Romeo's declarations of love to the level of mere cliché.[5] This
is made clear in Mercutio's mocking of Romeo's Petrarchan
conceits:

> Romeo! humours! madman! passion! lover!
> Appear thou in the likeness of a sigh;
> Speak but one rhyme and I am satisfied;
> Cry but 'Ay me!' pronounce but 'love'
>   and 'dove'. (2.1.7–10)

Although Shakespeare uses the irreverence of Mercutio to
make the connection between Romeo's unrequited love for
Rosaline and Petrarch's unrequited love for Laura, we need to
avoid the rash conclusion that Mercutio's voice is that of the
playwright. On the contrary, Mercutio's bawdy "realism" and
contempt for Renaissance romance does not enable him to
see or understand Romeo's "love" as coldly or clinically as he
and his many critical admirers seem to believe. Mercutio, as a
cynic, is even less capable of true love than is the love-sick
Romeo, and although he does not see it, he is even blinder to
the reality of love than is the besotted young man he ridi-
cules. He has no time for the numinous trappings of Petrarchan

---

[5] See, for instance, Crystal Downing, "A Rose by Any Other Name: The Plague
of Language in *Romeo and Juliet*", and Rebecca Munroe, "*Romeo and Juliet* and
the Petrarchan Love Poetry Tradition", both published in this edition.

love and, believing that the numinous is merely nebulous, dismisses the "heavenly" as having its head in the clouds.

For Mercutio, the very antithesis of the Petrarchan lover, love is ultimately synonymous with fornication. He sees no distinction between love and lust, the former being a circumscribed and euphemistic expression of the latter, and the latter being merely the honest expression of the former. When Mercutio dies, we do not doubt that he has "known" women, in the euphemistic sense of the word, but we also know that he has never truly known women as true lovers know them, or as husbands know them. We have no trouble believing that Mercutio has lost his virginity, but we suspect that he has never lost his heart. As Romeo says, "He jests at scars that never felt a wound" (2.2.1), a riposte that, though unheard by Mercutio, is as telling in its insightful accuracy as anything Mercutio has uttered from his huge arsenal of punning wit. In speaking of love, Mercutio speaks of something of which he knows nothing. Whereas Romeo's wandering and wayward heart has lost sight of true love, Mercutio's hardened heart has locked love out. Romeo is looking for love in the wrong places; Mercutio refuses to look for it at all. Since, to succumb to a cliché, there are none so blind as those who will not see, Mercutio is blinder to the reality of love than is the naïve and love-struck Romeo. It is not love that is blind but those who are blind to love.

Before we turn our attention to Juliet, the other "star-cross'd lover" at the center of the tragedy, let us pause for a moment in the company of the elusive Rosaline. All that we know of her is learned from the mouths of others. She is the object of Romeo's lovelorn desire and the subject of Mercutio's scorn. But who is she? The most important clue is given by Romeo in his discussion about her with Benvolio in the play's opening scene, most specifically in his plaintive disdain for her vow of chastity:

> [S]he'll not be hit
> With Cupid's arrow. She hath Dian's wit,
> And in strong proof of chastity well arm'd,

From Love's weak childish bow she lives unharm'd.
She will not stay the siege of loving terms,
Nor bide th' encounter of assailing eyes,
Nor ope her lap to saint-seducing gold. (1.1.206–12)

In these few pregnant lines we learn enough about Rosaline to know that she is not elusively unattainable in the same sense as Petrarch's Laura. She is not simply—or at any rate, she is not only—a poetic device. She is not a figment of idealized femininity, a personified abstraction of the ideal of *amour courtois*. She may remind us of Petrarch's Laura—or by a perverse leap of the imagination, of Dante's Beatrice—and no doubt Shakespeare means her to remind us of these idols of courtly love, but she is much more than this. She is quite clearly a woman of flesh and blood who has been forced to repel Romeo's evidently clumsy and unwelcome advances. The imagery that Romeo employs is that of warfare, of his having put her under siege. She resists "the siege of loving terms" and avoids the "encounter of assailing eyes". And when the lover's full frontal assault has been repelled, she shuns the subtle charms of bribery or the promise of worldly fortune, refusing to open her lap to "saint-seducing gold". The sexual imagery is entirely appropriate considering that Romeo's intentions seem to be entirely sexual. He scorns her desire to remain chaste and treats with dismissive contempt her apparent claim that her vow of chastity is connected to her Christian convictions. She cannot "merit bliss" (1.1.220) by making him despair. She cannot merit Heaven by sending him to Hell. These words are worth contemplating carefully because they offer a key to Romeo's character and to his notions of love. He is utterly self-absorbed, desiring to absorb his lover into his desire for self-gratification. Whereas true love is desiring the good of the other, Romeo desires that the other should feel good to him. He does not desire that his "love" go to Heaven, he does not want her to "merit bliss", if it means being refused what he wants. In these lines, Romeo reveals himself as totally self-centered, the epitome of the impetuous adolescent. Indeed, if he were not so young we would have no hesitation in dubbing him a contemptible cad. This is worth remembering because it is only a matter of hours before he first sets eyes on Juliet. Does Juliet cause a miraculous change in the young man, teaching him how to love truly, as romantic readers of the play believe, or does his residual selfishness and self-absorption contribute to the lovers' downfall?

Juliet is introduced to us, significantly, immediately after the self-absorbed discourse by Romeo that we have just discussed. No sooner has Romeo finished waxing wistful about his failure to seduce Rosaline (at the close of Act 1, scene 1) than we learn (in the opening lines of the following scene) of the woman who will take Rosaline's place as the object of his desire. It is also significant that Juliet, like Rosaline, is introduced in her absence when Capulet, her father, reminds Paris, her would-be suitor, that she is still a child:

> My child is yet a stranger in the world,
> She hath not seen the change of fourteen years;
> Let two more summers wither in their pride
> Ere we may think her ripe to be a bride. (1.2.8–11)

When Paris responds that "younger than she are happy mothers made" (12), Capulet's riposte is cutting: "And too soon marr'd are those so early made" (13).

To put the matter bluntly and frankly, Shakespeare makes it plain that Juliet is still a child, only thirteen years old, barely a teenager. This singularly crucial fact is all too often overlooked by modern critics, who bestow upon her an adulthood she does not possess.

The fact that Shakespeare is intent on stressing Juliet's immaturity is apparent in his making Juliet two years younger than her age in his source. In Brooke's *Tragicall Historye of Romeus and Juliet* she is almost sixteen, and in another English version of the tragedy that Shakespeare may have known, the translation of a novella by Matteo Bandello, she is almost eighteen. It is also noteworthy that in both these earlier versions the older Juliets were still considered too young to marry. And yet Shakespeare deliberately makes her even younger. His purpose for doing so is clearly that he wants us to see Juliet as a child who is thrown prematurely into an adult world in which she loses not only her innocence but her life. This is the heart of the tragedy.

Countering such a reading of the play, romantics will no doubt stress that the youth of the lovers is merely a device to highlight the unblemished purity of their true love. At the other extreme, cynical readers, taking their cue from Mercutio, will doubtless suggest that Shakespeare makes Juliet so young merely to show his male audience that Romeo is courting a true virgin. These two objections can be dismissed by closely scrutinizing the times in which Shakespeare was living and the moral and social conventions that prevailed in late Elizabethan England. Many social historians believe that children reached physical maturity, or puberty, later in sixteenth-century England than they do today. It is believed that girls matured at fourteen to fifteen, and boys at around sixteen.[6] As such, Juliet would have seemed even more of a child to Shakespeare's audience than she does to today's audiences. Youths under fifteen were still considered children, and early teenage marriages were rare indeed. Figures showing the age at first marriage during the period in which Shakespeare was writing indicate that only 6 percent of marriages were at the age of fifteen, and no figures are given for marriages below that age. Juliet was not yet fourteen when the action of the play takes place.[7] In the few cases on record in which children were married, they were not permitted to consummate their vows until they were much older.

---

[6] Lawrence Stone, *The Family, Sex and Marriage in England, 1500–1800* (New York: Harper, 1977), p. 512; Barbara Everett, *Young Hamlet: Essays on Shakespeare's Tragedies* (Oxford: Clarendon, 1989), p. 116; Ann Jennalie Cook, *Making a Match: Courtship in Shakespeare and His Society* (Princeton: Princeton University Press, 1991), pp. 17, 20; and J. Karl Franson, "'Too soon marr'd': Juliet's Age as Symbol in *Romeo and Juliet*", in *Papers on Language and Literature* 32, no. 3 (1996).

[7] Lawrence Stone, *The Crisis of the Aristocracy, 1558–1641* (Oxford: Clarendon, 1965), p. 654.

Popular manuals of health in sixteenth-century England cautioned against the permanent damage to a young woman's health that could be caused by early marriage and its consummation and by the childhood pregnancies that were its consequence. The grandmother of Anne Clopton, a contemporary of Shakespeare, opposed the proposed marriage of her thirteen-year-old granddaughter on the grounds of the "danger [that] might ensue to her very life from her extreme youth".[8] Such parental concern reflects Capulet's riposte to Paris that "too soon marr'd are those so early made", and it is surely significant that Shakespeare's own daughter Susanna was herself around Juliet's age when he was writing the play. As the father of a twelve-year-old daughter, Shakespeare's own perspective is that of a parent.

The general consensus in Elizabethan England was that marriage before sixteen was dangerous.[9] Elizabethan women married, on average, in their early to midtwenties, and men, on average, a few years later.[10] According to the historian Peter Laslett, who examined a thousand marriage licenses from the years immediately after Shakespeare wrote *Romeo and Juliet*, "the average age of ... Elizabethan and Jacobean brides was something like 24 and the average of bridegrooms was nearly 28."[11] The historian Christopher Hill noted that this is the oldest of any society known in history.[12] Shakespeare's own wife and his daughter Susanna conformed to the norms of Elizabethan society, marrying at about twenty-six and twenty-four, respectively, while his younger daughter, Judith, did not marry until she was thirty-one.

[8] Ibid., p. 656.

[9] Ibid., pp. 656–67.

[10] Peter Laslett, *The World We Have Lost: English Society before the Coming of Industry* (New York: Scribner's, 1965), pp. 81–86; Stone, *Family, Sex and Marriage in England*, pp. 49, 490; and Cook, *Making a Match*, pp. 265–67. The aristocracy married, on average, a little younger than the middle class and the poor, due to arranged marriages designed to secure an heiress or to seal a political alliance, but even among the aristocracy the average spousal age at marriage at the time Shakespeare wrote *Romeo and Juliet* was twenty-one or twenty-two.

[11] Laslett, *World We Have Lost*, p. 82.

[12] Christopher Hill, *The Collected Essays of Christopher Hill*, vol. 3, *People and Ideas in 17th Century England* (Brighton, England: Harvester, 1986), p. 195.

The literary critic J. Karl Franson concludes from this con-textual evidence that Shakespeare's audience would have been shocked at Juliet's age and the way in which the child was propelled, unprepared, into an adult world with which she was ill-equipped to cope: "That Capulet would offer his daughter to Paris despite her 'extreme youth' . . . must have been appall-ing to an Elizabethan."[13] Franson's overall conclusion is resoundingly and perceptively incisive. Juliet was "too soon marr'd" by the neglect or manipulation of callous and heart-less adults. At the play's tragic heart is the broken heart of a child.

Romantic readers of the play are blind to such contextual evidence. Following their hearts and forsaking and forswear-ing their heads, they see the "love at first sight" between Romeo and Juliet as one of the most beautiful things in the whole drama. It is as pure and passionate as it is impetuous and impul-sive. It is truly momentous, in the sense that it surrenders itself to the moment, and will not be assuaged by reason, temper-ance, or prudence. Such a love hurls itself heedlessly into the arms of the beloved, a headless heart hurtling toward a breath-lessly exhilarating consummation. Shakespeare, who invari-ably and unerringly perceives the human condition with the incisive insight of genius, understands the exhilaration of this sort of love, and from this moment onward, the whole action of the play accelerates. It is noteworthy, for instance, that Shake-speare condenses the whole drama into five breathless days, whereas in his source poem the action takes place over sev-eral months. The question is not whether Shakespeare under-stands such romantic passion; it is what he has to say about it.

In the first meeting between the two lovers, it is significant that Shakespeare selects sin as the prevailing metaphor for their first kiss. Unlike Rosaline, Juliet is clearly attracted by Romeo's charms and is torn between chaste decorum and erotic desire. As the mysterious stranger manipulates her words to serve his amorous purposes, bestowing the first kiss, the girl's struggle

---

[13] Franson, "'Too soon marr'd'".

with her conscience is strained to the limit. This kiss, almost certainly Juliet's first, is a new and strange experience, throwing her into confusion. Her conflicted emotions are aroused still further by Romeo's indecorous use of a religious image: "Thus from my lips by thine my sin is purg'd" (1.5.105). The metaphor of the "sinful kiss" is taken literally by the naïve Juliet, causing her to exclaim in alarm that she has indeed shared in a sinful act in permitting herself to be kissed by the stranger: "Then have my lips the sin that they have took" (106). Her sense of sin is no doubt heightened by the erotic pleasure the kiss has given her. Romeo, seizing the opportunity, manipulates her words once again to steal a second kiss: "Sin from my lips? O trespass sweetly urg'd! / Give me my sin again" (107–8).

Although romantic readers of this scene invariably bestow maturity on the thirteen-year-old, enabling her to play her part with a suave savoir faire belying her age, Shakespeare's use of the sin metaphor suggests a clear moral dimension to the exchange. The kiss does not merely transmit the sin metaphorically; it does so literally. The erotically charged Romeo has enflamed desire in the object of his advances, succeeding with Juliet where he had failed with the presumably more mature Rosaline.

The foregoing nonromantic reading of the lovers' first exchange seems to be vindicated by the words of the Chorus immediately after the scene we have just discussed:

> Now old desire doth in his death-bed lie,
> And young affection gapes to be his heir;
> That fair for which love groan'd for and would die,
> With tender Juliet match'd, is now not fair.
> Now Romeo is belov'd, and loves again,
> Alike bewitched by the charm of looks. (2 Prol. 1–6)

The voice of the Chorus, being impartial and aloof and therefore closest to the narrative voice of the playwright, makes no distinction between the nature of Romeo's love for Rosaline and that which he has for Juliet. The "old desire" for Rosaline may be dead, but the "young affection" for Juliet desires eagerly to be "his heir". One "love" has simply been replaced by another in its likeness. Romeo is "belov'd, and loves again, / Alike bewitched by the charm of looks". Again, no distinction is made between the earlier love and its heir. Indeed, the Chorus seems to be suggesting that there *is* no distinction. Romeo simply "loves again". He has not spurned false love for true but merely loves both women in the same way. In this sense the phrase "alike bewitched" seems to have a double meaning. Romeo and Juliet are "alike bewitched", i.e., bewitched by each other, but Romeo is also "alike bewitched" in that he was bewitched by Rosaline and Juliet alike. In both cases, he is bewitched by physical beauty, by "the charm of looks". And let us not forget that the love between Romeo and Juliet can be nothing but skin-deep and purely physical at this stage. Romeo and Juliet do not know each other. They do not even know each other's names. Romeo declares his "love" before he has even spoken a single word to his beloved. How can such love be anything but superficial, a bewitchment of the eye in response to great physical beauty? This, at any rate, seems to be the question that Shakespeare, via the Chorus, is asking.

The question is asked again, immediately, by Mercutio, in his savage lampooning of Petrarchan love (2.1.8–10) and in his disdain for the "gossip Venus" and for Cupid, "her purblind son", the latter of whom he regards as a swindler and confidence trickster (2.1.11–12).[14] Mercutio sees Romeo as a victim of Venus, struck by Cupid's duplicitous dart, and as such, struck witless by love: "Romeo! humours! madman! passion! lover!" (7). For Mercutio, "Romeo", "madman", and "lover" are synonyms. Responding to Mercutio's jesting, the soberminded Benvolio observes that Romeo is not so much a

---

[14] In some sources, Mercutio describes Venus' partially blind son as "Young Abraham Cupid" (2.1.13), an allusion to an "Abraham man", one of a class of beggars thrown into poverty by the dissolution of the monasteries by King Henry VIII in 1536. Such beggars, no longer able to obtain relief from religious houses, wandered the countryside feigning illness to obtain alms. Therefore, Mercutio is calling Cupid a beggarly con man.

madman as a blind man who is at home in the darkness of his passions: "Blind is his love, and best befits the dark" (2.1.32).

And so, with Mercutio's description of Romeo's madness, and Benvolio's lament at his blindness, and with the Chorus' suggestion that the young lover is still bewitched by the same enchantment that had overpowered him in the presence of Rosaline, we are prepared by Shakespeare for the breathless rush toward the tragic abyss, the self-destructive consequence of concupiscence. Throughout the remainder of the play, the palpable absence of the cardinal virtues of prudence and temperance paves the way for the denouement of the tragedy. The absence of such virtue in the lovers is exacerbated by its absence in other crucial characters, who, being older, are perhaps even more culpable than the play's principal protagonists. Friar Lawrence begins by giving sagacious advice but fails to practice what he preaches in his rash agreement to marry the lovers in secret and with undue haste; Capulet begins with a seeming desire to protect his child from a premature marriage but then tries to force her to marry Paris; the Nurse fails to support Juliet, even suggesting that her young charge proceed with the bigamous marriage to Paris. It is clear, therefore, that Juliet is betrayed by those who should have saved her from her own immature folly. This failure on the part of the adult characters serves as a moral counterpoint to the treacherous passions of youth. It is as though Shakespeare is illustrating that the young will go tragically astray if not restrained by the wisdom, virtue, and example of their elders. The final tragedy is that this lesson is learned by the Capulets and Montagues only in the wake of the deaths of their children. The lesson *is* learned, however, and the consequent restoration of peace provides a sad but consoling catharsis. Whether such a cathartic turn can be considered a happy ending is a moot point. It is, however, an ending that restores not only peace but sanity and moral equilibrium to the surviving protagonists, and this is surely a source of joy, even if a joy tinted with sorrow.

Ultimately, the peace that reigns at the end of *Romeo and Juliet* is much greater than the worldly and merely political peace that emerges in Verona. It is the peace that surpasses all understanding, as Saint Paul tells the Philippians (Phil 4:7); the peace that T. S. Eliot proclaims at the culmination and climax of *The Waste Land*; and the peace that descends on the so-called tragic climaxes of *Hamlet* and *King Lear*. Such peace is not of the sort that the world understands or desires. It is a peace that can be perceived only through the eyes of faith, a faith the world does not know and cannot offer, a faith that finds voice in the greatest art and finds the divine comedy in the midst of the greatest tragedies.

TEXTUAL NOTE

This edition of *Romeo and Juliet* is based upon the Second Quarto (1599), often known as the "good quarto" to distinguish it from the First Quarto (1597), or "bad quarto", which is generally believed to be a pirated edition. Many scholars believe that the Second Quarto was printed from Shakespeare's own manuscript, thereby establishing it beyond doubt as the authoritative text.

The Text of

ROMEO AND JULIET

DRAMATIS PERSONAE

Chorus
Escalus, Prince of Verona
Paris, a young nobleman, kinsman to the Prince
Montague, Capulet, heads of two houses at variance with each other
An Old Man of the Capulet family
Romeo, son to Montague
Mercuti, kinsman to the Prince, and friend to Romeo
Benvolio, nephew to Montague, and friend to Romeo
Tybalt, nephew to Lady Capulet
Friar Lawrence, Friar John, Franciscans
Balthasar, servant to Romeo
Sampson, Gregory, servants to Capulet
Peter, servant to Juliet's nurse
Abraham, servant to Montague
An Apothecary[1]
Three Musicians
An Officer
Lady Montague, wife to Montague
Lady Capulet, wife to Capulet
Juliet, daughter to Capulet
Nurse to Juliet
Citizens of Verona; Gentlemen and Gentlewomen of both houses; Maskers,[2] Torchbearers, Pages, Guards, Watchmen, Servants, and Attendants

---

[1] Apothecary: druggist.
[2] Maskers: those attending a masked ball.

The Scene: Verona and Mantua.

THE PROLOGUE

Enter Chorus.

Two households, both alike in dignity,[3]
In fair Verona, where we lay our scene,
From ancient grudge break to new mutiny,[4]
Where civil blood makes civil hands unclean.
From forth the fatal loins of these two foes   5
A pair of star-cross'd lovers take their life;
Whose misadventur'd[5] piteous overthrows
Doth with their death bury their parents' strife.
The fearful passage of their death-mark'd
    love,
And the continuance of their parents' rage,   10
Which, but their children's end, nought[6] could
    remove,
Is now the two hours' traffic of our stage;[7]
The which if you with patient ears attend,
What here shall miss, our toil shall strive to
    mend.   [*Exit.*]

---

[3] *dignity*: social rank, title.

[4] *mutiny*: violence, disorder, unlawful rebellion.

[5] *misadventur'd*: unlucky, unfortunate.

[6] *nought*: nothing.

[7] *two hours' traffic of our stage*: i.e., subject matter of our play (usually two hours in duration).

ACT 1

Scene 1. *Verona. A public place.*

*Enter Sampson and Gregory, of the house of Capulet,
with swords and bucklers*[8] *on.*

Sampson. Gregory, on my word, we'll not carry
coals.[9]

Gregory. No, for then we should be colliers.[10]

Sampson. I mean, an[11] we be in choler,[12] we'll draw.[13]

Gregory. Ay, while you live, draw your neck out
of collar.[14]   5

Sampson. I strike quickly, being moved.[15]

Gregory. But thou art not quickly moved to
strike.

Sampson. A dog of the house of Montague moves
me.

Gregory. To move is to stir, and to be valiant is
to stand; therefore, if thou art moved, thou
run'st away.   10

Sampson. A dog of that house shall move me to
stand. I will take the wall[16] of any man or maid of
Montague's.

---

[8] *bucklers*: small shields.
[9] *carry coals*: submit to insults.
[10] *colliers*: coal miners.
[11] *an*: if.
[12] *choler*: anger.
[13] *draw*: i.e., draw swords.
[14] *collar*: a hangman's noose.
[15] *moved*: angered.
[16] *the wall*: i.e., walk close to the wall, thereby forcing those walking in the
opposite direction into the street.

Gregory. That shows thee a weak slave; for the
   weakest goes to the wall.   *14*

Sampson. 'Tis true; and therefore women, being
   the weaker vessels, are ever thrust to the wall;
   therefore I will push Montague's men from the
   wall and thrust his maids to the wall.

Gregory. The quarrel is between our masters
   and us their men.   *20*

Sampson. 'Tis all one; I will show myself a tyrant.
   When I have fought with the men, I will be civil
   with the maids—I will cut off their heads.

Gregory. The heads of the maids?   *24*

Sampson. Ay, the heads of the maids, or their
   maidenheads;[17] take it in what sense thou wilt.   *26*

Gregory. They must take it in sense that feel it.

Sampson. Me they shall feel while I am able to
   stand; and 'tis known I am a pretty piece of
   flesh.

Gregory. 'Tis well thou art not fish; if thou
   hadst, thou hadst been poor-John.[18] Draw thy
   tool;[19] here comes two of the house of Montagues. *32*

   Enter two other Servants, Abraham and Balthasar.

Sampson. My naked weapon is out; quarrel,
   I will back thee.

Gregory. How? turn thy back and run?   *35*

Sampson. Fear me not.

---

[17] *maidenheads*: virginity.
[18] *poor-John*: small fish (poor man's fare).
[19] *tool*: weapon.

Gregory. No, marry;[20] I fear thee!

Sampson. Let us take the law of our sides;[21] let
  them begin.

Gregory. I will frown as I pass by, and let them
  take it as they list.   40

Sampson. Nay, as they dare. I will bite my thumb[22]
  at them, which is disgrace to them if they bear
  it.

Abraham. Do you bite your thumb at us, sir?

Sampson. I do bite my thumb, sir.   44

Abraham. Do you bite your thumb at us, sir?

Sampson. [*Aside to Gregory.*] Is the law of[23] our
  side, if I say ay?[24]

Gregory. [*Aside to Sampson.*] No.

Sampson. No, sir, I do not bite my thumb at you,
  sir; but I bite my thumb, sir.

Gregory. Do you quarrel, sir?   50

Abraham. Quarrel, sir! No, sir.

Sampson. But if you do, sir, I am for you. I serve
  as good a man as you.

Abraham. No better?

Sampson. Well, sir.   55

---

[20] *marry*: indeed (colloquial expression, literally meaning "by the Virgin Mary").
[21] *take the law of our sides*: keep the law on our side (i.e., by not provoking a quarrel).
[22] *I will bite my thumb*: To bite one's thumb is an insult, a gesture of contempt.
[23] *of*: on.
[24] *ay*: aye (i.e., yes).

Enter Benvolio.

Gregory. [*Aside to Sampson.*] Say 'better'; here
    comes one of my master's kinsmen.

Sampson. Yes, better, sir.

Abraham. You lie.   59

Sampson. Draw, if you be men. Gregory,
    remember thy swashing[25] blow.   [*They fight.*]

Benvolio. Part, fools!   [*Beats down their swords.*]
    Put up your swords; you know not what you do.   63

Enter Tybalt.

Tybalt. What, art thou drawn among these
      heartless hinds?[26]
    Turn thee, Benvolio; look upon thy death.   65

Benvolio. I do but keep the peace; put up thy
      sword,
    Or manage it to part these men with me.

Tybalt. What, drawn, and talk of peace! I hate
      the word,
    As I hate hell, all Montagues, and thee.

    Have at thee, coward!   [*They fight.*]   70

*Enter an Officer, and three or four Citizens with
clubs or partisans.*[27]

Officer. Clubs, bills,[28] and partisans! Strike; beat
    them down.

---

[25] *swashing*: violent, slashing.
[26] *heartless hinds*: cowardly rustics or laborers.
[27] *partisans*: spearlike weapons with a broad-bladed, double-edged head.
[28] *bills*: long-shafted weapons with a cleaverlike hook on one side and a spike
(or spikes) on the other.

Citizens. Down with the Capulets! Down with
the Montagues!

Enter Old Capulet in his gown, and his Wife.

Capulet. What noise is this? Give me my long
sword, ho!

Lady Capulet. A crutch, a crutch! Why call you
for a sword?

Capulet. My sword, I say! Old Montague is
come,   75
And flourishes his blade in spite[29] of me.

Enter Old Montague and his Wife.

Montague. Thou villain Capulet!—Hold me
not, let me go.

Lady Montague. Thou shalt not stir one foot to
seek a foe.

Enter Prince Escalus, with his Train.

Prince. Rebellious subjects, enemies to peace,
Profaners of this neighbour-stained steel—   80
Will they not hear? What, ho! you men, you
beasts,
That quench the fire of your pernicious rage
With purple fountains[30] issuing from your veins!
On pain of torture, from those bloody hands
Throw your mistempered[31] weapons to the
ground,   85
And hear the sentence of your moved[32] prince.

---

[29] *spite:* defiance.
[30] *purple fountains:* i.e., of blood.
[31] *mistempered:* (1) made (or tempered) hard in blood; (2) used with bad or
angry temper.
[32] *moved:* angry.

Three civil brawls, bred of an airy word,
By thee, old Capulet, and Montague,
Have thrice disturb'd the quiet of our streets
And made Verona's ancient citizens   90
Cast by[33] their grave beseeming[34] ornaments
To wield old partisans, in hands as old,
Cank'red[35] with peace, to part your cank'red[36] hate.
If ever you disturb our streets again,
Your lives shall pay the forfeit of the peace.   95
For this time all the rest depart away.
You, Capulet, shall go along with me;
And, Montague, come you this afternoon,
To know our farther pleasure in this case,
To old Free-town, our common judgment-
    place.   100
Once more, on pain of death, all men depart.

[*Exeunt all but Montague, his Wife, and Benvolio.*]

Montague. Who set this ancient quarrel new
    abroach?[37]
Speak, nephew; were you by when it began?

Benvolio. Here were the servants of your
    adversary
And yours, close fighting ere I did approach.   105
I drew to part them; in the instant came
The fiery Tybalt, with his sword prepar'd;
Which, as he breath'd defiance to my ears,
He swung about his head and cut the winds,
Who, nothing hurt withal,[38] hiss'd him in scorn.   110
While we were interchanging thrusts and blows,

---

[33] *by*: aside.
[34] *grave beseeming*: appropriately dignified.
[35] *Cank'red*: decayed.
[36] *cank'red*: malignant or infected.
[37] *new abroach*: newly opened, newly astir.
[38] *withal*: thereby.

Came more and more, and fought on part and
    part,[39]
Till the Prince came, who parted either part.

Lady Montague. O, where is Romeo? Saw you
    him to-day?
Right glad I am he was not at this fray.   115

Benvolio. Madam, an hour before the
    worshipp'd sun
Peer'd forth the golden window of the east,
A troubled mind drew me to walk abroad;
Where, underneath the grove of sycamore
That westward rooteth from this city side,   120
So early walking did I see your son.
Towards him I made; but he was ware[40] of me
And stole into the covert of the wood.
I, measuring his affections by my own,
Which then most sought where most might not
    be found,[41]   125
Being one too many by my weary self,
Pursu'd my humour, not pursuing his,[42]
And gladly shunn'd who gladly fled from me.

Montague. Many a morning hath he there been
    seen,
With tears augmenting the fresh morning's dew,   130
Adding to clouds more clouds with his deep
    sighs;
But all so soon as the all-cheering sun
Should in the farthest east begin to draw
The shady curtains from Aurora's[43] bed,

---

[39] *on part and part*: some on one side and some on the other.
[40] *ware*: aware.
[41] *most sought . . . found*: i.e., wanted most to be alone.
[42] *Pursu'd . . . pursuing his*: i.e., followed my own inclination by not asking
him about his mood.
[43] *Aurora's*: In classical mythology, Aurora is the goddess of the dawn.

Away from light steals home my heavy[44] son, 135
And private in his chamber pens himself,
Shuts up his windows, locks fair daylight out,
And makes himself an artificial[45] night.
Black and portentous must this humour[46] prove,
Unless good counsel may the cause remove. 140

Benvolio. My noble uncle, do you know the
cause?

Montague. I neither know it nor can learn of
him.

Benvolio. Have you importun'd him by any
means?

Montague. Both by myself and many other
friends.
But he, his own affections' counsellor, 145
Is to himself—I will not say how true;
But to himself so secret and so close,
So far from sounding[47] and discovery,
As is the bud bit with an envious[48] worm,
Ere he can spread his sweet leaves to the air, 150
Or dedicate his beauty to the sun.
Could we but learn from whence his sorrows
grow,
We would as willingly give cure as know.

Enter Romeo.

Benvolio. See where he comes. So please you
step aside;
I'll know his grievance or be much denied. 155

---

[44] *heavy*: melancholy, moody.
[45] *artificial*: i.e., unnatural.
[46] *humour*: mood.
[47] *sounding*: measuring and revealing the depth of his mood.
[48] *envious*: malign.

Montague. I would thou wert so happy[49] by thy
    stay
  To hear true shrift.[50] Come, madam, let's away.

                    [*Exeunt Montague and his Wife.*]

Benvolio. Good morrow,[51] cousin.

Romeo.   Is the day so young?

Benvolio. But new struck nine.

Romeo.   Ay me! sad hours seem long.
  Was that my father that went hence so fast?   *160*

Benvolio. It was. What sadness lengthens
    Romeo's hours?

Romeo. Not having that which having makes
    them short.

Benvolio. In love?

Romeo. Out—

Benvolio. Of love?   *165*

Romeo. Out of her favour where I am in love.

Benvolio. Alas that love,[52] so gentle in his view,[53]
  Should be so tyrannous and rough in proof![54]

Romeo. Alas that love, whose view is muffled
    still,[55]
  Should without eyes see pathways to his will!   *170*
  Where shall we dine? O me! What fray was
    here?

---

[49] *happy*: lucky.
[50] *shrift*: (Romeo's) confession.
[51] *morrow*: morning.
[52] *love*: Cupid, the classical god of love.
[53] *view*: appearance.
[54] *in proof*: in our experience of it.
[55] *muffled still*: always blindfolded. Cupid is often depicted as being blindfolded.

Yet tell me not, for I have heard it all.
Here's much to do with hate, but more with
    love.[56]
Why then, O brawling love! O loving hate!
O anything, of nothing first create![57] *175*
O heavy lightness! serious vanity!
Mis-shapen chaos of well-seeming forms!
Feather of lead, bright smoke, cold fire, sick
    health!
Still-waking sleep, that is not what it is!
This love feel I, that feel no love in this. *180*
Dost thou not laugh?

Benvolio.   No, coz,[58] I rather weep.

Romeo. Good heart, at what?

Benvolio.   At thy good heart's oppression.

Romeo. Why, such is love's transgression.
Griefs of mine own lie heavy in my breast,
Which thou wilt propagate,[59] to have it prest[60] *185*
With more of thine. This love that thou hast
    shown
Doth add more grief to too much of mine own.
Love is a smoke rais'd with the fume of sighs;
Being purg'd, a fire sparkling in lovers' eyes;
Being vex'd, a sea nourish'd with loving tears. *190*
What is it else? A madness most discreet,[61]

---

[56] *Here's . . . with love*: I.e., the combatants are so passionate about the cause of their quarrel that it is as if they are romantically infatuated. The following paradox of "loving hate" suggests the irony inherent in the love of one's own family leading to the hatred of another's.

[57] *O anything . . . create*: Romeo refers to God's creation of the world *ex nihilo*— out of nothing.

[58] *coz*: cousin (i.e., kinsman).

[59] *propagate*: increase.

[60] *prest*: combined or united.

[61] *discreet*: secret or discriminating.

A choking gall, and a preserving sweet.
Farewell, my coz.

Benvolio.   Soft![62] I will go along;
  An[63] if you leave me so, you do me wrong.

Romeo. Tut, I have lost myself; I am not here: 195
  This is not Romeo, he's some other where.

Benvolio. Tell me in sadness[64] who is that you
    love.

Romeo. What, shall I groan and tell thee?

Benvolio.   Groan! Why, no;
  But sadly[65] tell me who.

Romeo. Bid a sick man in sadness[66] make his will.   200
  Ah, word ill urg'd to one that is so ill!
  In sadness, cousin,[67] I do love a woman.

Benvolio. I aim'd so near when I suppos'd you
    lov'd.

Romeo. A right good markman! And she's fair I
    love.

Benvolio. A right fair mark,[68] fair coz, is soonest
    hit.   205

Romeo. Well, in that hit you miss: she'll not be
    hit
  With Cupid's arrow.[69] She hath Dian's wit,[70]

---

[62] *Soft*: wait.
[63] *An*: and.
[64] *in sadness*: truly or seriously.
[65] *sadly*: seriously.
[66] *in sadness*: (1) seriously; (2) in unhappiness.
[67] *cousin*: kinsman.
[68] *fair mark*: target easily seen.
[69] *Cupid's arrow*: In classical mythology, Cupid, the god of love, is usually depicted as a little boy with a bow and arrow.
[70] *Dian's wit*: In classical mythology, Diana (or Artemis) was a virgin goddess renowned as a huntress.

And in strong proof of chastity well arm'd,
From Love's weak childish bow she lives
   unharm'd.
She will not stay[71] the siege of loving terms,   *210*
Nor bide[72] th' encounter of assailing eyes,
Nor ope[73] her lap to saint-seducing gold.[74]
O, she is rich in beauty; only poor
That, when she dies, with beauty dies her store.[75]

Benvolio. Then she hath sworn that she will still[76]
   live chaste?   *215*

Romeo. She hath, and in that sparing makes huge
   waste;
For beauty, starv'd with her severity,
Cuts beauty off from all posterity.
She is too fair, too wise, wisely too fair,
To merit bliss[77] by making me despair.   *220*
She hath forsworn to love, and in that vow
Do I live dead that live to tell it now.

Benvolio. Be rul'd by me: forget to think of her.

Romeo. O, teach me how I should forget to
   think!

Benvolio. By giving liberty unto thine eyes.   *225*
   Examine other beauties.

Romeo.   'Tis the way
To call hers, exquisite, in question more.[78]

---

[71] *stay*: support, submit to.

[72] *bide*: abide.

[73] *ope*: open.

[74] *ope her lap . . . gold*: In classical mythology, the god Zeus seduced the princess Danae by coming into her lap as a shower of gold.

[75] *with beauty dies her store*: As she dies unmarried, her beauty will not be passed on (i.e., through the bearing of children). This analogy is carried further in the subsequent lines.

[76] *still*: always.

[77] *bliss*: i.e., heavenly bliss.

[78] *To call . . . in question more*: to bring her beauty into his mind even more.

These happy masks that kiss fair ladies' brows,
Being black, puts us in mind they hide the fair.
He that is strucken[79] blind cannot forget   230
The precious treasure of his eyesight lost.
Show me a mistress that[80] is passing fair,
What doth her beauty serve but as a note[81]
Where I may read who pass'd that passing fair?
Farewell; thou canst not teach me to forget.   235

Benvolio. I'll pay that doctrine or else die in
      debt.[82]   [*Exeunt.*]

Scene 2. A *street.*

Enter Capulet, County[83] Paris, and the Clown, his servant.

Capulet. But Montague is bound as well as I,
      In penalty alike; and 'tis not hard, I think,
      For men so old as we to keep the peace.

Paris. Of honourable reckoning[84] are you both,
      And pity 'tis you liv'd at odds so long.   5
      But now, my lord, what say you to my suit?

Capulet. But saying o'er what I have said before:
      My child is yet a stranger in the world,
      She hath not seen the change of fourteen years;
      Let two more summers wither in their pride   10
      Ere we may think her ripe to be a bride.

Paris. Younger than she are happy mothers
      made.

---

[79] *strucken:* struck.
[80] *that:* who.
[81] *note:* written reminder.
[82] *I'll pay . . . die in debt:* I will teach you (to forget) or else die trying.
[83] County: Count.
[84] *reckoning:* reputation.

Capulet. And too soon marr'd are those so early
 made.
 Earth hath swallowed all my hopes but she;[85]
 She is the hopeful lady of my earth.   15
 But woo her, gentle Paris, get her heart;
 My will to her consent is but a part.
 And, she agreed,[86] within her scope of choice
 Lies my consent and fair according[87] voice.
 This night I hold an old accustom'd[88] feast,   20
 Whereto I have invited many a guest,
 Such as I love; and you among the store,
 One more, most welcome, makes my number
  more.
 At my poor house look to behold this night
 Earth-treading stars[89] that make dark heaven
  light.   25
 Such comfort as do lusty[90] young men feel
 When well-apparell'd April on the heel
 Of limping winter treads, even such delight
 Among fresh female buds shall you this night
 Inherit[91] at my house. Hear all, all see,   30
 And like her most whose merit most shall be;
 Which on more view of many, mine, being one,
 May stand in number,[92] though in reck'ning
  none.[93]
 Come, go with me. [*To Servant, giving him a paper.*]
         Go, sirrah,[94] trudge about
 Through fair Verona; find those persons out   35

---

[85] *Earth hath swallowed . . . but she:* i.e., all of his other children are dead.
[86] *And, she agreed:* if she agrees.
[87] *according:* agreeing.
[88] *accustom'd:* established by custom.
[89] *Earth-treading stars:* i.e., young girls.
[90] *lusty:* vigorous, lively.
[91] *Inherit:* have.
[92] *in number:* as one in a group.
[93] *in reck'ning none:* not reckoned anything special.
[94] *sirrah:* term of address to inferiors.

Whose names are written there, and to them say
My house and welcome on their pleasure stay.[95]

> [*Exeunt Capulet and Paris.*]

Servant. Find them out whose names are
    written here! It is written that the shoemaker
    should meddle with his yard and the tailor with
    his last,[96] the fisher with his pencil and the
    painter with his nets;[97] but I am sent to find those
    persons whose names are here writ, and can
    never find[98] what names the writing person hath
    here writ. I must to the learned. In good time![99]   44

Enter Benvolio and Romeo.

Benvolio. Tut, man, one fire burns out another's
        burning,
    One pain is less'ned by another's anguish;
    Turn giddy, and be holp[100] by backward turning;[101]
    One desperate grief cures with another's
        languish.
    Take thou some new infection to thy eye,
    And the rank poison of the old will die.   50

Romeo. Your plantain leaf[102] is excellent for that.

Benvolio. For what, I pray thee?

Romeo.   For your broken[103] shin.

---

[95] *stay*: wait.
[96] *last*: a shoemaker's wooden model for shaping a shoe.
[97] *shoemaker . . . his nets*: scrambled version of a proverbial expression meaning that one should stick to what one knows.
[98] *find*: understand, make out.
[99] *In good time!* What luck! (He is cheering the arrival of "learned" men.)
[100] *holp*: helped.
[101] *backward turning*: turning in the opposite direction.
[102] *plantain leaf*: used medicinally to heal cuts or bruises.
[103] *broken*: scratched.

Benvolio. Why, Romeo, art thou mad?

Romeo. Not mad, but bound more than a
    madman is;
Shut up in prison, kept without my food,   55
Whipt and tormented, and—God-den,[104] good
    fellow.

Servant. God gi' go'den. I pray, sir, can you
    read?

Romeo. Ay, mine own fortune in my misery.

Servant. Perhaps you have learned it without
    book. But I pray, can you read anything you
    see?   60

Romeo. Ay, if I know the letters and the language.

Servant. Ye say honestly; rest you merry![105]

Romeo. Stay, fellow; I can read.
    [*He reads the list.*] 'Signior Martino and his wife
    and daughters; County Anselme and his
    beauteous sisters; the lady widow of Vitruvio;
    Signior Placentio and his lovely nieces;
    Mercutio and his brother Valentine; mine uncle
    Capulet, his wife, and daughters; my fair niece
    Rosaline and Livia; Signior Valentio and his
    cousin Tybalt; Lucio and the lively Helena.'   70
    A fair assembly. [*Gives back the paper.*] Whither
    should they come?

Servant. Up.

Romeo. Whither?

Servant. To supper. To our house.

Romeo. Whose house?   75

---

[104] *God-den:* good evening (good afternoon).
[105] *rest you merry:* colloquial phrase, literally meaning "may God keep you merry".

Servant. My master's.

Romeo. Indeed, I should have ask'd you that
          before.

Servant. Now I'll tell you without asking: my
          master is the great rich Capulet; and if you be
          not of the house of Montagues, I pray come and   80
          crush[106] a cup of wine. Rest you merry!   [*Exit.*]

Benvolio. At this same ancient[107] feast of Capulet's
          Sups the fair Rosaline whom thou so loves,
          With all the admired beauties of Verona.
          Go thither, and with unattainted[108] eye   85
          Compare her face with some that I shall show,
          And I will make thee think thy swan a crow.

Romeo. When the devout religion of mine eye
          Maintains such falsehood, then turn tears to
          fires;
          And these,[109] who, often drown'd, could never die,   90
          Transparent heretics, be burnt for liars!
          One fairer than my love! The all-seeing sun
          Ne'er saw her match since first the world begun.

Benvolio. Tut, you saw her fair, none else being
          by,
          Herself pois'd[110] with herself in either eye;   95
          But in that crystal scales[111] let there be weigh'd
          Your lady's love against some other maid
          That I will show you shining at this feast,
          And she shall scant[112] show well that now seems
          best.

---

[106] *crush:* drink.
[107] *ancient:* established by custom.
[108] *unattainted:* unbiased.
[109] *these:* i.e., his eyes.
[110] *pois'd:* balanced.
[111] *that crystal scales:* i.e., Romeo's eyes.
[112] *scant:* scarcely.

Romeo. I'll go along, no such sight to be shown,   *100*
    But to rejoice in splendour of mine own.[113]

[Handwritten: Juliet came and her mother wanted to talk privately but then lady Capulet

[Exeunt.]

[Handwritten: Lady Capulet told Nurse to get her daughter]

Scene 3. *Capulet's house.*

[Handwritten: told the Nurse to tell the council that she is not to]

Enter Lady Capulet and Nurse.

Lady Capulet. Nurse, where's my daughter?
    Call her forth to me.

Nurse. Now, by my maidenhead at twelve year
        old,
    I bade her come. What,[114] lamb! what, lady-bird!
    God forbid! Where's this girl? What, Juliet!

Enter Juliet.

Juliet. How now, who calls?   5

Nurse. Your mother.

Juliet. Madam, I am here. What is your will?

Lady Capulet. This is the matter. Nurse, give
        leave awhile,
    We must talk in secret. Nurse, come back again;
    I have rememb'red me, thou's[115] hear our counsel.   *10*
    Thou knowest my daughter's of a pretty age.

Nurse. Faith, I can tell her age unto an hour.

Lady Capulet. She's not fourteen.

---

[113] *mine own:* my own lady (i.e., Rosaline).
[114] *What:* colloquial expression demonstrative of impatience.
[115] *thou's:* thou shalt.

Nurse.   I'll lay fourteen of my teeth—
   And yet, to my teen[116] be it spoken, I have but
     four—
   She's not fourteen. How long is it now   15
   To Lammas-tide?[117] *feast*

Lady Capulet.   A fortnight and odd days.

Nurse. Even or odd, of all days in the year,
   Come Lammas Eve at night shall she be
     fourteen.
   Susan and she—God rest all Christian souls!—
   Were of an age.[118] Well, Susan is with God;   20
   She was too good for me. But, as I said,
   On Lammas Eve at night shall she be fourteen;
   That shall she, marry; I remember it well.
   'Tis since the earthquake[119] now eleven years;
   And she was wean'd—I never shall forget it—   25
   Of all the days of the year, upon that day;
   For I had then laid wormwood to my dug,[120]
   Sitting in the sun under the dove-house wall;
   My lord and you were then at Mantua.
   Nay, I do bear a brain. But, as I said,   30
   When it did taste the wormwood on the nipple
   Of my dug, and felt it bitter, pretty fool,
   To see it tetchy,[121] and fall out with the dug!
   Shake, quoth the dove-house.[122] 'Twas no need, I
     trow,[123]

---

[116] *teen*: sorrow, with a play on the word "ten" ("teen"), indicative of the number of teeth the Nurse lacks in order to swear as she wishes.

[117] *Lammas-tide*: English harvest festival on August 1.

[118] *of an age*: the same age.

[119] *earthquake*: usually associated with the English earthquake of 1580, perceived by many as an evil portent.

[120] *dug*: breast (placing wormwood, a bitter-tasting herb, on one's breast was a method of weaning children).

[121] *tetchy*: peevish, irritable.

[122] *Shake, quoth the dove-house*: She is addressing her own head, to demonstrate that her brain still works.

[123] *trow*: believe, think.

To bid me trudge.   35
And since that time it is eleven years;
For then she could stand high-lone;[124] nay, by th'
   rood,[125]
She could have run and waddled all about;
For even the day before, she broke her brow;[126]
And then my husband—God be with his soul!   40
'A[127] was a merry man—took up the child.
'Yea,' quoth he, 'dost thou fall upon thy face?
Thou wilt fall backward when thou hast more
   wit,
Wilt thou not, Jule?' And, by my holidam,[128]
The pretty wretch left crying, and said 'Ay'.   45
To see, now, how a jest shall come about!
I warrant, an I should live a thousand years,
I never should forget it: 'Wilt thou not, Jule?'
   quoth he;
And, pretty fool, it stinted,[129] and said 'Ay'.

Lady Capulet. Enough of this; I pray thee hold
   thy peace.   50

Nurse. Yes, madam. Yet I cannot choose but
   laugh
To think it should leave crying and say 'Ay'.
And yet, I warrant, it had upon it[130] brow
A bump as big as a young cock'rel's stone[131]—
A perilous knock; and it cried bitterly.   55
'Yea,' quoth my husband, 'fall'st upon thy face?

---

[124] *high-lone*: alone.
[125] *by th' rood*: colloquial expression, swearing "by the Cross".
[126] *brow*: forehead.
[127] *'A*: he.
[128] *by my holidam*: colloquial oath, literally "by my Holy Dame" (i.e., by the Virgin Mary).
[129] *stinted*: stopped (crying).
[130] *it*: its.
[131] *stone*: testical.

Thou wilt fall backward when thou comest to
    age;
Wilt thou not, Jule?' It stinted, and said 'Ay'.

Juliet. And stint thou too, I pray thee, nurse, say
    I.

Nurse. Peace, I have done. God mark thee to his
    grace!   60
Thou wast the prettiest babe that e'er I nurs'd;
An I might live to see thee married once,
I have my wish.

Lady Capulet. Marry,[132] that 'marry' is the very
    theme
I came to talk of. Tell me, daughter Juliet,   65
How stands your dispositions[133] to be married?

Juliet. It is an honour that I dream not of.

Nurse. An honour! Were not I thine only nurse,
I would say thou hadst suck'd wisdom from thy
    teat.

Lady Capulet. Well, think of marriage now.
    Younger than you,   70
Here in Verona, ladies of esteem,
Are made already mothers. By my count,
I was your mother much upon these years[134]
That you are now a maid. Thus, then, in brief:
The valiant Paris seeks you for his love.   75

Nurse. A man, young lady! lady, such a man
As all the world—why, he's a man of wax.[135]

Lady Capulet. Verona's summer hath not such a
    flower.

---

[132] *Marry:* indeed.

[133] *dispositions:* disposition, inclination.

[134] *much upon these years:* within the same length of time (i.e., at a younger age).

[135] *man of wax:* faultless or perfectly formed man.

Nurse. Nay, he's a flower; in faith, a very flower.

Lady Capulet. What say you? Can you love the
  gentleman?   80
 This night you shall behold him at our feast;
 Read o'er the volume of young Paris' face,
 And find delight writ there with beauty's pen;
 Examine every married lineament,[136]
 And see how one another lends content;[137] 85
 And what obscur'd in this fair volume lies
 Find written in the margent[138] of his eyes.
 This precious book of love, this unbound[139] lover,
 To beautify him, only lacks a cover.[140]
 The fish lives in the sea, and 'tis much pride 90
 For fair without the fair within to hide.[141]
 That book in many's eyes doth share the glory
 That in gold clasps locks in the golden story;
 So shall you share all that he doth possess,
 By having him making yourself no less. 95

Nurse. No less! Nay, bigger; women grow by
 men.

Lady Capulet. Speak briefly, can you like of[142]
 Paris' love?

Juliet. I'll look to like, if looking liking move;
 But no more deep will I endart[143] mine eye
 Than your consent gives strength to make it fly. 100

Enter a Servant.

---

[136] *married lineament:* harmonious feature.
[137] *one another lends content:* one enhances another.
[138] *margent:* margin.
[139] *unbound:* (1) without cover; (2) uncaught.
[140] *cover:* i.e., wife.
[141] *The fish . . . to hide:* I.e., the fair sea is even fairer because there are fair fish
in it.
[142] *like of:* be favorable to.
[143] *endart:* shoot a glance like a dart.

the people are arriving *and there* *aint enough food cause a nurse isnt heping*

Servant. Madam, the guests are come, supper
serv'd up, you call'd, my young lady ask'd for,
the nurse curs'd[144] in the pantry, and everything in
extremity.[145] I must hence to wait;[146] I beseech you,
follow straight.[147]

Lady Capulet. We follow thee. [Exit Servant.] 105
    Juliet, the County stays.[148]

Nurse. Go, girl, seek happy nights to happy days.

[Exeunt.]

Scene 4. A street.

Enter Romeo, Mercutio, Benvolio,
with five or six other Maskers; Torch-bearers.

Romeo. What, shall this speech be spoke for our
    excuse?[149] *What should our excuse be?*
Or shall we on without apology?

Benvolio. The date is out of such prolixity.[150]
    We'll have no Cupid hoodwink'd[151] with a scarf,
    Bearing a Tartar's painted bow of lath,[152]   5
    Scaring the ladies like a crow-keeper;[153]
    Nor no without-book prologue,[154] faintly spoke
    After the prompter, for our entrance;

[144] curs'd: i.e., because she is in the pantry and not helping.
[145] everything in extremity: extreme haste, extreme urgency.
[146] wait: serve.
[147] straight: directly.
[148] stays: is waiting.
[149] shall this speech . . . excuse? I.e., shall we speak a customary prepared speech
of introduction?
[150] The date . . . prolixity: I.e., such wordiness is unfashionable.
[151] hoodwink'd: blindfolded.
[152] Bearing a Tartar's painted bow of lath: carrying a painted oriental bow. A
lath is a thin length of wood.
[153] crow-keeper: boy tasked with scaring off crows.
[154] without-book prologue: memorized speech.

But, let them measure[155] us by what they will,
We'll measure them a measure,[156] and be gone.   10

Romeo. Give me a torch; I am not for this
    ambling;
    Being but heavy, I will bear the light.

Mercutio. Nay, gentle Romeo, we must have
    you dance.

Romeo. Not I, believe me. You have dancing
    shoes
    With nimble soles: I have a soul of lead
    So stakes me to the ground I cannot move.

Mercutio. You are a lover; borrow Cupid's
    wings
    And soar with them above a common bound.

Romeo. I am too sore enpierced with his shaft
    To soar with his light feathers; and so bound   20
    I cannot bound[157] a pitch[158] above dull woe.
    Under love's heavy burden do I sink.

Mercutio. And to sink in it should you burden
    love;
    Too great oppression for a tender thing.

Romeo. Is love a tender thing? It is too rough,   25
    Too rude, too boist'rous, and it pricks like
    thorn.

Mercutio. If love be rough with you, be rough
    with love;
    Prick love for pricking, and you beat love down.

---

[155] *measure*: judge.
[156] *measure them a measure*: dance one dance with them.
[157] *bound*: (1) leap; (2) limit.
[158] *pitch*: height from which a bird swoops to seize prey (falconry term).

Handwritten margin notes:
Romeo and Benvolio make it to me dance but Romeo doesn't want to 15 dance
Mercutio is encouraging
Romeo = O confindence
Mercutio tells Romeo to not fear love

Give me a case[159] to put my visage in.

                         [*Putting on a mask.*]

A visor[160] for a visor! What care I   30
What curious eye doth quote[161] deformities?
Here are the beetle brows[162] shall blush[163] for me.

Benvolio. Come, knock and enter; and no
       sooner in
But every man betake him to his legs.[164]

Romeo. A torch for me. Let wantons, light of
       heart,   35
Tickle the senseless rushes[165] with their heels;
For I am proverb'd with a grandsire phrase;[166]
I'll be a candle-holder[167] and look on;
The game was ne'er so fair,[168] and I am done.

Mercutio. Tut, dun's[169] the mouse, the constable's
       own word;[170]   40
If thou art Dun,[171] we'll draw thee from the mire
Of this sir-reverence[172] love, wherein thou stickest
Up to the ears. Come, we burn daylight,[173] ho!

---

[159] *case*: mask.

[160] *visor*: mask.

[161] *quote*: note, observe.

[162] *beetle brows*: bushy eyebrows.

[163] *blush*: (1) flush; (2) be grotesque.

[164] *betake him to his legs*: begin dancing.

[165] *rushes*: grasslike marsh plants whose stems were used for basket weaving and floor covering.

[166] *grandsire phrase*: old saying.

[167] *candle-holder*: attendant.

[168] *The game was ne'er so fair*: I.e., I have enjoyed dancing now as much as I ever shall.

[169] *dun's*: "Dun" means "dull", "drab", or "dark", associated with the dusk.

[170] *the constable's own word*: i.e., a curfew.

[171] *Dun*: common name for a horse, referring to a game called "Dun's in the Mire", which involves hauling a heavy log.

[172] *sir-reverence*: apologetic expression used before saying something potentially offensive, literally meaning "save your reverence".

[173] *burn daylight*: delay, waste time.

Romeo. Nay, that's not so.

Mercutio.   I mean, sir, in delay
    We waste our lights[174] in vain—like lights by day.   45
    Take our good meaning, for our judgment sits
    Five times in that[175] ere once in our five wits.[176]

Romeo. And we mean well in going to this mask;[177]
    But 'tis no wit[178] to go.

Mercutio.   Why, may one ask?

Romeo. I dreamt a dream to-night.[179]   50

Mercutio.   And so did I.

Romeo. Well, what was yours?

Mercutio.   That dreamers often lie.

Romeo. In bed asleep, while they do dream things
    true.

Mercutio. O, then I see Queen Mab[180] hath been
    with you.
    She is the fairies' midwife, and she comes
    In shape no bigger than an agate[181] stone   55
    On the fore-finger of an alderman,[182]
    Drawn with a team of little atomies[183]
    Athwart[184] men's noses as they lie asleep;

---

[174] *lights:* (1) torches; (2) mental faculties.

[175] *that:* i.e., our good meaning.

[176] *for our judgment . . . five wits:* since good judgment is found in our common senses five times more than our five senses.

[177] *mask:* masked ball.

[178] *'tis no wit:* it shows no discretion or wisdom.

[179] *to-night:* last night.

[180] *Queen Mab:* fairy queen with influence over people's dreams.

[181] *agate:* small, semiprecious stone.

[182] *alderman:* a co-opted member of an English county or borough council, next in dignity to the mayor.

[183] *atomies:* tiny creatures (as small as atoms).

[184] *Athwart:* crossing over from side to side.

Her waggon-spokes made of long spinners'[185] legs;
The cover, of the wings of grasshoppers;   60
Her traces, of the smallest spider's web;
Her collars, of the moonshine's wat'ry beams;
Her whip, of cricket's bone; the lash, of film;[186]
Her waggoner, a small grey-coated gnat,
Not half so big as a round little worm   65
Prick'd from the lazy finger of a maid.[187]
Her chariot is an empty hazel-nut,
Made by the joiner[188] squirrel or old grub,[189]
Time out o' mind[190] the fairies' coachmakers.
And in this state[191] she gallops night by night   70
Through lovers' brains, and then they dream of
     love;
O'er courtiers' knees, that dream on curtsies
     straight;
O'er lawyers' fingers, who straight dream on
     fees;
O'er ladies' lips, who straight on kisses dream,
Which oft the angry Mab with blisters plagues,   75
Because their breaths with sweetmeats[192] tainted
     are.
Sometime she gallops o'er a courtier's nose,
And then dreams he of smelling out a suit;[193]
And sometime comes she with a tithe-pig's[194] tail,
Tickling a parson's nose as 'a lies asleep,   80

---

[185] *spinners'*: spiders'.
[186] *film*: thin, fine filament.
[187] *worm . . . maid*: It was said that lazy maids had worms in their fingers.
[188] *joiner*: woodworker.
[189] *old grub*: probably a weevil.
[190] *Time out o' mind*: since time immemorial.
[191] *state*: pomp and stately array.
[192] *sweetmeats*: delicacies prepared with sugar.
[193] *smelling out a suit*: i.e., finding someone who will pay him to present a petition to the king.
[194] *tithe pig's*: A tithe pig is the tenth pig (supposed to be given to the parson as part of tithing).

Then dreams he of another benefice.[195]
Sometime she driveth o'er a soldier's neck,
And then dreams he of cutting foreign throats,
Of breaches, ambuscadoes,[196] Spanish blades,[197]
Of healths[198] five fathom deep; and then anon   85
Drums in his ear, at which he starts and wakes,
And, being thus frighted, swears a prayer or
   two,
And sleeps again. This is that very Mab
That plats the manes of horses in the night;
And bakes the elf-locks[199] in foul sluttish hairs,   90
Which once untangled much misfortune bodes.
This is the hag,[200] when maids lie on their backs,
That presses them and learns[201] them first to bear,
Making them women of good carriage.[202]
This is she—   95

Romeo.   Peace, peace, Mercutio, peace!
Thou talk'st of nothing.

Mercutio.   True, I talk of dreams,
Which are the children of an idle brain,
Begot of nothing but vain fantasy;[203]
Which is as thin of substance as the air,
And more inconstant than the wind, who woos   100
Even now the frozen bosom of the north,
And, being anger'd, puffs away from thence,
Turning his side to the dew-dropping south.

---

[195] *benefice*: ecclesial position with income and property, often given as a "gift" by local gentry.
[196] *ambuscadoes*: ambushes.
[197] *Spanish blades*: the most excellent swords.
[198] *healths*: toasts.
[199] *elf-locks*: hair tangled by elves.
[200] *hag*: nightmare or incubus.
[201] *learns*: teaches.
[202] *carriage*: (1) posture; (2) childbearing capacity.
[203] *fantasy*: misleading flight of fancy or imagination.

Benvolio. This wind you talk of blows us from
    ourselves:
    Supper is done, and we shall come too late.   105

Romeo. I fear, too early; for my mind misgives[204]
    Some consequence,[205] yet hanging in the stars,
    Shall bitterly begin his fearful date[206]
    With this night's revels and expire the term
    Of a despised life clos'd in my breast,   110
    By some vile forfeit of untimely death.[207]
    But He that hath the steerage of my course
    Direct my sail! On, lusty gentlemen.

Benvolio. Strike, drum.

> [*They march about the stage. Exeunt.*]

Scene 5. *Capulet's house.*

Enter the Maskers. Servants come forth with napkins.

Servant. Where's Potpan, that he helps not to
    take away? He shift a trencher![208] He scrape a
    trencher!

2 Servant. When good manners shall lie all in
    one or two men's hands, and they unwash'd too,
    'tis a foul thing.   4

Servant. Away with the join-stools,[209] remove the
    court-cubbert,[210] look to the plate. Good thou,

---

[204] *misgives:* doubts, fears.

[205] *consequence:* future event.

[206] *date:* duration (i.e., of the "consequence").

[207] *expire the term . . . untimely death:* The metaphor is of someone lending money while expecting that the borrower will forfeit the debt.

[208] *trencher:* wooden board or plate for carving or serving meat.

[209] *join-stools:* stools constructed by a joiner.

[210] *court-cubbert:* sideboard, often used to display china.

save me a piece of marchpane;[211] and as thou loves
me let the porter let in Susan Grindstone and
Nell. Antony, and Potpan!

2 Servant. Ay, boy, ready.   9

Servant. You are look'd for and call'd for, ask'd
   for and sought for, in the great chamber.

3 Servant. We cannot be here and there too.
   Cheerly, boys! Be brisk a while, and the longer
   liver take all!   [*Servants retire.*]

*Enter Capulet, with all the Guests and Gentlewomen to
the Maskers.*

Capulet. Welcome, gentlemen! Ladies that have
      their toes
   Unplagu'd with corns will have a bout[212] with you.   15
   Ah ha, my mistresses! which of you all
   Will now deny[213] to dance? She that makes dainty,[214]
   She I'll swear hath corns; am I come near ye
      now?[215]
   Welcome, gentlemen! I have seen the day
   That I have worn a visor[216] and could tell
   A whispering tale in a fair lady's ear,   20
   Such as would please. 'Tis gone, 'tis gone, 'tis
      gone!
   You are welcome, gentlemen. Come, musicians,
      play.
   A hall, a hall![217] give room; and foot it, girls.

                              [*Music plays, and they dance.*]

---

[211] *marchpane:* marzipan, a confection made of almonds, sugar, and egg white.
[212] *have a bout:* dance a turn.
[213] *deny:* refuse.
[214] *makes dainty:* hesitates, plays the coquette.
[215] *am I come near ye now?:* Have I come close to the truth?
[216] *visor:* mask.
[217] *A hall, a hall!* He is calling for the floor to be cleared.

More light, you knaves; and turn the tables up,[218]   25
And quench the fire, the room is grown too
    hot.
Ah, sirrah, this unlook'd-for sport[219] comes well.
Nay, sit, nay, sit, good cousin Capulet,
For you and I are past our dancing days.
How long is't now since last yourself and I   30
Were in a mask?

2 Capulet.   By'r Lady, thirty years.

Capulet. What, man? 'tis not so much, 'tis not so
    much.
'Tis since the nuptial of Lucentio,
Come Pentecost[220] as quickly as it will,
Some five and twenty years; and then we
    mask'd.   35

2 Capulet. 'Tis more, 'tis more: his son is elder,
    sir;
His son is thirty.

Capulet.   Will you tell me that?
His son was but a ward[221] two years ago.

Romeo. [*To a servant.*] What lady's that which
    doth enrich the hand
Of yonder knight?   40

Servant. I know not, sir.

Romeo. O, she doth teach the torches to burn
    bright!
It seems she hangs upon the cheek of night

---

[218] *turn the tables up*: I.e., move the tables out of the way to make room for dancing.

[219] *unlook'd-for sport*: unexpected fun.

[220] *Pentecost*: religious feast, seven weeks after Easter, commemorating the descent of the Holy Spirit upon the apostles.

[221] *ward*: minor.

As a rich jewel in an Ethiop's ear—
Beauty too rich for use, for earth too dear! 45
So shows a snowy dove trooping with crows
As yonder lady o'er her fellows shows.
The measure done, I'll watch her place of stand,
And, touching hers, make blessed my rude[222]
 hand.
Did my heart love till now? Forswear it, sight; 50
For I ne'er saw true beauty till this night.

Tybalt. This, by his voice, should be a Montague.
Fetch me my rapier, boy. What, dares the slave
Come hither, cover'd with an antic face,[223]
To fleer[224] and scorn at our solemnity? 55
Now, by the stock and honour of my kin,
To strike him dead I hold it not a sin.

Capulet. Why, how now, kinsman! Wherefore
 storm you so?

Tybalt. Uncle, this is a Montague, our foe;
A villain, that is hither come in spite 60
To scorn at our solemnity this night.

Capulet. Young Romeo, is it?

Tybalt.   'Tis he, that villain Romeo.

Capulet. Content thee, gentle coz, let him alone.
'A[225] bears him like a portly[226] gentleman;
And, to say truth, Verona brags of him 65
To be a virtuous and well-govern'd youth.
I would not for the wealth of all this town
Here in my house do him disparagement.[227]

---

[222] *rude*: rough.
[223] *antic face*: fantastic mask.
[224] *fleer*: jeer, laugh derisively.
[225] *'A*: he.
[226] *portly*: dignified, well-deported.
[227] *disparagement*: disrespect.

Therefore be patient, take no note of him;
It is my will; the which if thou respect,   70
Show a fair presence and put off these frowns,
An ill-beseeming semblance[228] for a feast.

Tybalt. It fits, when such a villain is a guest.
  I'll not endure him.

Capulet.   He shall be endur'd.
  What, goodman[229] boy! I say he shall. Go to;[230]   75
  Am I the master here or you? Go to.
  You'll not endure him! God shall mend my
    soul![231]
  You'll make a mutiny[232] among my guests!
  You will set cock-a-hoop![233] You'll be the man!

Tybalt. Why, uncle, 'tis a shame.

Capulet.   Go to, go to;   80
  You are a saucy boy. Is't so, indeed?
  This trick may chance to scathe[234] you. I know
    what:
  You must contrary me. Marry, 'tis time.—
  Well said, my hearts!—You are a princox;[235] go.
  Be quiet, or—More light, more light!—For
    shame!   85
  I'll make you quiet. What!—Cheerly, my hearts!

Tybalt. Patience perforce[236] with wilful choler[237]
    meeting

---

[228] *ill-beseeming semblance*: inappropriate appearance.
[229] *goodman*: someone below the rank of gentleman.
[230] *Go to*: colloquial exclamation, said impatiently.
[231] *God shall mend my soul*: colloquial exclamation, roughly meaning "indeed".
[232] *mutiny*: disturbance, uproar.
[233] *set cock-a-hoop*: be boastful or conceited (be "cock of the walk").
[234] *scathe*: harm, burn.
[235] *princox*: coxcomb, upstart.
[236] *perforce*: enforced.
[237] *choler*: anger.

Makes my flesh tremble in their different
    greeting.
I will withdraw; but this intrusion shall,
Now seeming sweet, convert to bitt'rest gall.   90

                                        [*Exit.*]

Romeo. [*To Juliet.*] If I profane with my
    unworthiest hand
    This holy shrine,[238] the gentle sin is this:
    My lips, two blushing pilgrims, ready stand
    To smooth that rough touch with a tender kiss.

Juliet. Good pilgrim, you do wrong your hand
    too much,   95
    Which mannerly devotion shows in this;
    For saints have hands that pilgrims' hands do
    touch,
    And palm to palm is holy palmers'[239] kiss.

Romeo. Have not saints lips, and holy palmers
    too?

Juliet. Ay, pilgrim, lips that they must use in
    pray'r.   100

Romeo. O, then, dear saint, let lips do what hands
    do!
    They pray; grant thou, lest faith turn to despair.

Juliet. Saints do not move, though grant for
    prayers' sake.

Romeo. Then move not while my prayer's effect I
    take.
    Thus from my lips by thine my sin is purg'd.   105

                                        [*Kissing her.*]

---

[238] *shrine*: i.e., Juliet's hand.
[239] *palmers'*: A palmer is a pilgrim carrying a palm leaf as a mark of his travels
to the Holy Land (providing the pun of the "palms" of Romeo and Juliet's hands).

Juliet. Then have my lips the sin that they have
　　took.

Romeo. Sin from my lips? O trespass sweetly
　　urg'd!
　Give me my sin again.　　　　　　　　[*Kissing her.*]

Juliet.　　　　　　　　　You kiss by th' book.²⁴⁰

Nurse. Madam, your mother craves a word with
　　you.

Romeo. What is her mother?

Nurse.　　　　　　　　　Marry, bachelor,
　Her mother is the lady of the house,
　And a good lady, and a wise and virtuous.
　I nurs'd her daughter that you talk'd withal.²⁴¹
　I tell you, he that can lay hold of her
　Shall have the chinks.²⁴²　　　　　　　　　　115

Romeo.　　　　　　Is she a Capulet?
　O dear account! my life is my foe's debt.

Benvolio. Away, be gone; the sport is at the best.

Romeo. Ay, so I fear; the more is my unrest.

Capulet. Nay, gentlemen, prepare not to be
　　gone;
　We have a trifling foolish banquet towards.²⁴³　　120
　Is it e'en so?²⁴⁴ Why, then I thank you all;
　I thank you, honest gentlemen; good night.
　More torches here! [*Exeunt Maskers.*] Come on
　　then, let's to bed.

---

²⁴⁰ *kiss by th' book*: i.e., take my words literally to gain more kisses.
²⁴¹ *withal*: with.
²⁴² *the chinks*: plenty of money ("chinking" coins).
²⁴³ *towards*: in preparation.
²⁴⁴ *Is it e'en so?* He notes that the maskers are leaving.

[handwritten margin note: nurse interrup. by telling Juliet mat her mom needs her. 110]

Ah, sirrah, by my fay,[245] it waxes late;
I'll to my rest.   125

[*Exeunt all but Juliet and Nurse.*]

Juliet. Come hither, nurse. What is yond
      gentleman?

Nurse. The son and heir of old Tiberio.

Juliet. What's he that now is going out of door?

Nurse. Marry, that I think be young Petruchio.

Juliet. What's he that follows there, that would
      not dance?   130

Nurse. I know not.

Juliet. Go ask his name.—If he be married,
   My grave is like to be my wedding bed.

Nurse. His name is Romeo, and a Montague;
   The only son of your great enemy.   135

Juliet. My only love sprung from my only hate!
   Too early seen unknown, and known too late!
   Prodigious[246] birth of love it is to me,
   That I must love a loathed enemy.

Nurse. What's this? What's this?

Juliet.   A rhyme I learnt even now
   Of one I danc'd withal.

                    [*One calls within, 'Juliet'.*]

Nurse.   Anon,[247] anon!   141
   Come, let's away; the strangers all are gone.

                                        [*Exeunt.*]

Handwritten annotations:
Juliet asked the nurse to find out Romeo's name and if he is married.
Juliet is still curious. Romeo is a Montague.

---

[245] *by my fay:* by my faith (generic oath).
[246] *Prodigious:* extraordinary, dangerous, of evil portent.
[247] *Anon:* at once.

ACT 2

Prologue.

Enter Chorus.

Now old desire doth in his death-bed lie,
And young affection gapes[1] to be his heir;
That fair[2] for which love groan'd for and would
    die,
With tender Juliet match'd, is now not fair.
Now Romeo is belov'd, and loves again,   5
Alike bewitched[3] by the charm of looks;
But to his foe suppos'd[4] he must complain,[5]
And she steal love's sweet bait from fearful
    hooks.
Being held a foe, he may not have access
To breathe such vows as lovers use[6] to swear;   10
And she as much in love, her means much less
To meet her new beloved any where.
But passion lends them power, time means, to
    meet,
Temp'ring extremities[7] with extreme sweet.[8]

                          [Exit.]

---

[1] *gapes*: is eager.
[2] *That fair*: i.e., Rosaline.
[3] *Alike bewitched*: I.e., both Romeo and Juliet are bewitched.
[4] *foe suppos'd*: i.e., because Juliet is a Capulet.
[5] *complain*: address his lover's suit, lament as a lover.
[6] *use*: are accustomed.
[7] *extremities*: difficulties.
[8] *extreme sweet*: extraordinary delights.

Scene 1. *A lane by the wall of Capulet's orchard.*

Enter Romeo.

Romeo. Can I go forward when my heart is here?
  Turn back, dull earth,[9] and find thy centre out.

[*He climbs the wall and leaps down within it.*]

Enter Benvolio with Mercutio.   Romeo runs forwrn

Benvolio. Romeo! my cousin, Romeo! Romeo!   Benvolio ang
                                                    merecutio

Mercutio.   He is wise,
  And, on my life, hath stol'n him home to bed.

Benvolio. He ran this way, and leapt this
          orchard wall.   5
  Call, good Mercutio.

Mercutio.   Nay, I'll conjure[10] too.
  Romeo! humours! madman! passion! lover!
  Appear thou in the likeness of a sigh;
  Speak but one rhyme and I am satisfied;
  Cry but 'Ay me!' pronounce but 'love' and
          'dove';   10
  Speak to my gossip[11] Venus[12] one fair word,
  One nickname for her purblind[13] son and heir,
  Young Adam Cupid,[14] he that shot so trim
  When King Cophetua lov'd the beggar-maid![15]
  He heareth not, he stirreth not, he moveth not;   15

---

[9] *dull earth*: i.e., his body.

[10] *conjure*: call up a spirit.

[11] *gossip*: crony, close companion.

[12] *Venus*: in classical mythology, the goddess of love.

[13] *purblind*: partially or wholly blind. Although the word is now defined as "partially blind", an archaic meaning was "wholly blind", as in "*pure* (or *purely*) blind". Figuratively, it also means dim-witted, or lacking in insight or understanding, a definition that adds a further disdainful dimension to Mercutio's words.

[14] *Adam Cupid*: the rascally god of love.

[15] *King Cophetua lov'd the beggar-maid*: reference to a sixteenth-century ballad.

The ape is dead,[16] and I must conjure him.
I conjure thee by Rosaline's bright eyes,
By her high forehead and her scarlet lip,
By her fine foot, straight leg, and quivering
thigh,
And the demesnes[17] that there adjacent lie,   20
That in thy likeness thou appear to us.

Benvolio. An[18] if he hear thee, thou wilt anger
him.

Mercutio. This cannot anger him: 'twould anger
him
To raise a spirit in his mistress' circle[19]
Of some strange nature, letting it there stand
Till she had laid it and conjur'd it down;
That were some spite.[20] My invocation
Is fair and honest: in his mistress' name,
I conjure only but to raise up him.

Benvolio. Come, he hath hid himself among
these trees   30
To be consorted[21] with the humorous[22] night:
Blind is his love, and best befits the dark.

Mercutio. If love be blind, love cannot hit the
mark.
Now will he sit under a medlar tree,
And wish his mistress were that kind of fruit   35
As maids call medlars[23] when they laugh alone.

---

[16] *The ape is dead*: I.e., Romeo is playing dead, like a performing ape.

[17] *demesnes*: region, domains.

[18] *An*: And.

[19] *circle*: i.e., circle drawn by a magician to conjure a spirit (potentially with a bawdy second meaning).

[20] *spite*: vexation.

[21] *consorted*: associated.

[22] *humorous*: (1) damp; (2) moody.

[23] *medlars*: small, brown, applelike fruit.

O Romeo, that she were, O that she were
An open et cetera,[24] thou a pop'rin pear![25]
Romeo, good night. I'll to[26] my truckle bed;[27]
This field-bed[28] is too cold for me to sleep.   40
Come, shall we go?

Benvolio.   Go, then; for 'tis in vain   *they give up*
To seek him here that means not to be found.   *and leave*

[*Exeunt.*]

Scene 2. *Capulet's orchard.*

Enter Romeo.

Romeo. He jests at scars that never felt a wound.

Enter Juliet above at a window.

But, soft! What light through yonder window
    breaks?
It is the east, and Juliet is the sun.
Arise, fair sun, and kill the envious moon,[29]
Who is already sick and pale with grief   5
That thou her maid art far more fair than she.
Be not her maid, since she is envious;
Her vestal livery[30] is but sick and green,[31]
And none but fools do wear it; cast it off.
It is my lady; O, it is my love!   10

---

[24] *open et cetera*: is "open-arse" in other texts, a reference to the colloquial name for the medlar fruit. Mercutio's tone is descending to that of crass crudity.

[25] *pop'rin pear*: a pear from Poperinghe in Flanders.

[26] *to*: go to.

[27] *truckle bed*: low bed on wheels.

[28] *field-bed*: i.e., the ground.

[29] *moon*: i.e., the goddess Diana (Diana is the patroness of virgins, so Juliet is her maid).

[30] *vestal livery*: maidenly appearance or apparel.

[31] *green*: (1) jealous; (2) suffering from "greensickness" (anemia particular to virgins).

O that she knew she were!
She speaks, yet she says nothing. What of that?
Her eye discourses; I will answer it.
I am too bold, 'tis not to me she speaks;
Two of the fairest stars in all the heaven,   15
Having some business, do entreat her eyes
To twinkle in their spheres[32] till they return.
What if her eyes were there, they in her head?
The brightness of her cheek would shame
    those stars,
As daylight doth a lamp; her eyes in heaven   20
Would through the airy region stream so
    bright
That birds would sing, and think it were not
    night.
See how she leans her cheek upon her hand!
O that I were a glove upon that hand,   25
That I might touch that cheek!

Juliet.   Ay me!

Romeo.   She speaks.
O, speak again, bright angel, for thou art
As glorious to this night, being o'er my head,
As is a winged messenger of heaven
Unto the white-upturned wond'ring eyes
Of mortals that fall back to gaze on him,   30
When he bestrides the lazy-pacing clouds
And sails upon the bosom of the air.

Juliet. O Romeo, Romeo! wherefore[33] art thou
    Romeo?
Deny thy father and refuse thy name;
Or, if thou wilt not, be but sworn my love,   35
And I'll no longer be a Capulet.

[32] *spheres*: orbits.
[33] *wherefore*: why.

Romeo. [*Aside.*] Shall I hear more, or shall I speak
    at this?

Juliet. 'Tis but thy name that is my enemy;
    Thou art thyself, though[34] not a Montague.
    What's Montague? It is nor hand, nor foot,   40
    Nor arm, nor face, nor any other part
    Belonging to a man. O, be some other name!
    What's in a name? That which we call a rose
    By any other name would smell as sweet;
    So Romeo would, were he not Romeo call'd,   45
    Retain that dear perfection which he owes[35]
    Without that title. Romeo, doff[36] thy name;
    And for thy name, which is no part of thee,
    Take all myself.

Romeo.   I take thee at thy word:
    Call me but love, and I'll be new baptiz'd;   50
    Henceforth I never will be Romeo.

Juliet. What man art thou, that, thus bescreen'd
    in night,
    So stumblest on my counsel?

Romeo.   By a name
    I know not how to tell thee who I am:
    My name, dear saint, is hateful to myself,   55
    Because it is an enemy to thee;
    Had I it written, I would tear the word.

Juliet. My ears have yet not drunk a hundred
    words
    Of thy tongue's uttering, yet I know the sound:
    Art thou not Romeo, and a Montague?   60

Romeo. Neither, fair maid, if either thee dislike.

---

[34] *though*: even if you were.
[35] *owes*: owns.
[36] *doff*: discard.

Juliet. How cam'st thou hither, tell me, and
      wherefore?
   The orchard walls are high and hard to climb;
   And the place death, considering who thou art,
   If any of my kinsmen find thee here.   65

Romeo. With love's light wings did I o'er-perch[37]
      these walls,
   For stony limits cannot hold love out;
   And what love can do, that dares love attempt.
   Therefore thy kinsmen are no stop to me.

Juliet. If they do see thee, they will murder thee.   70

Romeo. Alack, there lies more peril in thine eye
   Than twenty of their swords; look thou but
      sweet,
   And I am proof[38] against their enmity.

Juliet. I would not for the world they saw thee
      here.

Romeo. I have night's cloak to hide me from their
      eyes;   75
   And but[39] thou love me, let them find me here.
   My life were better ended by their hate
   Than death prorogued[40] wanting of thy love.

Juliet. By whose direction found'st thou out this
      place?

Romeo. By love, that first did prompt me to
      enquire;   80
   He lent me counsel, and I lent him eyes.
   I am no pilot; yet, wert thou as far

---

[37] *o'er-perch*: fly over.
[38] *proof*: protected.
[39] *And but*: if only.
[40] *prorogued*: delayed, postponed.

As that vast shore wash'd with the farthest sea,
I should adventure[41] for such merchandise.

Juliet. Thou knowest the mask of night is on my
          face,   85
Else would a maiden blush bepaint my cheek
For that which thou hast heard me speak to-
          night.
Fain would I dwell on form, fain, fain deny
What I have spoke; but farewell compliment![42]
Dost thou love me? I know thou wilt say ay,
And I will take thy word; yet, if thou swear'st,
Thou mayst prove false; at lovers' perjuries
They say Jove[43] laughs. O gentle Romeo,
If thou dost love, pronounce it faithfully.
Or, if thou think'st I am too quickly won,   95
I'll frown, and be perverse,[44] and say thee nay,
So thou wilt woo; but else, not for the world.
In truth, fair Montague, I am too fond;[45]
And therefore thou mayst think my haviour[46]
          light;
But trust me, gentleman, I'll prove more true   100
Than those that have more cunning to be
          strange.[47]
I should have been more strange, I must
          confess,
But that thou overheard'st, ere I was ware,
My true love's passion. Therefore pardon me,
And not impute this yielding to light love,   105
Which the dark night hath so discovered.[48]

---

[41] *adventure*: risk a journey.
[42] *compliment*: courtesy.
[43] *Jove*: in classical mythology, the king of the gods.
[44] *perverse*: contrary.
[45] *fond*: foolishly tender, affectionate.
[46] *haviour*: behavior.
[47] *strange*: aloof, reserved.
[48] *discovered*: revealed.

Romeo. Lady, by yonder blessed moon I vow,
    That tips with silver all these fruit-tree tops—

Juliet. O, swear not by the moon, th' inconstant
    moon,
    That monthly changes in her circled orb,   *110*
    Lest that thy love prove likewise variable.

Romeo. What shall I swear by?

Juliet.   Do not swear at all;
Or, if thou wilt, swear by thy gracious self,
Which is the god of my idolatry,
And I'll believe thee.

Romeo.   If my heart's dear love—   *115*

Juliet. Well, do not swear. Although I joy in
    thee,   *Juliet leaves Romeo*
    I have no joy of this contract to-night: *unsatisfied*
    It is too rash, too unadvis'd, too sudden;
    Too like the lightning, which doth cease to be
    Ere one can say 'It lightens'. Sweet, good night!   *120*
    This bud of love, by summer's ripening breath,
    May prove a beauteous flow'r when next we
        meet.
    Good night, good night! As sweet repose and
        rest
    Come to thy heart as that within my breast!

Romeo. O, wilt thou leave me so unsatisfied?   *125*

Juliet. What satisfaction canst thou have to-
    night?

Romeo. Th' exchange of thy love's faithful vow
    for mine.

Juliet. I gave thee mine before thou didst request
    it;
    And yet I would it were to give again.

Handwritten note: Juliet comes back to confront Romeo about being unintrusive

Romeo. Wouldst thou withdraw it? For what
    purpose, love?

Juliet. But to be frank,[49] and give it thee again.
    And yet I wish but for the thing I have.
    My bounty[50] is as boundless as the sea,
    My love as deep: the more I give to thee,
    The more I have, for both are infinite.   135

                    [*Nurse calls within.*]

    I hear some noise within. Dear love, adieu!—
    Anon, good nurse!—Sweet Montague, be true.
    Stay but a little, I will come again.   [*Exit.*]

Romeo. O blessed, blessed night! I am afeard,
    Being in night, all this is but a dream,   140
    Too flattering-sweet to be substantial.

Re-enter Juliet above.

Juliet. Three words, dear Romeo, and good night
    indeed.
    If that thy bent[51] of love be honourable,
    Thy purpose marriage, send me word
      tomorrow,
    By one that I'll procure to come to thee,   145
    Where and what time thou wilt perform the rite;
    And all my fortunes at thy foot I'll lay,
    And follow thee, my lord, throughout the
      world.

Handwritten note: Juliet leaves for a min to not get caught while Romeo reassures.

Nurse. [*Within.*] Madam!

Juliet. I come anon.—But if thou meanest not
    well,   150
    I do beseech thee—

Nurse. [*Within.*] Madam!

[49] *frank:* generous.
[50] *bounty:* capacity for giving.
[51] *bent:* aim, purpose.

Juliet.   By and by,[52] I come—
  To cease thy suit, and leave me to my grief.
  To-morrow will I send.

Romeo.   So thrive my soul—

Juliet. A thousand times good night!   [*Exit.*]

Romeo. A thousand times the worse, to want thy
    light.   155
  Love goes toward love as school-boys from their
    books;
  But love from love, toward school with heavy
    looks.

Re-enter Juliet above.

[handwritten: mm plan to meet up again at night mi next day]

Juliet. Hist! Romeo, hist!—O for a falc'ner's
    voice,
  To lure this tassel-gentle[53] back again!
  Bondage is hoarse, and may not speak aloud;[54]   160
  Else would I tear the cave where Echo[55] lies,
  And make her airy tongue more hoarse than
    mine
  With repetition of my Romeo's name.
  Romeo!

Romeo. It is my soul that calls upon my name.   165
  How silver-sweet sound lovers' tongues by
    night,
  Like softest music to attending[56] ears!

---

[52] *By and by:* at once, soon.
[53] *tassel-gentle:* gentle male hawk (from the falconry term "tiercel").
[54] *Bondage . . . speak aloud:* I.e., as Juliet is in her father's house, she must whisper when speaking to Romeo.
[55] *Echo:* In classical mythology, the nymph Echo was cursed so that she could not speak freely, but could only repeat the words of others. Her unrequited love for the vain Narcissus made her wander alone until she wasted away into a mere echoing voice.
[56] *attending:* attentive.

Juliet. Romeo!

Romeo.   My dear?

Juliet.   At what o'clock to-morrow
    Shall I send to thee?

Romeo.   By the hour of nine.

Juliet. I will not fail. 'Tis twenty years till then.   170
    I have forgot why I did call thee back.

Romeo. Let me stand here till thou remember it.

Juliet. I shall forget, to have thee still stand
        there,
    Rememb'ring how I love thy company.

Romeo. And I'll still stay, to have thee still forget,   175
    Forgetting any other home but this.

Juliet. 'Tis almost morning. I would have thee
        gone;
    And yet no farther than a wanton's[57] bird,
    That lets it hop a little from her hand,
    Like a poor prisoner in his twisted gyves,[58]   180
    And with a silk thread plucks it back again,
    So loving-jealous of his liberty.

Romeo. I would I were thy bird.

Juliet.   Sweet, so would I.
    Yet I should kill thee with much cherishing.
    Good night, good night! Parting is such sweet
        sorrow   185
    That I shall say good night till it be morrow.[59]

                                                    [*Exit.*]

---

[57] *wanton's*: A wanton is an undisciplined, capricious child.
[58] *gyves*: fetters.
[59] *morrow*: morning.

Romeo. Sleep dwell upon thine eyes, peace in thy
    breast!
    Would I were sleep and peace, so sweet to rest!
    Hence will I to my ghostly father's[60] cell,
    His help to crave and my dear hap[61] to tell.   190

                                              [*Exit.*]

they both depart any Juliet goes to bed after a long night of talking

Scene 3. *Friar Lawrence's cell.*

Enter *Friar Lawrence with a basket.*

Friar Lawrence. The gray-ey'd morn smiles on
    the frowning night,
    Check'ring the eastern clouds with streaks of
    light;

Friar Lawrence is introducing the reader and is picking flowers.

    And fleckel'd[62] darkness like a drunkard reels
    From forth day's path and Titan's fiery wheels.[63]
    Now, ere the sun advance his burning eye   5
    The day to cheer and night's dank dew to dry,
    I must up-fill this osier cage[64] of ours
    With baleful[65] weeds and precious-juiced flowers.
    The earth that's nature's mother is her tomb;
    What is her burying grave, that is her womb.   10
    And from her womb children of divers kind
    We sucking on her natural bosom find;
    Many for many virtues excellent,
    None but for some, and yet all different.
    O, mickle[66] is the powerful grace that lies   15
    In plants, herbs, stones, and their true qualities;

[60] *ghostly father's*: spiritual father's (i.e., confessor's).
[61] *dear hap*: good fortune or news.
[62] *fleckel'd*: spotted.
[63] *Titan's fiery wheels*: in classical mythology, the wheels of the sun's chariot
(the sun was said to be drawn in a chariot across the sky).
[64] *osier cage*: willow basket.
[65] *baleful*: evil or poisonous.
[66] *mickle*: much, great.

For nought so vile that on the earth doth live
But to the earth some special good doth give;
Nor aught so good but, strain'd[67] from that fair
    use,
Revolts from true birth,[68] stumbling on abuse: *20*
Virtue itself turns vice, being misapplied,
And vice sometime's by action dignified.[69]

Enter Romeo.

Within the infant rind[70] of this weak flower
Poison hath residence, and medicine[71] power;
For this, being smelt, with that part cheers each
    part;[72]   *25*
Being tasted, slays all senses with the heart.
Two such opposed kings encamp them still[73]
In man as well as herbs—grace and rude will;
And where the worser is predominant,
Full soon the canker[74] death eats up that plant.   *30*

Romeo. Good morrow, father!   *romeo player*

Friar Lawrence.   Benedicite![75]   *Lawrence*
What early tongue so sweet saluteth me?
Young son, it argues a distempered head[76]
So soon to bid good morrow to thy bed.
Care keeps his watch in every old man's eye,   *35*
And where care lodges sleep will never lie;
But where unbruised youth with unstuff'd[77] brain

[67] *strain'd*: constrained, diverted, sidetracked.
[68] *revolts from true birth*: rebels against its proper purpose.
[69] *dignified*: made worthy.
[70] *infant rind*: tender, young bark.
[71] *medicine*: medicinal.
[72] *cheers each part*: i.e., stimulates or delights every part of the body.
[73] *still*: always.
[74] *canker*: cankerworm.
[75] *Benedicite*: Latin blessing.
[76] *distempered head*: troubled mind.
[77] *unstuff'd*: untroubled.

Doth couch his limbs, there golden sleep doth
  reign.
Therefore thy earliness doth me assure
Thou art uprous'd with some distemp'rature; 40
Or if not so, then here I hit it right—
Our Romeo hath not been in bed to-night.

Romeo. That last is true; the sweeter rest was
  mine.

Friar Lawrence. God pardon sin! Wast thou
  with Rosaline?

Romeo. With Rosaline, my ghostly father? No; 45
  I have forgot that name, and that name's woe.

Friar Lawrence. That's my good son; but where
  hast thou been then?

Romeo. I'll tell thee ere thou ask it me again.
  I have been feasting with mine enemy;
  Where, on a sudden, one hath wounded me   50
  That's by me wounded; both our remedies
  Within thy help and holy physic[78] lies.
  I bear no hatred, blessed man, for, lo,
  My intercession likewise steads[79] my foe.

Friar Lawrence. Be plain, good son, and
  homely in thy drift;[80]   55
  Riddling[81] confession finds but riddling shrift.[82]

Romeo. Then plainly know my heart's dear love
  is set
  On the fair daughter of rich Capulet.
  As mine on hers, so hers is set on mine;

[78] *physic*: medicine or remedy.
[79] *steads*: helps, benefits.
[80] *homely in thy drift*: plain in your speech.
[81] *riddling*: puzzling.
[82] *shrift*: absolution.

[Handwritten margin notes:
Lawrence wonders why Romeo isn't in bed
Lawrence is curious of when Romeo has been he thinks he been w/ Rosaline
Romeo tells Lawrence abt Juliet and how she is a Capulet and that he wants to see her]

And all combin'd,[83] save what thou must combine   60
By holy marriage. When, and where, and how,
We met, we woo'd, and made exchange of vow,
I'll tell thee as we pass; but this I pray,
That thou consent to marry us to-day.

Friar Lawrence. Holy Saint Francis! What a
     change is here!   65
Is Rosaline, that thou didst love so dear,
So soon forsaken? Young men's love, then, lies
Not truly in their hearts, but in their eyes.
Jesu Maria, what a deal of brine[84]
Hath wash'd thy sallow cheeks for Rosaline!
How much salt water thrown away in waste,
To season[85] love, that of it doth not taste!
The sun not yet thy sighs from heaven clears,
Thy old groans yet ring in mine ancient ears;
Lo, here upon thy cheek the stain doth sit   75
Of an old tear that is not wash'd off yet.
If e'er thou wast thyself, and these woes thine,
Thou and these woes were all for Rosaline.
And art thou chang'd? Pronounce this sentence,
     then:
Women may fall, when there's no strength[86] in
     men.   80

Romeo. Thou chid'st me oft for loving Rosaline.

Friar Lawrence. For doting, not for loving,
     pupil mine.

Romeo. And bad'st me bury love.

Friar Lawrence.   Not in a grave
     To lay one in, another out to have.

---

[83] *combin'd*: (1) brought into unity; (2) settled.
[84] *brine*: salt water (i.e., tears).
[85] *season*: (1) preserve; (2) flavor.
[86] *strength*: fortitude, constancy (i.e., moral strength specifically).

Romeo. I pray thee chide me not; her I love now   85
  Doth grace for grace and love for love allow;
  The other did not so.

Friar Lawrence.   O, she knew well
  Thy love did read by rote that could not spell.[87]
  But come, young waverer, come, go with me,
  In one respect I'll thy assistant be;
  For this alliance may so happy prove
  To turn your households' rancour[88] to pure love.

Romeo. O, let us hence; I stand[89] on sudden haste.

Friar Lawrence. Wisely and slow; they stumble
      that run fast.   [*Exeunt.*]

Scene 4. *A street.*

Enter Benvolio and Mercutio.

Mercutio. Where the devil should this Romeo
    be?
  Came he not home to-night?

Benvolio. Not to his father's; I spoke with his
    man.

Mercutio. Why, that same pale hard-hearted
    wench, that Rosaline,
  Torments him so that he will sure run mad.   5

Benvolio. Tybalt, the kinsman to old Capulet,
  Hath sent a letter to his father's house.

Mercutio. A challenge, on my life.

Benvolio. Romeo will answer[90] it.

---

[87] *by rote that could not spell:* by rote memorization only, not with understanding.
[88] *rancour:* bitterness, resentment.
[89] *stand:* insist.
[90] *answer:* accept.

2.4.

Mercutio. Any man that can write may answer a
letter.

Benvolio. Nay, he will answer the letter's
master, how he dares, being dared.

Mercutio. Alas, poor Romeo, he is already dead:
stabb'd with a white wench's black eye; run
through the ear with a love-song; the very pin[91] of
his heart cleft with the blind bow-boy's butt-
shaft.[92] And is he a man to encounter Tybalt?   17

Benvolio. Why, what is Tybalt?

Mercutio. More than Prince of Cats.[93] O, he's the
courageous captain of compliments.[94] He fights as
you sing prick-song:[95] keeps time, distance, and
proportion; he rests his minim rests,[96] one, two,
and the third in your bosom; the very butcher of
a silk button,[97] a duellist, a duellist; a gentleman
of the very first house,[98] of the first and second
cause.[99] Ah, the immortal passado![100] the punto
reverso![101] the hay![102]—   26

Benvolio. The what?

Mercutio. The pox of such antic, lisping,
affecting fantasticoes;[103] these new tuners of

---

[91] *pin:* center (of a target).
[92] *blind bow-boy's butt-shaft:* blunt arrow fired by the blind god of love, Cupid.
[93] *Prince of Cats:* Variants of Tybalt's name were given to a cat in a medieval tale.
[94] *captain of compliments:* master of all the formal courtesies and rules of dueling.
[95] *prick-song:* (1) from a text; (2) with attention to accuracy.
[96] *rests his minim rests:* i.e., pays attention to minor details (minim rests are the shortest rests in musical notation).
[97] *button:* i.e., on his opponent's shirt.
[98] *house:* rank.
[99] *first and second cause:* grounds for offense and for administering a challenge (dueling terms).
[100] *passado:* lunge or forward thrust.
[101] *punto reverso:* backhanded thrust.
[102] *hay:* cry when a thrust goes home (in Italian, *hai*).
[103] *fantasticoes:* fops.

accent!—'By Jesu, a very good blade! a very tall[104]
man! a very good whore!' Why, is not this a
lamentable thing, grandsire, that we should be
thus afflicted with these strange flies, these
fashion-mongers, these pardon me's,[105] who stand
so much on the new form[106] that they cannot sit at
ease on the old bench? O, their bones,[107] their
bones!   35

Enter Romeo.

Benvolio. Here comes Romeo, here comes
  Romeo.

Mercutio. Without his roe,[108] like a dried herring.
  O flesh, flesh, how art thou fishified! Now is he
  for the numbers[109] that Petrarch flow'd in; Laura,[110]
  to his lady, was a kitchen-wench—marry, she
  had a better love to berhyme her; Dido,[111] a
  dowdy;[112] Cleopatra,[113] a gipsy;[114] Helen and Hero,[115]
  hildings[116] and harlots; Thisbe,[117] a gray eye[118] or so,

[104] *tall*: brave.

[105] *pardon me's*: affected people who adopt foreign phrases (*perdona mi* is Italian for "forgive me").

[106] *form*: (1) fashion; (2) bench.

[107] *bones*: pun on the French *bon*, meaning "good".

[108] *Without his roe*: (1) as an exhausted fish that has spawned its eggs (roe); (2) literally emaciated, with his name stripped of "Ro" (leaving only "meo").

[109] *numbers*: metrics, poetry.

[110] *Laura*: the beloved of the Italian poet Petrarch.

[111] *Dido*: in classical mythology, the queen of Carthage, deserted by her lover Aeneas, Prince of Troy.

[112] *dowdy*: drab woman.

[113] *Cleopatra*: Cleopatra VII Thea Philopator (69–30 B.C.), the Egyptian pharaoh central to Shakespeare's *Antony and Cleopatra*.

[114] *gipsy*: deceitful woman (gypsies were commonly believed to be Egyptian).

[115] *Helen and Hero*: In ancient mythology, Helen was the beautiful wife of Menelaus; her affair with Paris was the central cause of the Trojan War. Hero was the beloved of Leander; their romance ended in tragedy.

[116] *hildings*: good-for-nothings.

[117] *Thisbe*: In ancient mythology, Thisbe was the beloved of Pyramus; their romance ended in tragedy.

[118] *gray eye*: i.e., gleam in the eye.

but not to the purpose—Signior Romeo, bon
jour! There's a French salutation to your French
slop.[119] You gave us the counterfeit fairly last
night.   45

Romeo. Good morrow to you both. What
counterfeit did I give you?

Mercutio. The slip,[120] sir, the slip; can you not
conceive?[121]

Romeo. Pardon, good Mercutio; my business was
great, and in such a case as mine a man may
strain courtesy.   50

Mercutio. That's as much as to say, such a case[122]
as yours constrains a man to bow in the hams.

Romeo. Meaning, to curtsy.

Mercutio. Thou hast most kindly hit[123] it.

Romeo. A most courteous exposition.   55

Mercutio. Nay, I am the very pink[124] of courtesy.

Romeo. Pink for flower.

Mercutio. Right.

Romeo. Why, then is my pump[125] well flower'd.   59

Mercutio. Sure wit! Follow me this jest now till
thou hast worn out thy pump, that, when the
single sole of it is worn, the jest may remain,
after the wearing, solely singular.[126]

---

[119] *slop*: loose-fitting breeches.
[120] *slip*: (1) escape; (2) counterfeit coin.
[121] *conceive*: understand.
[122] *case*: (1) situation; (2) physical condition.
[123] *kindly hit*: politely interpreted.
[124] *pink*: perfection.
[125] *pump*: shoe.
[126] *solely singular*: (1) single-soled (i.e., weak); (2) uniquely unique.

Romeo. O single-sol'd jest, solely singular for the
singleness!

Mercutio. Come between us, good Benvolio; my
wits faints.

Romeo. Swits[127] and spurs, swits and spurs; or I'll
cry a match.[128]   68

Mercutio. Nay, if our wits run the wild-goose
chase,[129] I am done; for thou hast more of the wild
goose in one of thy wits than, I am sure, I have
in my whole five. Was I with you there for the
goose?[130]   72

Romeo. Thou wast never with me for anything
when thou wast not there for the goose.[131]

Mercutio. I will bite thee by the ear for that jest.   75

Romeo. Nay, good goose, bite not.[132]

Mercutio. Thy wit is a very bitter sweeting;[133] it is
a most sharp sauce.

Romeo. And is it not then well serv'd in to a sweet
goose?[134]

Mercutio. O, here's a wit of cheveril,[135] that
stretches from an inch narrow to an ell[136] broad!

---

[127] *Swits*: switches.
[128] *cry a match*: claim the victory.
[129] *wild-goose chase*: game where riders follow a lead horse across the countryside.
[130] *goose*: i.e., end of the chase.
[131] *goose*: prostitute.
[132] *good goose, bite not*: proverbial phrase begging mercy.
[133] *sweeting*: variety of sweet apple.
[134] *sweet goose*: tender goose.
[135] *cheveril*: kid leather, easily stretched.
[136] *ell*: unit of measurement (roughly forty-five inches).

Romeo. I stretch it out for that word 'broad',   81
which, added to the goose, proves thee far and
wide a broad[137] goose.   84

Mercutio. Why, is not this better now than
groaning for love? Now art thou sociable, now
art thou Romeo; now art thou what thou art by
art as well as by nature; for this drivelling love is
like a great natural[138] that runs lolling[139] up and
down to hide his bauble[140] in a hole.

Benvolio. Stop there, stop there.

Mercutio. Thou desirest me to stop in my tale
against the hair.[141]

Benvolio. Thou wouldst else have made thy tale
large.[142]

Mercutio. O, thou art deceiv'd: I would have
made it short; for I was come to the whole depth
of my tale, and meant, indeed, to occupy the
argument[143] no longer.   96

Romeo. Here's goodly gear![144]

Enter Nurse and her man, Peter.

Mercutio. A sail, a sail!

Benvolio. Two, two; a shirt and a smock.[145]

Nurse. Peter!   100

---

[137] *broad*: indecent, indelicate, countrified.
[138] *natural*: fool.
[139] *lolling*: with tongue hanging out.
[140] *bauble*: trinket.
[141] *against the hair*: in a rough or disagreeable manner.
[142] *large*: indecent.
[143] *occupy the argument*: discuss or address the matter.
[144] *gear*: stuff.
[145] *a shirt and a smock*: i.e., a man and a woman.

Peter. Anon.

Nurse. My fan, Peter.

[handwritten note: Nurse comes to look for Romeo, by asking Romeo himself.]

Mercutio. Good Peter, to hide her face; for her
fan's the fairer face. 104

Nurse. God ye good morrow, gentlemen.

Mercutio. God ye good den, fair gentlewoman.

Nurse. Is it good den?

Mercutio. 'Tis no less, I tell ye; for the bawdy
hand of the dial is now upon the prick[146] of noon.

Nurse. Out upon you! What a man are you? 110

Romeo. One, gentlewoman, that God hath made
himself to mar.

Nurse. By my troth, it is well said. 'For himself to
mar' quoth 'a![147] Gentlemen, can any of you tell
me where I may find the young Romeo? 115

Romeo. I can tell you; but young Romeo will be
older when you have found him than he was
when you sought him. I am the youngest of that
name, for fault of a worse.[148]

Nurse. You say well. 120

Mercutio. Yea, is the worst well? Very well took,[149]
i' faith;[150] wisely, wisely.

Nurse. If you be he, sir, I desire some confidence
with[151] you. 124

---

[146] *prick*: point (as on a clock).
[147] *quoth 'a*: indeed (literally, "said he").
[148] *for fault of a worse*: parody of "for want of a better".
[149] *took*: taken, understood.
[150] *i' faith*: truly (literally, "in faith").
[151] *some confidence with*: to confide in.

Benvolio. She will indite[152] him to some supper.

Mercutio. A bawd,[153] a bawd, a bawd! So ho![154]

Romeo. What hast thou found?

Mercutio. No hare, sir; unless a hare,[155] sir, in a
lenten pie,[156] that is something stale and hoar[157] ere it
be spent.   [*He walks by them and sings.*]

> An old hare hoar,
> And an old hare hoar,   130
> Is very good meat in Lent;
> But a hare that is hoar
> Is too much for a score,
> When it hoars ere it be spent.   135

Romeo, will you come to your father's? We'll to
dinner thither.

Romeo. I will follow you.

Mercutio. Farewell, ancient lady; farewell,
[*Sings.*] lady, lady, lady.[158]   140

>   [*Exeunt Mercutio and Benvolio.*]

Nurse. I pray you, sir, what saucy merchant was
this that was so full of his ropery?[159]

Romeo. A gentleman, nurse, that loves to hear
himself talk, and will speak more in a minute
than he will stand to in a month.

---

[152] *indite*: invite.
[153] *bawd*: woman who tends a house of ill repute.
[154] *So ho!* hunting cry when the quarry is sighted.
[155] *hare*: prostitute.
[156] *lenten pie*: rabbit pie.
[157] *hoar*: moldy, with a pun on "whore" that becomes more obvious in the following lines.
[158] *lady, lady, lady*: refrain from the ballad "Chaste Susanna".
[159] *ropery*: roguery, rascally talk.

Nurse. An 'a speak anything against me, I'll take
him down, an 'a were lustier than he is, and
twenty such Jacks; and if I cannot, I'll find those
that shall. Scurvy knave! I am none of his flirt-
gills;[160] I am none of his skains-mates.[161] And thou
must stand by too, and suffer every knave to use
me at his pleasure?   151

Peter. I saw no man use you at his pleasure; if I
had, my weapon should quickly have been out, I
warrant you. I dare draw as soon as another
man, if I see occasion in a good quarrel, and the
law on my side.   155

Nurse. Now, afore God, I am so vex'd that every
part about me quivers. Scurvy knave!—Pray
you, sir, a word; and as I told you, my young
lady bid me enquire you out; what she bid me
say I will keep to myself. But first let me tell ye,
if ye should lead her in a fool's paradise,[162] as they
say, it were a very gross kind of behaviour, as
they say; for the gentlewoman is young; and,
therefore, if you should deal double with her,
truly it were an ill thing to be off'red to any
gentlewoman, and very weak[163] dealing.

Romeo. Nurse, commend me to thy lady and
mistress. I protest unto thee—

Nurse. Good heart, and, i' faith, I will tell her as
much. Lord, Lord! she will be a joyful woman.

Romeo. What wilt thou tell her, nurse? Thou dost
not mark me.   171

---

[160] *flirt-gills:* loose or flirtatious women.
[161] *skains-mates:* cutthroat companions.
[162] *lead her in a fool's paradise:* seduce her.
[163] *weak:* unmanly, unscrupulous.

Nurse. I will tell her, sir, that you do protest;
  which, as I take it, is a gentleman-like offer.

Romeo. Bid her devise
  Some means to come to shrift this afternoon;   *175*
  And there she shall at Friar Lawrence' cell
  Be shriv'd and married. Here is for thy pains.

Nurse. No, truly, sir; not a penny.

Romeo. Go to; I say you shall.

Nurse. This afternoon, sir? Well, she shall be
    there.   *180*

Romeo. And stay, good nurse—behind the abbey
    wall
  Within this hour my man shall be with thee,
  And bring thee cords made like a tackled stair;[164]
  Which to the high top-gallant[165] of my joy
  Must be my convoy[166] in the secret night.   *185*
  Farewell; be trusty, and I'll quit[167] thy pains.
  Farewell; commend me to thy mistress.

Nurse. Now God in heaven bless thee!—
    Hark you, sir.

Romeo. What say'st thou, my dear nurse?

Nurse. Is your man secret? Did you ne'er hear say   *190*
  Two may keep counsel, putting one away?

Romeo. I warrant thee my man's as true as steel.

Nurse. Well, sir. My mistress is the sweetest lady
  —Lord, Lord! when 'twas a little prating thing!
  O, there is a nobleman in town, one Paris, that

---

[164] *tackled stair*: rope ladder.
[165] *top-gallant*: summit (the top-gallant mast and sail appear above the topmast of a ship).
[166] *convoy*: conveyance.
[167] *quit*: reward.

would fain lay knife aboard;[168] but she, good soul,
had as lief[169] see a toad, a very toad, as see him. I
anger her sometimes, and tell her that Paris is
the properer man; but, I'll warrant you, when I
say so she looks as pale as any clout[170] in the versal[171]
world. Doth not rosemary[172] and Romeo begin
both with a letter?   201

Romeo. Ay, nurse; what of that? Both with an R.

Nurse. Ah, mocker! that's the dog's name.[173] R is for
the—no, I know it begins with some other
letter. And she hath the prettiest sententious[174] of
it, of you and rosemary, that it would do you
good to hear it.

Romeo. Commend me to thy lady.   207

Nurse. Ay, a thousand times.—Peter!

Peter. Anon.

Nurse. [*Handing him her fan.*] Before and apace.

                                                    [*Exeunt.*]

Scene 5. *Capulet's orchard.*

Enter Juliet.

Juliet. The clock struck nine when I did send the
    nurse;
In half an hour she promis'd to return.

---

[168] *lay knife aboard*: lay claim to (Juliet).
[169] *had as lief*: would rather or would prefer.
[170] *clout*: cloth, piece of clothing.
[171] *versal*: whole, entire.
[172] *rosemary*: an herb given as a token of remembrance between lovers and
for the dead. The connection with Romeo is, therefore, portentous.
[173] *that's the dog's name*: The R sound sounds like the growl of a dog.
[174] *sententious*: sentences, pithy sayings.

Perchance she cannot meet him—that's not so.
O, she is lame! Love's heralds should be
    thoughts,
Which ten times faster glide than the sun's
    beams
Driving back shadows over louring hills;
Therefore do nimble-pinion'd[175] doves draw Love,
And therefore hath the wind-swift Cupid wings.
Now is the sun upon the highmost hill
Of this day's journey; and from nine till twelve   10
Is three long hours, yet she is not come.
Had she affections and warm youthful blood,
She would be as swift in motion as a ball;
My words would bandy[176] her to my sweet love,
And his to me.   15
But old folks—many feign as[177] they were dead;
Unwieldy, slow, heavy, and pale as lead.

Enter Nurse and Peter.

O God, she comes! O honey nurse, what news?
Hast thou met with him? Send thy man away.

Nurse. Peter, stay at the gate.   [*Exit Peter.*]   20

Juliet. Now, good sweet nurse—O Lord, why
    look'st thou sad?
Though news be sad, yet tell them merrily;
If good, thou shamest the music of sweet news
By playing it to me with so sour a face.

Nurse. I am aweary, give me leave a while;   25
Fie, how my bones ache! What a jaunce[178] have I
    had!

---

[175] *nimble-pinion'd*: swift-winged.
[176] *bandy*: speed (toss back and forth).
[177] *feign as*: pretend as if.
[178] *jaunce*: jaunt, fatiguing walk.

Juliet. I would thou hadst my bones and I thy
    news.
  Nay, come, I pray thee speak; good, good nurse,
    speak.

Nurse. Jesu, what haste? Can you not stay[179] a
    while?
  Do you not see that I am out of breath?

Juliet. How art thou out of breath, when thou
    hast breath
  To say to me that thou art out of breath?
  The excuse that thou dost make in this delay
  Is longer than the tale thou dost excuse.
  Is thy news good or bad? Answer to that;   35
  Say either, and I'll stay the circumstance.[180]
  Let me be satisfied, is't good or bad?

Nurse. Well, you have made a simple[181] choice; you
  know not how to choose a man. Romeo! no, not
  he; though his face be better than any man's, yet
  his leg excels all men's; and for a hand, and a
  foot, and a body, though they be not to be talk'd
  on, yet they are past compare. He is not the
  flower of courtesy, but I'll warrant him as gentle
  as a lamb. Go thy ways, wench; serve God.
  What, have you din'd at home?

Juliet. No, no. But all this did I know before.   46
  What says he of our marriage? What of that?

Nurse. Lord, how my head aches! What a head
    have I!
  It beats as it would fall in twenty pieces.
  My back a[182] t' other side—ah, my back, my back!   50

---

[179] *stay*: wait.
[180] *stay the circumstance*: wait for the details.
[181] *simple*: foolish.
[182] *a*: on.

Handwritten notes: Nurse trys to distract Juliet cause she doesnt want to answer

Beshrew[183] your heart for sending me about
To catch my death with jaunving up and down!

Juliet. I' faith, I am sorry that thou art not well.
Sweet, sweet, sweet nurse, tell me, what says my
love?   54

Nurse. Your love says like an honest gentleman,
and a courteous, and a kind, and a handsome,
and, I warrant, a virtuous—Where is your
mother?

Handwritten notes: Nurse beigns to tell Juliet but then distracts her again asking where her mother is

Juliet. Where is my mother! Why, she is within;
Where should she be? How oddly thou repliest!
'Your love says like an honest gentleman,
Where is your mother?'   60

Nurse.   O God's lady dear!
Are you so hot?[184] Marry, come up, I trow;[185]
Is this the poultice for my aching bones?
Henceforward, do your messages yourself.

Juliet. Here's such a coil![186] Come, what says
Romeo?   65

Nurse. Have you got leave to go to shrift[187] to-day?

Juliet. I have.

Nurse. Then hie you hence to Friar Lawrence'
cell;
There stays a husband to make you a wife.
Now comes the wanton blood up in your
cheeks;
They'll be in scarlet straight[188] at any news.
Hie you to church; I must another way,

Handwritten notes: Nurse finally tells Juliet that Romeo wants to make her his wife then they are both excited.

---

[183] *Beshrew*: generic oath (literally, "curse").
[184] *hot*: angry.
[185] *I trow*: indeed.
[186] *coil*: commotion, disturbance.
[187] *shrift*: confession.
[188] *straight*: straightway, directly.

To fetch a ladder, by the which your love
Must climb a bird's nest soon when it is dark.
I am the drudge,[189] and toil in your delight;   75
But you shall bear the burden soon at night.
Go; I'll to dinner; hie you to the cell.

Juliet. Hie to high fortune! Honest nurse,
    farewell.   [*Exeunt.*]

Scene 6. *Friar Lawrence's cell.*

Enter Friar Lawrence and Romeo.

Friar Lawrence. So smile the heavens upon this
    holy act
That after-hours with sorrow chide us not!

Romeo. Amen, amen! But come what sorrow can,
It cannot countervail[190] the exchange of joy
That one short minute gives me in her sight.   5
Do thou but close our hands with holy words,
Then love-devouring death do what he dare;
It is enough I may but call her mine.

Friar Lawrence. These violent delights have
    violent ends,
And in their triumph die; like fire and powder,   10
Which, as thy kiss, consume. The sweetest
    honey
Is loathsome in his own deliciousness,
And in the taste confounds the appetite.
Therefore love moderately: long love doth so;
Too swift arrives as tardy as too slow.   15

Enter Juliet.

---

[189] *drudge:* person doing menial labor.
[190] *countervail:* equal, match.

Here comes the lady. O, so light a foot
Will ne'er wear out the everlasting flint.[191]
A lover may bestride the gossamer[192]
That idles in the wanton[193] summer air
And yet not fall, so light is vanity.[194]

Juliet. Good even to my ghostly confessor.

Friar Lawrence. Romeo shall thank thee,
  daughter, for us both.

Juliet. As much to him,[195] else is his thanks too
  much.

Romeo. Ah, Juliet, if the measure of thy joy
Be heap'd like mine, and that thy skill be more
To blazon[196] it, then sweeten with thy breath
This neighbour air, and let rich music's tongue
Unfold the imagin'd happiness that both
Receive in either by this dear encounter.

Juliet. Conceit, more rich in matter than in
  words,   30
Brags of his substance, not of ornament.[197]
They are but beggars that can count their worth;
But my true love is grown to such excess
I cannot sum up sum of half my wealth.

Friar Lawrence. Come, come with me, and we
  will make short work;   35
For, by your leaves, you shall not stay alone
Till holy church incorporate two in one.

[*Exeunt.*]

---

[191] *so light . . . everlasting flint:* I.e., Juliet's footsteps are so light that they are lighter than waterdrops, which can wear away stones.

[192] *gossamer:* cobweb.

[193] *wanton:* capricious.

[194] *vanity:* transitory earthly pleasure.

[195] *As much to him:* I.e., Juliet gives the same greeting to Romeo.

[196] *blazon:* declare, set forth, celebrate.

[197] *Conceit . . . not of ornament:* I.e., true understanding has its own substantial depth; it is not made up of merely superficial words.

ACT 3

Scene 1. *A public place.*

Enter Mercutio, Benvolio, Page, and Servants.

Benvolio. I pray thee, good Mercutio, let's retire.
    The day is hot, the Capulets abroad,
    And if we meet we shall not scape a brawl;
    For now, these hot days, is the mad blood
      stirring.

Mercutio. Thou art like one of these fellows   5
    that, when he enters the confines of a tavern,
    claps me his sword upon the table, and says
    'God send me no need of thee!' and by the
    operation of the second cup[1] draws him on the
    drawer,[2] when, indeed, there is no need.

Benvolio. Am I like such a fellow?   10

Mercutio. Come, come, thou art as hot a Jack in
    thy mood as any in Italy; and as soon moved to
    be moody,[3] and as soon moody to be moved.[4]

Benvolio. And what to?   14

Mercutio. Nay, an there were two such, we
    should have none shortly, for one would kill the
    other. Thou! why, thou wilt quarrel with a man
    that hath a hair more or a hair less in his beard
    than thou hast. Thou wilt quarrel with a man for
    cracking nuts, having no other reason but
    because thou hast hazel eyes. What eye but such

---

[1] *by the operation . . . cup*: by the time the second cup of alcohol has its effect.
[2] *draws him on the drawer*: draws his sword on the waiter who is serving him in the tavern.
[3] *moody*: angry, annoyed.
[4] *moody to be moved*: quick-tempered, ready for a quarrel.

an eye would spy out such a quarrel? Thy head
is as full of quarrels as an egg is full of meat; and
yet thy head hath been beaten as addle[5] as an egg
for quarrelling. Thou hast quarrell'd with a man
for coughing in the street, because he hath
wakened thy dog that hath lain asleep in the
sun. Didst thou not fall out with a tailor for
wearing his new doublet[6] before Easter? With
another for tying his new shoes with old riband?[7]
And yet thou wilt tutor me from quarrelling![8]   29

Benvolio. An I were so apt to quarrel as thou art,
any man should buy the fee simple[9] of my life for
an hour and a quarter.

Mercutio. The fee simple! O simple![10]

Enter Tybalt and Others.

Benvolio. By my head, here comes the Capulets.

Mercutio. By my heel, I care not.   35

Tybalt. Follow me close, for I will speak to them.
Gentlemen, good den; a word with one of you.

Mercutio. And but one word with one of us?
Couple it with something; make it a word and a
blow.

Tybalt. You shall find me apt enough to that, sir,
an you will give me occasion.   41

Mercutio. Could you not take some occasion
without giving?

Tybalt. Mercutio, thou consortest with Romeo.

---

[5] *addle*: muddled, scrambled, perhaps also rotten.
[6] *doublet*: close-fitting sleeveless jacket.
[7] *riband*: ribbon.
[8] *tutor me from quarrelling*: teach me how to keep from quarreling.
[9] *fee simple*: absolute possession, form of freehold ownership.
[10] *simple*: stupid, feeble, or foolish.

Mercutio. Consort!¹¹ What, dost thou make us
   minstrels? An thou make minstrels of us, look
   to hear nothing but discords. Here's my
   fiddlestick;¹² here's that shall make you dance.
   Zounds,¹³ consort!   47

Benvolio. We talk here in the public haunt of
    men;
   Either withdraw unto some private place,
   Or reason coldly of your grievances,   50
   Or else depart; here all eyes gaze on us.

Mercutio. Men's eyes were made to look, and let
    them gaze;
   I will not budge for no man's pleasure, I.

Enter Romeo.

Tybalt. Well, peace be with you, sir. Here comes
    my man.¹⁴

Mercutio. But I'll be hang'd, sir, if he wear your
    livery.¹⁵   55
   Marry, go before to field,¹⁶ he'll be your follower;
   Your worship in that sense may call him man.

Tybalt. Romeo, the love I bear thee can afford
   No better term than this: thou art a villain.¹⁷

Romeo. Tybalt, the reason that I have to love thee   60
   Doth much excuse the appertaining¹⁸ rage
   To such a greeting. Villain am I none;
   Therefore, farewell; I see thou knowest me not.

---

¹¹ *Consort:* (1) keep company; (2) a company of musicians.

¹² *fiddlestick:* bow for a fiddle (here, referring to his sword).

¹³ *Zounds:* vague oath (literally, an abbreviation of "by God's wounds").

¹⁴ *man:* i.e., rightful opponent (taken by Mercutio to mean "manservant").

¹⁵ *livery:* distinctive clothes, denoting a servant's allegiance to his master.

¹⁶ *field:* field for dueling.

¹⁷ *villain:* low fellow.

¹⁸ *appertaining:* appropriate or proper to.

Tybalt. Boy, this shall not excuse the injuries
 That thou hast done me; therefore turn and
  draw.   65

Romeo. I do protest I never injur'd thee,
 But love thee better than thou canst devise[19]
 Till thou shalt know the reason of my love;
 And so, good Capulet—which name I tender[20]
 As dearly as mine own—be satisfied. 70

Mercutio. O calm, dishonourable, vile
  submission!
 Alla stoccata[21] carries it away. [*Draws.*]

 Tybalt, you rat-catcher, will you walk?[22]

Tybalt. What wouldst thou have with me?

Mercutio. Good King of Cats, nothing but one
 of your nine lives; that I mean to make bold
 withal, and, as you shall use me hereafter, dry-
 beat[23] the rest of the eight. Will you pluck your
 sword out of his pilcher[24] by the ears? Make
 haste, lest mine be about your ears ere it be out. 79

Tybalt. I am for you.   [*Draws.*]

Romeo. Gentle Mercutio, put thy rapier up.

Mercutio. Come, sir, your passado.[25] [*They fight.*]

Romeo. Draw, Benvolio; beat down their
  weapons.
 Gentlemen, for shame, forbear this outrage!
 Tybalt! Mercutio! the Prince expressly hath 85

---

[19] *devise*: imagine.
[20] *tender*: value.
[21] *Alla stoccata*: at the thrust (fencing term, used here as a name for Tybalt).
[22] *walk*: step aside (to fight).
[23] *dry-beat*: beat severely, thrash.
[24] *pilcher*: scabbard.
[25] *passado*: lunge.

Forbid this bandying[26] in Verona streets.
Hold, Tybalt! Good Mercutio!

[*Tybalt under Romeo's arm thrusts Mercutio in, and flies
with his friends.*]

Mercutio.   I am hurt.
A plague a[27] both your houses! I am sped.[28]
Is he gone and hath nothing?

Benvolio.   What, art thou hurt?

Mercutio. Ay, ay, a scratch, a scratch; marry, 'tis
    enough.   90
Where is my page? Go, villain, fetch a surgeon.

                                        [*Exit Page.*]
Romeo. Courage, man; the hurt cannot be much.   92

Mercutio. No, 'tis not so deep as a well, nor so
    wide as a church door, but 'tis enough, 'twill
    serve. Ask for me to-morrow, and you shall find
    me a grave[29] man. I am peppered,[30] I warrant, for
    this world. A plague a both your houses!
    Zounds, a dog, a rat, a mouse, a cat, to scratch a
    man to death! A braggart, a rogue, a villain, that
    fights by the book of arithmetic![31] Why the devil
    came you between us? I was hurt under your
    arm.   100

Romeo. I thought all for the best.

Mercutio. Help me into some house, Benvolio,
    or I shall faint.
A plague a both your houses!

---

[26] *bandying*: exchange (of insults and provocations).
[27] *a*: on.
[28] *sped*: wounded, done for.
[29] *grave*: (1) serious; (2) ready for the grave.
[30] *peppered*: overseasoned (ready for death).
[31] *by the book of arithmetic*: by formal rules.

They have made worms' meat of me.   104
I have it,[32] and soundly too—Your houses!

[*Exeunt Mercutio and Benvolio.*]

Romeo. This gentleman, the Prince's near ally,[33]
My very[34] friend, hath got this mortal hurt
In my behalf; my reputation stain'd
With Tybalt's slander—Tybalt, that an hour
Hath been my cousin. O sweet Juliet,   110
Thy beauty hath made me effeminate,
And in my temper soft'ned valour's steel![35]

Re-enter Benvolio.

Benvolio. O Romeo, Romeo, brave Mercutio is
    dead!
That gallant spirit hath aspir'd[36] the clouds,
Which too untimely here did scorn the earth.   115

Romeo. This day's black fate on moe[37] days doth
    depend;[38]
This but begins the woe others must end.

Re-enter Tybalt.

Benvolio. Here comes the furious Tybalt back
    again.

Romeo. Alive in triumph and Mercutio slain!
Away to heaven respective lenity,[39]   120
And fire-ey'd fury be my conduct[40] now!
Now, Tybalt, take the 'villain' back again

---

[32] *I have it*: I.e., I have had it; I am finished.
[33] *ally*: kinsman.
[34] *very*: true.
[35] *in my temper . . . steel*: softened my steel-like, valorous side.
[36] *aspir'd*: i.e., aspired to reach.
[37] *moe*: more.
[38] *depend*: hang over.
[39] *respective lenity*: discriminating mercy.
[40] *conduct*: guide.

That late thou gav'st me; for Mercutio's soul
Is but a little way above our heads,
Staying for thine to keep him company.   125
Either thou or I, or both, must go with him.

Tybalt. Thou, wretched boy, that didst consort
        him here,
Shalt with him hence.

Romeo.   This shall determine that.

                        [*They fight; Tybalt falls.*]

Benvolio. Romeo, away, be gone.
The citizens are up, and Tybalt slain.   130
Stand not amaz'd. The Prince will doom thee
        death
If thou art taken. Hence, be gone, away!

Romeo. O, I am fortune's fool![41]

Benvolio.   Why dost thou stay?

                        [*Exit Romeo.*]

Enter Citizens.

1 Citizen. Which way ran he that kill'd
        Mercutio?
Tybalt, that murderer, which way ran he?   135

Benvolio. There lies that Tybalt.

1 Citizen.   Up, sir, go with me;
I charge thee in the Prince's name, obey.

*Enter Prince, attended; Montague, Capulet, their Wives,
and All.*

Prince. Where are the vile beginners of this fray?

---

[41] *fool:* plaything, dupe.

Benvolio. O noble Prince, I can discover[42] all
   The unlucky manage[43] of this fatal brawl:
   There lies the man, slain by young Romeo,   *140*
   That slew thy kinsman, brave Mercutio.

Lady Capulet. Tybalt, my cousin! O my
     brother's child!
   O Prince! O husband! O, the blood is spill'd
   Of my dear kinsman! Prince, as thou art true,   *145*
   For blood of ours shed blood of Montague.
   O cousin, cousin!

Prince. Benvolio, who began this bloody fray?

Benvolio. Tybalt, here slain, whom Romeo's
     hand did slay;
   Romeo that spoke him fair, bid him bethink   *150*
   How nice[44] the quarrel was, and urg'd[45] withal
   Your high displeasure. All this, uttered
   With gentle breath, calm look, knees humbly
     bow'd,
   Could not take truce with the unruly spleen[46]
   Of Tybalt, deaf to peace, but that he tilts[47]   *155*
   With piercing steel at bold Mercutio's breast;
   Who, all as hot, turns deadly point to point,
   And, with a martial scorn, with one hand beats
   Cold death aside, and with the other sends
   It back to Tybalt, whose dexterity   *160*
   Retorts it. Romeo he cries aloud
   'Hold, friends! friends, part!' and, swifter than
     his tongue,
   His agile arm beats down their fatal points,

---

[42] *discover*: reveal.
[43] *manage*: course, management.
[44] *nice*: trivial.
[45] *urg'd*: mentioned.
[46] *spleen*: anger, ill nature.
[47] *tilts*: thrusts.

And 'twixt them rushes; underneath whose arm
An envious[48] thrust from Tybalt hit the life   165
Of stout Mercutio; and then Tybalt fled;
But by and by comes back to Romeo,
Who had but newly entertain'd[49] revenge,
And to't they go like lightning; for ere I
Could draw to part them was stout Tybalt slain;   170
And as he fell did Romeo turn and fly.
This is the truth, or let Benvolio die.

Lady Capulet. He is a kinsman to the Montague,
Affection makes him false, he speaks not true;
Some twenty of them fought in this black strife,   175
And all those twenty could but kill one life.
I beg for justice, which thou, Prince, must give:
Romeo slew Tybalt, Romeo must not live.

Prince. Romeo slew him; he slew Mercutio.
Who now the price of his dear blood doth owe?   180

Montague. Not Romeo, Prince; he was
    Mercutio's friend;
His fault concludes but what the law should
    end,
The life of Tybalt.

Prince.   And for that offence,
Immediately we do exile him hence.
I have an interest in your hate's proceeding,   185
My blood[50] for your rude brawls doth lie
    a-bleeding;
But I'll amerce[51] you with so strong a fine
That you shall all repent the loss of mine.
I will be deaf to pleading and excuses,

[48] *envious*: spiteful, full of enmity.
[49] *entertain'd*: contemplated, considered.
[50] *My blood*: i.e., his kinsman Mercutio.
[51] *amerce*: punish monetarily.

Nor tears nor prayers shall purchase out abuses;   190
Therefore use none. Let Romeo hence in haste,
Else when he is found that hour is his last.
Bear hence this body, and attend our will:⁵²
Mercy but murders, pardoning those that kill.

[*Exeunt.*]

Scene 2. *Capulet's orchard.*

Enter Juliet.

Juliet. Gallop apace, you fiery-footed steeds⁵³
Towards Phoebus' lodging;⁵⁴ such a waggoner⁵⁵
As Phaethon⁵⁶ would whip you to the west,
And bring in cloudy night immediately.
Spread thy close curtain, love-performing night,   5
That runaways'⁵⁷ eyes may wink,⁵⁸ and Romeo
Leap to these arms, untalk'd of and unseen.
Lovers can see to do their amorous rites
By their own beauties; or if love be blind,
It best agrees with night. Come, civil night,   10
Thou sober-suited matron, all in black,
And learn me how to lose a winning match,
Play'd for a pair of stainless maidenhoods;
Hood⁵⁹ my unmann'd⁶⁰ blood, bating⁶¹ in my cheeks,

---

⁵² *attend our will*: respect my decision (using the royal plural).

⁵³ *fiery-footed steeds*: horses who draw the chariot of the sun god.

⁵⁴ *Towards Phoebus' lodging*: i.e., beneath the horizon.

⁵⁵ *waggoner*: driver (as of a wagon).

⁵⁶ *Phaethon*: in classical mythology, Phoebus' son, who tended the horses that drew the sun chariot. One day Phaethon drove the horses himself, with tragic results.

⁵⁷ *runaways'*: i.e., referring to the horses.

⁵⁸ *wink*: close.

⁵⁹ *Hood*: cover with a hood (falconry term).

⁶⁰ *unmann'd*: (1) untamed; (2) husbandless.

⁶¹ *bating*: fluttering.

With thy black mantle, till strange[62] love, grown
    bold,   15
Think true love acted simple modesty.
Come, night; come, Romeo; come, thou day in
    night;
For thou wilt lie upon the wings of night
Whiter than new snow on a raven's back.
Come, gentle night, come, loving black-brow'd
    night,   20
Give me my Romeo; and, when he shall die,
Take him and cut him out in little stars,
And he will make the face of heaven so fine
That all the world will be in love with night,
And pay no worship to the garish sun.   25
O, I have bought the mansion of a love,
But not possess'd it; and though I am sold,
Not yet enjoy'd. So tedious is this day
As is the night before some festival
To an impatient child that hath new robes,   30
And may not wear them. O, here comes my
    nurse,

Enter Nurse with cords.[63]

And she brings news; and every tongue that
    speaks
But Romeo's name speaks heavenly eloquence.
Now, nurse, what news? What hast thou
    there? The cords
That Romeo bid thee fetch?

Nurse.   Ay, ay, the cords.   35

                           [Throws them down.]

Juliet. Ay, me! what news? Why dost thou wring
    thy hands?

---

[62] *strange*: unfamiliar.
[63] *cords*: rope ladder.

Nurse. Ah, well-a-day![64] he's dead, he's dead, he's
    dead.
  We are undone, lady, we are undone.
  Alack the day! he's gone, he's kill'd, he's dead.

Juliet. Can heaven be so envious?

Nurse.   Romeo can,   40
  Though heaven cannot. O Romeo, Romeo!
  Who ever would have thought it? Romeo!

Juliet. What devil art thou that dost torment me
    thus?
  This torture should be roar'd in dismal hell.
  Hath Romeo slain himself? Say thou but 'Ay',   45
  And that bare vowel I shall poison more
  Than the death-darting eye of cockatrice.[65]
  I am not I if there be such an 'I';
  Or those eyes shut that makes thee answer 'I'.
  If he be slain, say 'I'; or if not, 'No';   50
  Brief sounds determine of my weal[66] or woe.

Nurse. I saw the wound, I saw it with mine eyes—
  God save the mark![67]—here on his manly breast.
  A piteous corse,[68] a bloody piteous corse;
  Pale, pale as ashes, all bedaub'd in blood,   55
  All in gore-blood. I swounded[69] at the sight.

Juliet. O, break, my heart! poor bankrupt, break
    at once!
  To prison, eyes; ne'er look on liberty.
  Vile earth,[70] to earth resign;[71] end motion here;
  And thou and Romeo press one heavy bier!   60

[64] *well-a-day*: alas.
[65] *cockatrice*: mythical creature like a basilisk (fabled to kill by its glance).
[66] *weal*: happiness.
[67] *God save the mark*: colloquial expression of distress, perhaps to avert a bad omen.
[68] *corse*: corpse.
[69] *swounded*: swooned.
[70] *Vile earth*: i.e., her own body.
[71] *resign*: resign yourself, return.

Nurse. O Tybalt, Tybalt, the best friend I had!
　　O courteous Tybalt! honest gentleman!
　　That ever I should live to see thee dead!

Juliet. What storm is this that blows so contrary?
　　Is Romeo slaught'red, and is Tybalt dead?　　　　65
　　My dearest cousin and my dearer lord?
　　Then, dreadful trumpet, sound the general
　　　　doom;[72]
　　For who is living if those two are gone?

Nurse. Tybalt is gone, and Romeo banished;
　　Romeo that kill'd him, he is banished.　　　　70

Juliet. O God! Did Romeo's hand shed Tybalt's
　　blood?

Nurse. It did, it did; alas the day, it did!

Juliet. O serpent heart, hid with a flow'ring face!
　　Did ever dragon keep so fair a cave?
　　Beautiful tyrant! fiend angelical!　　　　75
　　Dove-feather'd raven! wolfish-ravening lamb!
　　Despised substance of divinest show!
　　Just opposite to what thou justly seem'st,
　　A damned saint, an honourable villain!
　　O nature, what hadst thou to do in hell,　　　　80
　　When thou didst bower the spirit of a fiend
　　In mortal paradise of such sweet flesh?
　　Was ever book containing such vile matter
　　So fairly bound? O, that deceit should dwell
　　In such a gorgeous palace!

Nurse.　　　　　　　　　There's no trust,　　　85
　　No faith, no honesty in men; all perjur'd,
　　All forsworn, all naught,[73] all dissemblers.

---

[72] *dreadful trumpet . . . doom:* A trumpet will sound on the Day of Judgment
(when the general judgment will take place).

[73] *all naught:* all nought, all as nothing, worthless, useless.

Ah, where's my man? Give me some aqua vitae.[74]
These griefs, these woes, these sorrows, make
   me old.
Shame come to Romeo!

Juliet.   Blister'd be thy tongue   90
   For such a wish! He was not born to shame:
   Upon his brow shame is asham'd to sit;
   For 'tis a throne where honour may be crown'd
   Sole monarch of the universal earth.
   O, what a beast was I to chide at him!   95

Nurse. Will you speak well of him that kill'd your
   cousin?

Juliet. Shall I speak ill of him that is my
   husband?
   Ah, poor my lord, what tongue shall smooth thy
   name,
   When I, thy three-hours wife, have mangled
   it?
   But wherefore, villain, didst thou kill my
   cousin?   100
   That villain cousin would have kill'd my
   husband.
   Back, foolish tears, back to your native spring;
   —Your tributary drops belong to woe,
   Which you, mistaking, offer up to joy.
   My husband lives that Tybalt would have slain,   105
   And Tybalt's dead that would have slain my
   husband.
   All this is comfort; wherefore weep I then?
   Some word there was, worser than Tybalt's
   death,
   That murd'red me; I would forget it fain,   110
   But, O, it presses to my memory

---

[74] *aqua vitae*: alcoholic spirits.

Like damned guilty deeds to sinners' minds:
'Tybalt is dead, and Romeo banished'.
That 'banished', that one word 'banished'
Hath slain ten thousand Tybalts. Tybalt's death
Was woe enough, if it had ended there;   *115*
Or if sour woe delights in fellowship
And needly will be rank'd with[75] other griefs,
Why followed not, when she said 'Tybalt's
   dead',
Thy father or thy mother, nay, or both,
Which modern[76] lamentation might have mov'd?   *120*
But, with a rear-ward[77] following Tybalt's death,
'Romeo is banished'—to speak that word
Is father, mother, Tybalt, Romeo, Juliet,
All slain, all dead. 'Romeo is banished'—
There is no end, no limit, measure, bound,   *125*
In that word's death; no words can that woe
   sound.
Where is my father and my mother, nurse?

Nurse. Weeping and wailing over Tybalt's corse.
   Will you go to them? I will bring you thither.

Juliet. Wash they his wounds with tears!
   Mine shall be spent,   *130*
When theirs are dry, for Romeo's banishment.
Take up those cords. Poor ropes, you are
   beguil'd,
Both you and I, for Romeo is exil'd;
He made you for a highway to my bed,
But I, a maid, die maiden-widowed.   *135*
Come, cords; come, nurse; I'll to my wedding-
   bed;
And death, not Romeo, take my maiden-head!

---

[75] *needly will be rank'd with*: needs must be accompanied or united by.
[76] *modern*: commonplace, ordinary.
[77] *rear-ward*: rear guard.

Nurse. Hie to your chamber; I'll find Romeo
  To comfort you. I wot[78] well where he is.   *140*
  Hark ye, your Romeo will be here at night.
  I'll to him; he is hid at Lawrence' cell.

Juliet. O, find him! give this ring to my true
    knight,
  And bid him come to take his last farewell.

                              [*Exeunt.*]

            Scene 3. *Friar Lawrence's cell.*

              Enter Friar Lawrence.

Friar Lawrence. Romeo, come forth; come
  forth, thou fearful[79] man;

  Affliction is enamour'd of thy parts,[80]
  And thou art wedded to calamity.

Enter Romeo.

Romeo. Father, what news? What is the Prince's
    doom?[81]
  What sorrow craves acquaintance at my hand   5
  That I yet know not?

Friar Lawrence.   Too familiar
  Is my dear son with such sour company;
  I bring thee tidings of the Prince's doom.

Romeo. What less than doomsday[82] is the Prince's
    doom?

---

[78] *wot*: know.
[79] *fearful*: frightened.
[80] *parts*: attractive qualities.
[81] *doom*: judgment, final decision.
[82] *doomsday*: i.e., Romeo's death.

Friar Lawrence. A gentler judgment vanish'd[83]
    from his lips—   10
  Not body's death, but body's banishment.

Romeo. Ha, banishment! Be merciful, say 'death';
  For exile hath more terror in his look,
  Much more than death. Do not say
    'banishment'.

Friar Lawrence. Here from Verona art thou
    banished.   15
  Be patient, for the world is broad and wide.

Romeo. There is no world without Verona walls,
  But purgatory, torture, hell itself.
  Hence banished is banish'd from the world,
  And world's exile is death. Then 'banished'   20
  Is death mis-term'd; calling death 'banished',
  Thou cut'st my head off with a golden axe,
  And smilest upon the stroke that murders me.

Friar Lawrence. O deadly sin! O rude
    unthankfulness!
  Thy fault our law calls death; but the kind
    Prince,   25
  Taking thy part, hath rush'd[84] aside the law,
  And turn'd that black word death to
    banishment.
  This is dear mercy, and thou seest it not.

Romeo. 'Tis torture, and not mercy; heaven is
    here
  Where Juliet lives, and every cat, and dog,   30
  And little mouse, every unworthy thing,
  Live here in heaven and may look on her;
  But Romeo may not. More validity,[85]

---

[83] *vanish'd*: escaped.
[84] *rush'd*: pushed.
[85] *validity*: value, worth.

More honourable state, more courtship[86] lives
In carrion flies than Romeo. They may seize   35
On the white wonder of dear Juliet's hand,
And steal immortal blessing from her lips;
Who, even in pure and vestal[87] modesty,
Still blush, as thinking their own kisses sin;
But Romeo may not—he is banished.   40
This may flies do, when I from this must fly;
They are free men, but I am banished.
And sayest thou yet that exile is not death?
Hadst thou no poison mix'd, no sharp-ground
    knife,
No sudden mean[88] of death, though ne'er so
    mean,[89]   45
But 'banished' to kill me—'banished'?
O friar, the damned use that word in hell;
Howling attends it; how hast thou the heart,
Being a divine, a ghostly confessor,
A sin-absolver, and my friend profess'd,   50
To mangle me with that word 'banished'?

Friar Lawrence. Thou fond[90] mad man, hear me
    a little speak.

Romeo. O, thou wilt speak again of banishment.

Friar Lawrence. I'll give thee armour to keep
    off that word;
Adversity's sweet milk, philosophy,   55
To comfort thee, though thou art banished.

Romeo. Yet[91] 'banished'? Hang up philosophy;
    Unless philosophy can make a Juliet,

---

[86] *courtship*: opportunity for courting.
[87] *vestal*: virginal.
[88] *mean*: means.
[89] *mean*: lowly.
[90] *fond*: foolish.
[91] *Yet*: still.

Displant a town, reverse a prince's doom,
It helps not, it prevails not. Talk no more.   60

Friar Lawrence. O, then I see that madmen
    have no ears.

Romeo. How should they, when that wise men
    have no eyes?

Friar Lawrence. Let me dispute[92] with thee of
    thy estate.[93]

Romeo. Thou canst not speak of that thou dost
    not feel.
    Wert thou as young as I, Juliet thy love,   65
    An hour but married, Tybalt murdered,
    Doting like me, and like me banished,
    Then mightst thou speak, then mightst thou
        tear thy hair,
    And fall upon the ground, as I do now,
    Taking the measure[94] of an unmade grave.   70

                        [*Knocking within.*]

Friar Lawrence. Arise; one knocks. Good
    Romeo, hide thyself.

Romeo. Not I; unless the breath of heart-sick
    groans,
    Mist-like, enfold me from the search of eyes.

                        [*Knocking.*]

Friar Lawrence. Hark how they knock! Who's
    there? Romeo, arise;
    Thou wilt be taken.—Stay awhile.—Stand up;   75

---

[92] *dispute*: discuss.
[93] *estate*: situation.
[94] *Taking the measure*: i.e., measuring by stretching his body out on the ground.

[*Knocking.*] Run to my study.—By and by.[95]—
   God's will,
What simpleness[96] is this!—I come, I come.

                              [*Knocking.*]

Who knocks so hard? Whence come you?
   What's your will?

Nurse. [*Within.*] Let me come in and you shall
   know my errand;
I come from Lady Juliet.

Friar Lawrence.   Welcome, then.   80

Enter Nurse.

Nurse. O holy friar, O, tell me, holy friar,
   Where's my lady's lord, where's Romeo?

Friar Lawrence. There on the ground, with his
   own tears made drunk.

Nurse. O, he is even in my mistress' case,
   Just in her case!

Friar Lawrence. O woeful sympathy!
   Piteous predicament!

Nurse.   Even so lies she,   85
   Blubb'ring and weeping, weeping and
      blubb'ring.
   Stand up, stand up; stand, an you be a man;
   For Juliet's sake, for her sake, rise and stand;
   Why should you fall into so deep an O?[97]   90

Romeo. Nurse!

---

[95] *By and by*: just a moment (said to whoever is knocking on the door).
[96] *simpleness*: foolishness (referring to Romeo on the ground).
[97] *O*: moan or cry.

Nurse. Ah, sir! ah, sir! Well, death's the end of
    all.

Romeo. Spakest thou of Juliet? How is it with
    her?
    Doth not she think me an old murderer,
    Now I have stain'd the childhood of our joy   95
    With blood remov'd but little from her own?
    Where is she? and how doth she? and what says
    My conceal'd lady[98] to our cancell'd love?

Nurse. O, she says nothing, sir, but weeps and
    weeps;
    And now falls on her bed, and then starts up,   100
    And Tybalt calls; and then on Romeo cries,
    And then down falls again.

Romeo.   As if that name,
    Shot from the deadly level[99] of a gun,
    Did murder her; as that name's cursed hand
    Murder'd her kinsman. O, tell me, friar, tell me,   105
    In what vile part of this anatomy
    Doth my name lodge? Tell me that I may sack[100]
    The hateful mansion.   [*Drawing his sword.*]

Friar Lawrence.   ~~stop your~~ Hold thy desperate hand.
             are you
    Art thou a man? Thy form cries out thou art:
    Thy tears are womanish; thy wild acts denote   110
    The unreasonable[101] fury of a beast.   your acting
    Unseemly[102] woman in a seeming man!   like a girl or
    And ill-beseeming beast in seeming both![103]   an animal
    Thou hast amaz'd me. By my holy order,

---

[98] *conceal'd lady*: secret wife (i.e., Juliet).

[99] *level*: aim.

[100] *sack*: plunder, loot.

[101] *unreasonable*: irrational, lacking human reason.

[102] *Unseemly*: indecorous, unbecoming.

[103] *ill-beseeming . . . seeming both*: i.e., inappropriate to both men and women in resembling a brute animal so much.

character or attitude

I thought thy disposition better temper'd. *made*   *115*
Hast thou slain Tybalt? Wilt thou slay thyself? *Killed*
And slay thy lady that in thy life lives, *Juliet*
By doing damned hate upon thyself? = *suicide*
Why railest thou on thy birth, the heaven, and *yell at*
    earth?   *Family*
Since birth, and heaven, and earth,[104] all three do
    meet *you*   *soul*   *body* *(Gen. 2)*   *120*
In thee at once; which thou at once wouldst
    lose.[105] *abandon*
Fie, fie! thou shamest thy shape, thy love, thy
    wit;
Which,[106] like a usurer, abound'st in all,
And usest none in that true use indeed
Which should bedeck[107] thy shape, thy love, thy
    wit.   *125*
Thy noble shape is but a form of wax,
Digressing from the valour of a man;[108]
Thy dear love sworn but hollow perjury,
Killing that love which thou hast vow'd to
    cherish;
Thy wit, that ornament to shape and love,   *130*
Misshapen in the conduct[109] of them both,
Like powder in a skilless soldier's flask,[110]
Is set afire by thine own ignorance,
And thou dismemb'red with thine own defence.[111]
What, rouse thee, man! Thy Juliet is alive,   *135*
For whose dear sake thou wast but lately dead;[112]

---

[104] *birth, and heaven, and earth*: i.e., family origin, soul, and body.

[105] *lose*: abandon.

[106] *Which*: who.

[107] *bedeck*: do honor to, decorate.

[108] *valour of a man*: i.e., manly qualities.

[109] *conduct*: management.

[110] *flask*: i.e., for gunpowder.

[111] *dismemb'red with thine own defence*: I.e., Romeo is unreasonable, divided from his intellect, which would properly guide and defend him.

[112] *wast but lately dead*: i.e., just recently declared yourself dead.

There art thou happy.[113] Tybalt would kill thee,
But thou slewest Tybalt; there art thou happy
   too.
The law, that threat'ned death, becomes thy
   friend,
And turns it to exile; there art thou happy.   140
A pack of blessings lights upon thy back;
Happiness courts thee in her best array;
But, like a misbehav'd and sullen wench,
Thou pout'st upon thy fortune and thy love.
Take heed, take heed, for such die miserable.   145
Go, get thee to thy love, as was decreed,
Ascend her chamber, hence and comfort her.
But look thou stay not till the watch be set,
For then thou canst not pass to Mantua,
Where thou shalt live till we can find a time   150
To blaze[114] your marriage, reconcile your friends,
Beg pardon of the Prince, and call thee back
With twenty hundred thousand times more joy
Than thou went'st forth in lamentation.
Go before, nurse; commend me to thy lady;   155
And bid her hasten all the house to bed,
Which heavy sorrow makes them apt unto;
Romeo is coming.

Nurse. O Lord, I could have stay'd here all the
   night
To hear good counsel; O, what learning is!   160
My lord, I'll tell my lady you will come.

Romeo. Do so, and bid my sweet prepare to
   chide.

Nurse. Here, sir, a ring she bid me give you, sir.
Hie you, make haste, for it grows very late.

                                 [*Exit.*]

---

[113] *happy*: fortunate.
[114] *blaze*: announce publicly.

Romeo. How well my comfort is reviv'd by this!   *165*

Friar Lawrence. Go hence; good night; and
        here stands all your state:[115]
    Either be gone before the watch be set,
    Or by the break of day disguis'd from hence.
    Sojourn in Mantua; I'll find out your man,
    And he shall signify from time to time   *170*
    Every good hap to you that chances here.
    Give me thy hand. 'Tis late; farewell; good night.

Romeo. But that a joy past joy calls out on me,
    It were a grief so brief to part with thee.
    Farewell.   [*Exeunt.*]

                Scene 4. *Capulet's house.*

            Enter Capulet, Lady Capulet, and Paris.

Capulet. Things have fall'n out, sir, so unluckily
    That we have had no time to move[116] our
        daughter.
    Look you, she lov'd her kinsman Tybalt dearly,
    And so did I. Well, we were born to die.
    'Tis very late; she'll not come down tonight.   *5*
    I promise[117] you, but for your company,
    I would have been abed an hour ago.

Paris. These times of woe afford no time to woo.
    Madam, good night; commend me to your
        daughter.

Lady Capulet. I will, and know her mind early
        to-morrow;   *10*
    To-night she's mew'd up[118] to her heaviness.

---

[115] *here stands all your state*: I.e., this is your situation.
[116] *move*: persuade.
[117] *promise*: assure.
[118] *mew'd up*: caged up (a mew is a cage for molting hawks).

Capulet. Sir Paris, I will make a desperate tender[119]
    Of my child's love. I think she will be rul'd
    In all respects by me; nay, more, I doubt it not.
    Wife, go you to her ere you go to bed;   15
    Acquaint her here of my son Paris' love
    And bid her, mark you me,[120] on Wednesday
        next—
    But, soft! what day is this?

Paris.   Monday, my lord.

Capulet. Monday! ha, ha![121] Well, Wednesday is
    too soon,
    A[122] Thursday let it be; a Thursday, tell her,   20
    She shall be married to this noble earl.
    Will you be ready? Do you like this haste?
    We'll keep no great ado[123]—a friend or two;
    For, hark you, Tybalt being slain so late,
    It may be thought we held him carelessly,[124]   25
    Being our kinsman, if we revel much;
    Therefore we'll have some half a dozen friends,
    And there an end. But what say you to
        Thursday?

Paris. My lord, I would that Thursday were to-
    morrow.

Capulet. Well, get you gone; a Thursday be it
    then.   30
    Go you to Juliet ere you go to bed;
    Prepare her, wife, against[125] this wedding-day.
    Farewell, my lord. Light to my chamber, ho!

---

[119] *desperate tender*: bold or risky offer.
[120] *mark you me*: attend to what I say.
[121] *ha, ha!* Capulet says this reflectively, not necessarily with amusement.
[122] *A*: on.
[123] *keep no great ado*: make no great fuss.
[124] *held him carelessly*: did not care deeply about him.
[125] *against*: in preparation for.

Afore me,[126] it is so very very late
That we may call it early by and by.[127]   35
Good night.   [*Exeunt.*]

Scene 5. *Capulet's orchard.*

Enter Romeo and Juliet, aloft.

Juliet. Wilt thou be gone? It is not yet near day;
   It was the nightingale, and not the lark,
   That pierc'd the fearful[128] hollow of thine ear;
   Nightly she sings on yond pomegranate tree.
   Believe me, love, it was the nightingale.   5

Romeo. It was the lark, the herald of the morn,
   No nightingale. Look, love, what envious
      streaks
   Do lace the severing clouds in yonder east;
   Night's candles[129] are burnt out, and jocund day
   Stands tiptoe on the misty mountain tops.   10
   I must be gone and live, or stay and die.

Juliet. Yond light is not daylight; I know it, I:
   It is some meteor that the sun exhales
   To be to thee this night a torch-bearer,
   And light thee on thy way to Mantua;   15
   Therefore stay yet; thou need'st not to be gone.

Romeo. Let me be ta'en, let me be put to death;
   I am content, so thou wilt have it so.
   I'll say yon grey is not the morning's eye,
   'Tis but the pale reflex[130] of Cynthia's brow;[131]   20

---

[126] *Afore me*: indeed (light oath).
[127] *by and by*: soon.
[128] *fearful*: feeling fear.
[129] *Night's candles*: i.e., the stars.
[130] *reflex*: reflection.
[131] *Cynthia's brow*: the edge of the moon. In classical mythology, Cynthia was one of the names of the goddess of the moon.

Nor that is not the lark whose notes do beat
The vaulty heaven so high above our heads.
I have more care[132] to stay than will to go.
Come death, and welcome! Juliet wills it so.
How is't, my soul? Let's talk—it is not day.   25

Juliet. It is, it is; hie hence, be gone, away!
It is the lark that sings so out of tune,
Straining harsh discords and unpleasing sharps.
Some say the lark makes sweet division;[133]
This doth not so, for she divideth us.   30
Some say the lark and loathed toad change eyes;
O, now I would they had chang'd voices too!
Since arm from arm that voice doth us affray,[134]
Hunting thee hence with hunts-up[135] to the day.
O, now be gone! More light and light it grows.   35

Romeo. More light and light—more dark and
      dark our woes!

Enter Nurse.

Nurse. Madam!

Juliet. Nurse?

Nurse. Your lady mother is coming to your
      chamber.
The day is broke; be wary, look about.   [*Exit.*]   40

Juliet. Then, window, let day in and let life out.

Romeo. Farewell, farewell! One kiss, and I'll
      descend.   [*He goeth down.*]

---

[132] *care:* desire.
[133] *division:* melody (i.e., division of notes).
[134] *affray:* frighten, cause us to brawl interiorly.
[135] *hunts-up:* morning song used to wake huntsmen (also addressed to a newly married bride).

Juliet. Art thou gone so, love—lord, ay,
     husband, friend!
   I must hear from thee every day in the hour,
   For in a minute there are many days;   45
   O, by this count I shall be much in years[136]
   Ere I again behold my Romeo!

Romeo. Farewell!
   I will omit no opportunity
   That may convey my greetings, love, to thee.   50

Juliet. O, think'st thou we shall ever meet again?

Romeo. I doubt it not; and all these woes shall
     serve
   For sweet discourses in our times to come.

Juliet. O, God, I have an ill-divining[137] soul!
   Methinks I see thee, now thou art below,   55
   As one dead in the bottom of a tomb;
   Either my eyesight fails or thou look'st pale.

Romeo. And trust me, love, in my eye so do you;
   Dry[138] sorrow drinks our blood. Adieu, adieu!

                           [*Exit below.*]

Juliet. O Fortune. Fortune! all men call thee
     fickle.   60
   If thou art fickle, what dost thou[139] with him
   That is renown'd for faith? Be fickle, Fortune;
   For then, I hope, thou wilt not keep him long,
   But send him back.

Lady Capulet. [*Within.*] Ho, daughter! are you
     up?

---

[136] *much in years*: much older.
[137] *ill-divining*: with special insight for evil, foreseeing evil.
[138] *Dry*: thirsty.
[139] *what dost thou*: what business do you have.

Juliet. Who is't that calls? It is my lady mother. 65
 Is she not down[140] so late, or up so early?
 What unaccustom'd cause procures her hither?

Enter Lady Capulet.

Lady Capulet. Why, how now, Juliet!

Juliet.   Madam, I am not well.

Lady Capulet. Evermore weeping for your
 cousin's death?
 What, wilt thou wash him from his grave with
  tears? 70
 An if thou couldst, thou couldst not make him
  live;
 Therefore have done. Some grief shows much of
  love;
 But much of grief shows still some want of wit.

Juliet. Yet let me weep for such a feeling loss.[141]

Lady Capulet. So shall you feel the loss, but not
 the friend 75
 Which you weep for.

Juliet.   Feeling so the loss,
 I cannot choose but ever weep the friend.

Lady Capulet. Well, girl, thou weep'st not so
 much for his death
 As that the villain lives which slaughter'd him.

Juliet. What villain, madam?

Lady Capulet.   That same villain, Romeo. 80

Juliet. [*Aside.*] Villain and he be many miles
 asunder!—

---

[140] *down*: in bed.
[141] *feeling loss*: strongly felt loss.

God pardon him! I do, with all my heart;
And yet no man like he doth grieve my heart.

Lady Capulet. That is because the traitor
    murderer lives.

Juliet. Ay, madam, from the reach of these my
    hands.   85
  Would none but I might venge my cousin's
    death.

Lady Capulet. We will have vengeance for it,
    fear thou not;
  Then weep no more. I'll send to one in Mantua—
  Where that same banish'd runagate[142] doth live—
  Shall give him such an unaccustom'd dram[143]   90
  That he shall soon keep Tybalt company;
  And then I hope thou wilt be satisfied.

Juliet. Indeed I never shall be satisfied
  With Romeo till I behold him—dead—
  Is my poor heart so for a kinsman vex'd.   95
  Madam, if you could find out but a man
  To bear a poison, I would temper[144] it,
  That Romeo should, upon receipt thereof,
  Soon sleep in quiet. O, how my heart abhors
  To hear him nam'd, and cannot come to him,   100
  To wreak[145] the love I bore my cousin Tybalt
  Upon his body that hath slaughter'd him!

Lady Capulet. Find thou the means, and I'll find
    such a man.
  But now I'll tell thee joyful tidings, girl.

Juliet. And joy comes well in such a needy time.   105
  What are they, beseech your ladyship?

---

[142] *runagate*: fugitive, renegade.
[143] *dram*: small draught (of poison).
[144] *temper*: (1) mix; (2) weaken.
[145] *wreak*: (1) avenge; (2) give full bent to.

Lady Capulet. Well, well, thou hast a careful[146]
　　father, child;
　One who, to put thee from thy heaviness,
　Hath sorted out[147] a sudden day of joy
　That thou expects not, nor I look'd not for.   *110*

Juliet. Madam, in happy time,[148] what day is that?

Lady Capulet. Marry, my child, early next
　　Thursday morn
　The gallant, young, and noble gentleman,
　The County Paris, at Saint Peter's Church,
　Shall happily make thee there a joyful bride.   *115*

Juliet. Now, by Saint Peter's Church, and Peter
　　too,
　He shall not make me there a joyful bride.
　I wonder at this haste, that I must wed
　Ere he that should be husband comes to woo.
　I pray you tell my lord and father, madam,   *120*
　I will not marry yet; and when I do, I swear
　It shall be Romeo, whom you know I hate,
　Rather than Paris. These are news indeed!

Lady Capulet. Here comes your father; tell him
　　so yourself,
　And see how he will take it at your hands.   *125*

Enter Capulet and Nurse.

Capulet. When the sun sets, the air doth drizzle
　　dew;
　But for the sunset of my brother's son
　It rains downright.
　How now! a conduit,[149] girl? What, still in tears?
　Evermore show'ring? In one little body   *130*

---

[146] *careful*: caring, solicitous, vigilant.
[147] *sorted out*: selected, arranged.
[148] *in happy time*: most opportunely.
[149] *conduit*: water pipe.

Thou counterfeit'st a bark, a sea, a wind;
For still thy eyes, which I may call the sea,
Do ebb and flow with tears. The bark[150] thy body
   is,
Sailing in this salt flood; the winds thy sighs,
Who, raging with thy tears, and they with them,   135
Without a sudden[151] calm will overset
Thy tempest-tossed body. How now, wife!
Have you delivered to her our decree?

Lady Capulet. Ay, sir; but she will none, she
   gives you thanks.[152]
I would the fool were married to her grave!   140

Capulet. Soft! take me with you,[153] take me with
   you, wife.
How will she none? Doth she not give us
   thanks?
  Is she not proud? Doth she not count her blest,
Unworthy as she is, that we have wrought[154]
So worthy a gentleman to be her bride-groom?   145

Juliet. Not proud you have, but thankful that
   you have.
Proud can I never be of what I hate,
But thankful even for hate that is meant love.

Capulet. How how, how how, chopt logic![155] What
   is this?
'Proud'—and 'I thank you'—and 'I thank you
   not'—   150
And yet 'not proud'? Mistress minion,[156] you,

---

[150] *bark*: ship, boat.

[151] *sudden*: immediate.

[152] *she will . . . thanks*: she will have none of it, thank you.

[153] *take me with you*: help me to understand you (take me with you in understanding).

[154] *wrought*: arranged for.

[155] *chopt logic*: sophistry, subtle argumentation.

[156] *Mistress minion*: minx, spoiled hussy.

Thank me no thankings, nor proud me no
　　prouds,
But fettle[157] your fine joints 'gainst Thursday next,
To go with Paris to Saint Peter's Church,
Or I will drag thee on a hurdle[158] thither.　　　　　*155*
Out, you green-sickness[159] carrion! Out, you
　　baggage![160]
You tallow-face!

Lady Capulet. Fie, fie! what, are you mad?

Juliet. Good father, I beseech you on my knees,
　　Hear me with patience but to speak a word.

Capulet. Hang thee, young baggage! disobedient
　　wretch!　　　　　　　　　　　　　　　　　　　*160*
　I tell thee what—get thee to church a Thursday,
　Or never after look me in the face.
　Speak not, reply not, do not answer me;
　My fingers itch. Wife, we scarce thought us blest
　That God had lent us but this only child;　　　　　*165*
　But now I see this one is one too much,
　And that we have a curse in having her.
　Out on her, hilding![161]

Nurse.　　　　　　　　　　God in heaven bless her!
　You are to blame, my lord, to rate[162] her so.

Capulet. And why, my Lady Wisdom? Hold
　　your tongue,　　　　　　　　　　　　　　　　　*170*
　Good Prudence; smatter[163] with your gossips, go.

Nurse. I speak no treason.

---

[157] *fettle*: prepare, make ready.
[158] *hurdle*: frame or sledge that carries prisoners to the place of execution.
[159] *green-sickness*: anemic.
[160] *baggage*: strumpet, loose woman.
[161] *hilding*: good-for-nothing.
[162] *rate*: berate, scold.
[163] *smatter*: chatter.

Capulet.   O, God-i-goden![164]

Nurse. May not one speak?

Capulet.   Peace, you mumbling fool!
  Utter your gravity o'er a gossip's bowl,
  For here we need it not.

Lady Capulet.   You are too hot.   175

Capulet. God's bread![165] it makes me mad:
  Day, night, hour, tide, time, work, play,
  Alone, in company, still my care hath been
  To have her match'd; and having now provided
  A gentleman of noble parentage,   180
  Of fair demesnes,[166] youthful, and nobly train'd,
  Stuff'd, as they say, with honourable parts,
  Proportion'd as one's thought would wish a
    man—
  And then to have a wretched puling[167] fool,
  A whining mammet,[168] in her fortune's tender,[169]   185
  To answer 'I'll not wed, I cannot love,
  I am too young, I pray you pardon me'!
  But, an[170] you will not wed, I'll pardon you.
  Graze where you will, you shall not house with
    me.
  Look to't, think on't; I do not use to jest.[171]   190
  Thursday is near; lay hand on heart, advise:[172]
  An[173] you be mine, I'll give you to my friend;

---

[164] *God-i-goden*: God give you good evening (i.e., "get on with you").
[165] *God's bread*: colloquial oath, literally swearing by the Holy Eucharist.
[166] *demesnes*: domains, manorial lands.
[167] *puling*: whining, whimpering.
[168] *mammet*: puppet, idol.
[169] *in her fortune's tender*: when she is offered (tendered) good fortune.
[170] *an*: if.
[171] *do not use to jest*: do not usually make jokes.
[172] *advise*: consider.
[173] An: if.

An you be not, hang, beg, starve, die in the
  streets,
For, by my soul, I'll ne'er acknowledge thee,
Nor what is mine shall never do thee good.   195
Trust to't, bethink you, I'll not be forsworn.

                                                    [*Exit.*]

Juliet. Is there no pity sitting in the clouds
  That sees into the bottom of my grief?
  O, sweet my mother, cast me not away!
  Delay this marriage for a month, a week;   200
  Or, if you do not, make the bridal bed
  In that dim monument where Tybalt lies.

Lady Capulet. Talk not to me, for I'll not speak
  a word;
  Do as thou wilt, for I have done with thee.

                                                    [*Exit.*]

Juliet. O God!—O nurse! how shall this be
  prevented?   205
  My husband is on earth, my faith[174] in heaven;
  How shall that faith return again to earth,
  Unless that husband send it me from heaven
  By leaving earth?[175] Comfort me, counsel me.
  Alack, alack, that heaven should practise
    stratagems   210
  Upon so soft a subject as myself!
  What say'st thou! Hast thou not a word of joy?
  Some comfort, nurse.

Nurse.   Faith, here it is:
  Romeo is banished; and all the world to nothing[176]

---

[174] *faith*: nuptial vow recorded.
[175] By *leaving earth*: i.e., by dying.
[176] *all the world to nothing*: stakes in a gamble.

That he dares ne'er come back to challenge[177] you;   215
Or, if he do, it needs must be by stealth.
Then, since the case so stands as now it doth,
I think it best you married with the County.
O, he's a lovely gentleman!
Romeo's a dishclout[178] to him; an eagle, madam,   220
Hath not so green, so quick, so fair an eye
As Paris hath. Beshrew[179] my very heart,
I think you are happy in this second match,
For it excels your first; or, if it did not,
Your first is dead, or 'twere as good he were   225
As living here and you no use of him.

Juliet. Speak'st thou from thy heart?

Nurse. And from my soul too, else beshrew them
    both.

Juliet. Amen!

Nurse. What?   230

Juliet. Well, thou hast comforted me marvellous
    much.
    Go in; and tell my lady I am gone,
    Having displeas'd my father, to Lawrence' cell
    To make confession, and to be absolv'd.

Nurse. Marry, I will; and this is wisely done.   235

                                                [*Exit.*]

Juliet. Ancient damnation![180] O most wicked fiend!
    Is it more sin to wish me thus forsworn,[181]

---

[177] *challenge*: claim.
[178] *dishclout*: dishcloth.
[179] *Beshrew*: generic oath (literally, "curse").
[180] *Ancient damnation*: (1) damned old woman; (2) old devil.
[181] *forsworn*: i.e., to break her marriage vow.

Or to dispraise my lord with that same tongue
Which she hath prais'd him with above compare
So many thousand times? Go, counsellor;   *240*
Thou and my bosom henceforth shall be twain.[182]
I'll to the friar to know his remedy;
If all else fail, myself have power to die.   [*Exit.*]

[182] *Thou . . . shall be twain*: I.e., I shall henceforth separate you from my counsel or trust.

ACT 4

Scene 1. *Friar Lawrence's cell.*

Enter Friar Lawrence and County Paris.

Friar Lawrence. On Thursday, sir? The time is
    very short.

Paris. My father Capulet will have it so,
  And I am nothing slow to slack his haste.[1]

Friar Lawrence. You say you do not know the
    lady's mind;
  Uneven[2] is the course; I like it not.   5

Paris. Immoderately she weeps for Tybalt's
    death,
  And therefore have I little talk'd of love;
  For Venus smiles not in a house of tears.
  Now, sir, her father counts it dangerous
  That she do give her sorrow so much sway,   10
  And in his wisdom hastes our marriage,
  To stop the inundation of her tears;
  Which, too much minded[3] by herself alone,[4]
  May be put from her by society.   15
  Now do you know the reason of this haste.

Friar Lawrence. [*Aside.*] I would I knew not
    why it should be slow'd.—
  Look, sir, here comes the lady toward my cell.

Enter Juliet.

Paris. Happily met, my lady and my wife!

---

[1] *I am . . . haste:* I.e., I am not slow in any way as I would not slow his haste.
[2] *Uneven:* irregular, arbitrary.
[3] *minded:* thought about.
[4] *by herself alone:* when she is alone.

Juliet. That may be, sir, when I may be a wife.

Paris. That may be must be, love, on Thursday
     next.   20

Juliet. What must be shall be.

Friar Lawrence.   That's a certain text.

Paris. Come you to make confession to this
     father?

Juliet. To answer that, I should confess to you.

Paris. Do not deny to him that you love me.

Juliet. I will confess to you that I love him.   25

Paris. So will ye, I am sure, that you love me.

Juliet. If I do so, it will be of more price
     Being spoke behind your back than to your face.

Paris. Poor soul, thy face is much abus'd with
     tears.

Juliet. The tears have got small victory by that,   30
     For it was bad enough before their spite.⁵

Paris. Thou wrong'st it more than tears with that
     report.

Juliet. That is no slander, sir, which is a truth;
     And what I spake, I spake it to my face.

Paris. Thy face is mine, and thou hast sland'red
     it.   35

Juliet. It may be so, for it is not mine own.
     Are you at leisure, holy father, now,
     Or shall I come to you at evening mass?

---

⁵ *before their spite*: i.e., before they marred it (i.e., her face).

Friar Lawrence. My leisure serves me, pensive
    daughter, now.
My lord, we must entreat the time alone.[6]   40

Paris. God shield[7] I should disturb devotion!
    Juliet, on Thursday early will I rouse ye;
    Till then, adieu, and keep this holy kiss.   [*Exit.*]

Juliet. O, shut the door, and when thou hast
    done so,
Come weep with me—past hope, past cure, past
    help.   45

Friar Lawrence. O, Juliet, I already know thy
    grief;
It strains me past the compass of my wits.
I hear thou must, and nothing may prorogue[8] it,
On Thursday next be married to this County.

Juliet. Tell me not, friar, that thou hear'st of this,   50
    Unless thou tell me how I may prevent it;
If, in thy wisdom, thou canst give no help,
Do thou but call my resolution wise.
And with this knife I'll help it presently.[9]
God join'd my heart and Romeo's, thou our
    hands;   55
And ere this hand, by thee to Romeo's seal'd,
Shall be the label[10] to another deed,[11]
Or my true heart with treacherous revolt
Turn to another, this shall slay them both.
Therefore, out of thy long-experienc'd time,   60
Give me some present counsel; or, behold,
'Twixt my extremes and me this bloody knife

---

[6] *entreat the time alone*: ask that we be left alone for this time.

[7] *God shield*: God forbid (colloquial oath).

[8] *prorogue*: delay, postpone.

[9] *presently*: at once.

[10] *label*: bearer of the seal.

[11] *deed*: (1) act; (2) legal document.

Shall play the umpire, arbitrating that
Which the commission[12] of thy years and art
Could to no issue of true honour bring.   65
Be not so long to speak; I long to die,
If what thou speak'st speak not of remedy.

Friar Lawrence. Hold, daughter; I do spy a
    kind of hope,
Which craves as desperate an execution
As that is desperate which we would prevent.   70
If, rather than to marry County Paris,
Thou hast the strength of will to slay thyself,
Then is it likely thou wilt undertake
A thing like death to chide away this shame,
That cop'st[13] with death himself to scape from it;   75
And, if thou dar'st, I'll give thee remedy.

Juliet. O, bid me leap, rather than marry Paris,
From off the battlements of any tower,
Or walk in thievish ways,[14] or bid me lurk
Where serpents are; chain me with roaring
    bears,   80
Or hide me nightly in a charnel house,[15]
O'er-cover'd quite with dead men's rattling
    bones,
With reeky[16] shanks and yellow chapless[17] skulls;
Or bid me go into a new-made grave,
And hide me with a dead man in his shroud—   85
Things that, to hear them told, have made me
    tremble—
And I will do it without fear or doubt,
To live an unstain'd wife to my sweet love.

---

[12] *commission*: authority.
[13] *cop'st*: copes, grapples, contends.
[14] *thievish ways*: pathways infested with thieves.
[15] *charnel house*: building or vault in which corpses or bones are piled.
[16] *reeky*: damp, reeking.
[17] *chapless*: jawless.

Friar Lawrence. Hold, then; go home, be
      merry, give consent
      To marry Paris. Wednesday is to-morrow;   *90*
      To-morrow night look that thou lie alone,
      Let not the nurse lie with thee in thy chamber.
      Take thou this vial, being then in bed,
      And this distilled liquor drink thou off;
      When presently through all thy veins shall run   *95*
      A cold and drowsy humour;[18] for no pulse
      Shall keep his native[19] progress, but surcease;[20]
      No warmth, no breath, shall testify thou livest;
      The roses in thy lips and cheeks shall fade
      To paly[21] ashes, thy eyes' windows[22] fall,   *100*
      Like death when he shuts up the day of life;
      Each part, depriv'd of supple government,[23]
      Shall, stiff and stark and cold, appear like death;
      And in this borrow'd likeness of shrunk death
      Thou shalt continue two and forty hours,   *105*
      And then awake as from a pleasant sleep.
      Now, when the bridegroom in the morning
            comes
      To rouse thee from thy bed, there art thou dead.
      Then, as the manner of our country is,
      In thy best robes, uncovered on the bier,   *110*
      Thou shalt be borne to that same ancient vault
      Where all the kindred of the Capulets lie.
      In the meantime, against[24] thou shalt awake,
      Shall Romeo by my letters know our drift,[25]
      And hither shall he come; and he and I   *115*
      Will watch thy waking, and that very night

---

[18] *humour*: fluid.
[19] *native*: natural.
[20] *surcease*: stop, desist from action.
[21] *paly*: pale.
[22] *windows*: i.e., lids.
[23] *supple government*: capacity of motion.
[24] *against*: before.
[25] *drift*: purpose.

Shall Romeo bear thee hence to Mantua.
And this shall free thee from this present shame,
If no inconstant toy²⁶ nor womanish fear
Abate thy valour in the acting it.   *120*

Juliet. Give me, give me! O, tell not me of fear!

Friar Lawrence. Hold; get you gone, be strong
    and prosperous
In this resolve. I'll send a friar with speed
To Mantua, with my letters to thy lord.

Juliet. Love give me strength! and strength shall
    help afford.   *125*
    Farewell, dear father!   [*Exeunt.*]

Scene 2. *Capulet's house.*

*Enter Capulet, Lady Capulet, Nurse,
and two or three Servingmen.*

Capulet. So many guests invite as here are writ.

                            [*Exit a Servingman.*]

Sirrah, go hire me twenty cunning²⁷ cooks.

Servant. You shall have none ill, sir; for I'll try²⁸ if
    they can lick their fingers.

Capulet. How canst thou try them so?   *5*

Servant. Marry, sir, 'tis an ill cook that cannot
    lick his own fingers;²⁹ therefore he that cannot
    lick his fingers goes not with me.

²⁶ *inconstant toy*: whim.
²⁷ *cunning*: skilled.
²⁸ *try*: test.
²⁹ *'tis an ill cook . . . fingers*: I.e., the skill of cooks is demonstrated by whether
they are willing to test their own cooking.

Capulet. Go, be gone.   [*Exit second Servant.*]

We shall be much unfurnish'd[30] for this time.   10
What, is my daughter gone to Friar Lawrence?

Nurse. Ay, forsooth.[31]

Capulet. Well, he may chance to do some good
    on her:
A peevish self-will'd harlotry it is.

Enter Juliet.

Nurse. See where she comes from shrift with
    merry look.   15

Capulet. How now, my headstrong! Where have
    you been gadding?[32]

Juliet. Where I have learnt me to repent the sin
Of disobedient opposition
To you and your behests; and am enjoin'd[33]
By holy Lawrence to fall prostrate here,   20
To beg your pardon. Pardon, I beseech you.
Henceforward I am ever rul'd by you.

Capulet. Send for the County; go tell him of this.
I'll have this knot knit up to-morrow morning.

Juliet. I met the youthful lord at Lawrence' cell,   25
And gave him what becomed[34] love I might,
Not stepping o'er the bounds of modesty.

Capulet. Why, I am glad on't; this is well—stand
    up—
This is as't should be. Let me see the County;
Ay, marry, go, I say, and fetch him hither.   30

---

[30] *unfurnish'd*: unprovisioned, unsupplied, unprepared.
[31] *forsooth*: yes, indeed.
[32] *gadding*: wandering.
[33] *enjoin'd*: ordered, directed.
[34] *becomed*: becoming, proper, appropriate.

Now, afore God, this reverend holy friar,
All our whole city is much bound to him.

Juliet. Nurse, will you go with me into my closet[35]
To help me sort such needful ornaments
As you think fit to furnish me to-morrow?   35

Lady Capulet. No, not till Thursday; there is
          time enough.

Capulet. Go, nurse, go with her. We'll to church
          to-morrow.   [*Exeunt Juliet and Nurse.*]

Lady Capulet. We shall be short in our
          provision;
     'Tis now near night.

Capulet.   Tush, I will stir about,
And all things shall be well, I warrant thee, wife.   40
Go thou to Juliet, help to deck up her;
I'll not to bed to-night; let me alone.
I'll play the huswife[36] for this once. What, ho!
They are all forth; well, I will walk myself
To County Paris, to prepare up him   45
Against[37] to-morrow. My heart is wondrous light
Since this same wayward girl is so reclaim'd.

                              [*Exeunt.*]

Scene 3. *Juliet's chamber.*

Enter Juliet and Nurse.

Juliet. Ay, those attires are best; but, gentle
          nurse,
     I pray thee, leave me to myself to-night,

---

[35] *closet*: small room, private chamber.
[36] *huswife*: housewife.
[37] *Against*: for, in anticipation of.

For I have need of many orisons[38]
To move the heavens to smile upon my state,[39]
Which well thou knowest is cross[40] and full of
   sin.   5

Enter Lady Capulet.

Lady Capulet. What, are you busy, ho? Need
   you my help?

Juliet. No, madam; we have cull'd[41] such
   necessaries
As are behoveful[42] for our state[43] to-morrow.
So please you, let me now be left alone,
And let the nurse this night sit up with you;   10
For I am sure you have your hands full all
In this so sudden business.

Lady Capulet.   Good night.
   Get thee to bed, and rest; for thou hast need.

               [*Exeunt Lady Capulet and Nurse.*]

Juliet. Farewell! God knows when we shall meet
   again.
I have a faint[44] cold fear thrills through my veins,   15
That almost freezes up the heat of life;
I'll call them back again to comfort me.   *nervous*
Nurse!—What should she do here?   *has to be*
My dismal scene I needs must act alone.   *strong*
Come, vial.   20
What if this mixture do not work at all?

---

[38] *orisons:* prayers.

[39] *state:* situation.

[40] *cross:* unfavorable, perverse.

[41] *cull'd:* selected, collected.

[42] *behoveful:* necessary, expedient.

[43] *state:* pomp.

[44] *faint:* cold, causing faintness.

Shall I be married, then, to-morrow morning?
No, no; this shall forbid it. Lie thou there.

[*Laying down her dagger.*]

What if it be a poison which the friar
Subtly hath minist'red to have me dead,   25
Lest in this marriage he should be dishonour'd,
Because he married me before to Romeo?
I fear it is; and yet methinks it should not,
For he hath still[45] been tried[46] a holy man.
How if, when I am laid into the tomb,   30
I wake before the time that Romeo
Come to redeem me? There's a fearful point.
Shall I not then be stifled in the vault,
To whose foul mouth no healthsome air
    breathes in,
And there die strangled ere my Romeo comes?   35
Or, if I live, is it not very like
The horrible conceit[47] of death and night,
Together with the terror of the place—
As in a vault, an ancient receptacle
Where for this many hundred years the bones   40
Of all my buried ancestors are pack'd;
Where bloody Tybalt, yet but green in earth,[48]
Lies fest'ring in his shroud; where, as they say,
At some hours in the night spirits resort—
Alack, alack, is it not like that I,   45
So early waking—what with loathsome smells,
And shrieks like mandrakes'[49] torn out of the
    earth,

---

[45] *still*: always.
[46] *tried*: proved.
[47] *conceit*: thought.
[48] *green in earth*: newly buried.
[49] *mandrakes'*: A mandrake is a plant the root of which resembles the human body (the plant is supposed to shriek when uprooted, bringing death or madness to those who hear it).

That living mortals, hearing them, run mad—
O, if I wake, shall I not be distraught,[50]
Environed with[51] all these hideous fears,   *50*
And madly play with my forefathers' joints,
And pluck the mangled Tybalt from his
      shroud,
And, in this rage, with some great kinsman's
      bone,
As with a club, dash out my desp'rate brains?
O, look! methinks I see my cousin's ghost   *55*
Seeking out Romeo, that did spit his body
Upon a rapier's point. Stay, Tybalt, stay.
Romeo, I come. This do I drink to thee.

[*She drinks and falls upon her bed within the curtains.*]

Scene 4. *Capulet's house.*

Enter Lady Capulet and Nurse.

Lady Capulet. Hold, take these keys, and fetch
      more spices, nurse.

Nurse. They call for dates and quinces in the
      pastry.[52]

Enter Capulet.

Capulet. Come, stir, stir, stir! The second cock
      hath crow'd,
  The curfew bell[53] hath rung, 'tis three o'clock.
  Look to the bak'd meats,[54] good Angelica;[55]   5
  Spare not for cost.

[50] *distraught*: driven mad.
[51] *Environed with*: surrounded by.
[52] *pastry*: room where pastry is made.
[53] *curfew bell*: bell rung in the evening and the morning to signal the beginning and end of curfew.
[54] *bak'd meats*: meat pies.
[55] *Angelica*: i.e., the Nurse.

Nurse.   Go, you cot-quean,[56] go,
   Get you to bed; faith, you'll be sick to-morrow
   For this night's watching.[57]

Capulet. No, not a whit; what! I have watch'd
      ere now
   All night for lesser cause, and ne'er been sick.   10

Lady Capulet. Ay, you have been a mouse-hunt[58]
      in your time;
   But I will watch you from such watching now.

                    [*Exeunt Lady Capulet and Nurse.*]

Capulet. A jealous-hood,[59] a jealous-hood!

*Enter three or four Servants with spits and logs and
baskets.*

                                   Now, fellow,
      What is there?

1 Fellow. Things for the cook, sir; but I know
      not what.   15

Capulet. Make haste, make haste.   [*Exit 1 Fellow.*]

   Sirrah, fetch drier logs;
   Call Peter; he will show thee where they are.

2 Fellow. I have a head, sir, that will find out
      logs,[60]
   And never trouble Peter for the matter.

---

[56] *cot-quean*: man who takes the place of a housewife.

[57] *watching*: staying awake.

[58] *mouse-hunt*: night prowler, woman chaser (asserting that his "lesser cause" was a woman).

[59] *jealous-hood*: jealous person, someone conditioned and formed by jealousy. ("Hood" seems to be employed in the sense in which it is used as a suffix, e.g., as in "manhood". In Middle English, "hood", in this sense, was an independent noun.)

[60] *a head . . . logs*: a head with an affinity for logs (i.e., a head made of wood).

Capulet. Mass,[61] and well said; a merry whoreson,[62]
    ha!   20
    Thou shalt be logger-head.[63]   *[Exit 2 Fellow.]*

    Good faith, 'tis day;
    The County will be here with music straight,
    For so he said he would. *[Play music.]* I hear
        him near.
    Nurse! Wife! What, ho! What, nurse, I say!

Re-enter Nurse.

    Go waken Juliet, go and trim her up;   25
    I'll go and chat with Paris. Hie, make haste,
    Make haste. The bridegroom he is come
        already.
    Make haste, I say.   *[Exeunt.]*

Scene 5. *Juliet's chamber.*

Enter Nurse.

Nurse. Mistress! What, mistress! Juliet! Fast,[64] I
    warrant her, she.
    Why, lamb! Why, lady! Fie, you slug-a-bed![65]
    Why, love, I say! madam! sweetheart! Why,
        bride!
    What, not a word? You take your penny-worths[66]
        now;
    Sleep for a week; for the next night, I warrant,   5
    The County Paris hath set up his rest[67]
    That you shall rest but little. God forgive me!

---

[61] *Mass*: colloquial oath (literally, "by the Mass").
[62] *whoreson*: rascal (literally, the son of a prostitute).
[63] *logger-head*: blockhead.
[64] *Fast*: fast asleep.
[65] *slug-a-bed*: sleepyhead.
[66] *penny-worths*: small portions (i.e., short naps).
[67] *set up his rest*: firmly resolved, arranged.

Marry, and amen. How sound is she asleep!
I needs must wake her. Madam, madam,
    madam!
Ay, let the County take you in your bed;   10
He'll fright you up, i' faith. Will it not be?

                              [*Draws the curtains.*]

What, dress'd, and in your clothes, and down[68]
    again!
I must needs wake you. Lady! lady! lady!
Alas, alas! Help, help! my lady's dead!
O well-a-day[69] that ever I was born!   15
Some aqua-vitae,[70] ho! My lord! My lady!

Enter Lady Capulet.

Lady Capulet. What noise is here?

Nurse.   O lamentable day!

Lady Capulet. What is the matter?

Nurse.   Look, look! O heavy day!

Lady Capulet. O me, O me! My child, my only
    life,
Revive, look up, or I will die with thee!   20
  Help, help! Call help.

Enter Capulet.

Capulet. For shame, bring Juliet forth; her lord
    is come.

Nurse. She's dead, deceas'd, she's dead; alack the
    day!

---

[68] *down*: lying down, in bed.
[69] *well-a-day*: alas.
[70] *aqua-vitae*: alcoholic spirits.

Lady Capulet. Alack the day, she's dead, she's
 dead, she's dead!

Capulet. Ha! let me see her. Out, alas! she's cold; 25
 Her blood is settled,[71] and her joints are stiff.
 Life and these lips have long been separated.
 Death lies on her like an untimely frost
 Upon the sweetest flower of all the field.

Nurse. O lamentable day!

Lady Capulet.   O woeful time! 30

Capulet. Death, that hath ta'en her hence to
 make me wail,
 Ties up my tongue and will not let me speak.

Enter Friar Lawrence and County Paris, with Musicians.

Friar Lawrence. Come, is the bride ready to go
 to church?

Capulet. Ready to go, but never to return.
 O son, the night before thy wedding day 35
 Hath Death lain with thy wife. There she lies,
 Flower as she was, deflowered by him.[72]
 Death is my son-in-law, Death is my heir;
 My daughter he hath wedded; I will die,
 And leave him all; life, living, all is Death's. 40

Paris. Have I thought long to see this morning's
 face,
 And doth it give me such a sight as this?

Lady Capulet. Accurs'd, unhappy, wretched,
 hateful day!
 Most miserable hour that e'er time saw
 In lasting labour of his pilgrimage! 45

---

[71] *is settled*: has stopped flowing; i.e., there is no pulse.
[72] *deflowered by him*: i.e., having lost her virginity to him.

But one, poor one, one poor and loving child,
But one thing to rejoice and solace in,
And cruel Death hath catch'd it from my sight!

Nurse. O woe! O woeful, woeful, woeful day!
Most lamentable day, most woeful day   50
That ever, ever, I did yet behold!
O day! O day! O day! O hateful day!
Never was seen so black a day as this.
O woeful day, O woeful day!

Paris. Beguil'd, divorced, wronged, spited, slain!   55
Most detestable Death, by thee beguil'd,
By cruel cruel thee quite overthrown!
O love! O life!—not life, but love in death!

Capulet. Despis'd, distressed, hated, martyr'd,
    kill'd!—
Uncomfortable[73] time, why cam'st thou now   60
To murder, murder our solemnity?
O child! O child! my soul, and not my child!
Dead art thou; alack, my child is dead,
And with my child my joys are buried.

Friar Lawrence. Peace, ho, for shame!
    Confusion's cure lives not   65
In these confusions. Heaven and yourself
Had part in this fair maid; now heaven hath all,
And all the better is it for the maid.
Your part in her you could not keep from death,
But heaven keeps his part in eternal life.   70
The most you sought was her promotion,[74]
For 'twas your heaven she should be advanc'd;
And weep ye now, seeing she is advanc'd
Above the clouds, as high as heaven itself?

---

[73] *Uncomfortable*: discomforting, unhappy, unlucky.
[74] *promotion*: advancement in rank.

O, in this love,[75] you love your child so ill   75
That you run mad, seeing that she is well.[76]
She's not well married that lives married long,
But she's best married that dies married young.
Dry up your tears, and stick your rosemary[77]
On this fair corse, and, as the custom is,   80
In all her best array bear her to church;
For though fond nature[78] bids us all lament,
Yet nature's tears are reason's merriment.

Capulet. All things that we ordained festival[79]
     Turn from their office to black funeral: 85
     Our instruments to melancholy bells,
     Our wedding cheer to a sad burial feast,
     Our solemn hymns to sullen dirges change;
     Our bridal flowers serve for a buried corse;
     And all things change them to the contrary.   90

Friar Lawrence. Sir, go you in; and, madam, go
     with him;
     And go, Sir Paris. Every one prepare
     To follow this fair corse unto her grave.
     The heavens do lour[80] upon you for some ill;
     Move them no more by crossing their high will.   95

[*Exeunt all but Nurse and Musicians.*]

1 Musician. Faith, we may put up our pipes and
     be gone.

Nurse. Honest good fellows, ah, put up, put up;
     For well you know this is a pitiful case.[81]   [*Exit.*]

---

[75] *in this love*: i.e., in the desire for her social advancement.
[76] *well*: i.e., in Heaven.
[77] *rosemary*: evergreen herb, signifying remembrance.
[78] *fond nature*: foolish human nature.
[79] *ordained festival*: i.e., prepared for the wedding.
[80] *lour*: frown, scowl.
[81] *case*: (1) situation or state of affairs; (2) case for a musical instrument.

1 Musician. Ay, by my troth, the case may be
    amended.

Enter Peter.

Peter. Musicians, O, musicians, 'Heart's ease',
    'Heart's ease'! O, an you will have me live, play
    'Heart's ease'.

1 Musician. Why 'Heart's ease'?

Peter. O, musicians, because my heart itself plays
    'My heart is full of woe'. O, play me some merry
    dump[82] to comfort me.   105

1 Musician. Not a dump we! 'Tis no time to play
    now.

Peter. You will not, then?

1 Musician. No.

Peter. I will then give it you soundly.

1 Musician. What will you give us?   110

Peter. No money, on my faith, but the gleek.[83] I
    will give[84] you the minstrel.

1 Musician. Then will I give you the serving-
    creature.

Peter. Then will I lay the serving-creature's
    dagger on your pate.[85] I will carry[86] no crotchets:[87]
    I'll re you, I'll fa[88] you; do you note[89] me?   116

---

[82] *dump*: tune.
[83] *gleek*: gibe, gesture of contempt.
[84] *give*: call.
[85] *pate*: head.
[86] *carry*: endure, submit to.
[87] *crotchets*: (1) notions, whims; (2) quarter notes.
[88] *re . . . fa*: Re and fa are musical notes.
[89] *note*: understand.

1 Musician. An[90] you re us and fa us, you note us.[91]

2 Musician. Pray you put up your dagger, and
put out[92] your wit.

Peter. Then have at you with my wit! I will dry-
beat you with an iron wit, and put up my iron
dagger. Answer me like men.

'When griping grief the heart doth wound
    And doleful dumps the mind oppress,
Then music with her silver sound'—[93]   125

Why 'silver sound'? Why 'music with her silver
sound'? What say you, Simon Catling?[94]

1 Musician. Marry, sir, because silver hath a
sweet sound.

Peter. Pretty! What say you, Hugh Rebeck?[95]   130

2 Musician. I say 'silver sound' because
musicians sound for silver.

Peter. Pretty too! What say you, James
Soundpost?[96]

3 Musician. Faith, I know not what to say.

Peter. O, I cry you mercy,[97] you are the singer; I
will say for you. It is 'music with her silver
sound' because musicians have no gold for
sounding.   137

---

[90] *An*: if.
[91] *note us*: set us to music.
[92] *put out*: display.
[93] *When griping grief . . . sound*: lines taken from "In Commendation of Music",
from Richard Edwards' 1576 *The Paradise of Dainty Devices*.
[94] *Catling*: lute or fiddle string made out of cat gut.
[95] *Rebeck*: three-stringed fiddle.
[96] *Soundpost*: part of the internal workings of a violin.
[97] *cry you mercy*: beg your pardon.

'Then music with her silver sound
   With speedy help doth lend redress.'

                                [*Exit.*]

1 Musician. What a pestilent knave is this same!

2 Musician. Hang him, Jack! Come, we'll in here;
   tarry[98] for the mourners, and stay dinner.

                                [*Exeunt.*]

[98] *tarry*: wait.

ACT 5

Scene 1. *Mantua. A street.*

Enter Romeo.

Romeo. If I may trust the flattering[1] truth of sleep,
  My dreams presage[2] some joyful news at hand.
  My bosom's lord[3] sits lightly in his throne,
  And all this day an unaccustom'd spirit
  Lifts me above the ground with cheerful
    thoughts.   5
  I dreamt my lady came and found me dead—
  Strange dream, that gives a dead man leave to
    think!—
  And breath'd such life with kisses in my lips   } dream
  That I reviv'd, and was an emperor.
  Ah me! how sweet is love itself possess'd.   10
  When but love's shadows[4] are so rich in joy!

Enter Balthasar, Romeo's man.

  News from Verona! How now, Balthasar!
  Dost thou not bring me letters from the friar?
  How doth my lady? Is my father well?
  How fares my Juliet? That I ask again,   15
  For nothing can be ill if she be well.

Balthasar. Then she is well, and nothing can be
    ill.
  Her body sleeps in Capels' monument,[5]
  And her immortal part with angels lives.
  I saw her laid low in her kindred's vault,   20

---

[1] *flattering*: illusory.
[2] *presage*: foretell, predict.
[3] *bosom's lord*: love or literally the heart.
[4] *shadows*: dreams.
[5] *Capels' monument*: i.e., the Capulet family tomb.

129

And presently took post[6] to tell it you.
O, pardon me for bringing these ill news,
Since you did leave it for my office,[7] sir.

Romeo. Is it e'en so? Then I defy you, stars.
Thou knowest my lodging: get me ink and
   paper,   25
And hire post-horses; I will hence to-night.

Balthasar. I do beseech you, sir, have patience;
Your looks are pale and wild, and do import[8]
Some misadventure.

Romeo.   Tush, thou art deceiv'd;
Leave me, and do the thing I bid thee do.   30
Hast thou no letters to me from the friar?

Balthasar. No, my good lord.

Romeo.   No matter; get thee gone,
And hire those horses; I'll be with thee straight.

                             [*Exit Balthasar.*]

Well, Juliet, I will lie with thee to-night.
Let's see for means. O mischief, thou art swift
To enter in the thoughts of desperate men!   35
I do remember an apothecary,
And hereabouts 'a dwells, which late I noted
In tatt'red weeds,[9] with overwhelming[10] brows,
Culling of simples.[11] Meagre were his looks;   40
Sharp misery had worn him to the bones;
And in his needy shop a tortoise hung,
An alligator stuff'd, and other skins

---

[6] *took post*: traveled swiftly by horses hired from a post office.
[7] *office*: duty.
[8] *import*: suggest.
[9] *weeds*: clothing.
[10] *overwhelming*: overhanging.
[11] *Culling of simples*: gathering medicinal herbs.

Of ill-shap'd fishes; and about his shelves
A beggarly account[12] of empty boxes,   45
Green earthen pots, bladders, and musty seeds,
Remnants of packthread, and old cakes of
    roses,[13]
Were thinly scattered, to make up a show.
Noting this penury, to myself I said
'An if a man did need a poison now,   50
Whose sale is present death in Mantua,
Here lives a caitiff[14] wretch would sell it him'.
O, this same thought did but forerun my need;
And this same needy man must sell it me.
As I remember, this should be the house.   55
Being holiday, the beggar's shop is shut.
What, ho! Apothecary!

Enter Apothecary.

Apothecary. Who calls so loud?

Romeo. Come hither, man. I see that thou art
    poor.
Hold, there is forty ducats; let me have
A dram of poison, such soon-speeding gear[15]   60
As will disperse itself through all the veins
That the life-weary taker may fall dead,
And that the trunk[16] may be discharg'd of breath
As violently as hasty powder fir'd
Doth hurry from the fatal cannon's womb.   65

Apothecary. Such mortal drugs I have; but
    Mantua's law
Is death to any he that utters[17] them.

---

[12] *A beggarly account*: few in number or little in worth.
[13] *cakes of roses*: dried and pressed rose petals.
[14] *caitiff*: miserable, wretched.
[15] *soon-speeding gear*: fast-acting stuff.
[16] *trunk*: body.
[17] *utters*: dispenses, sells.

Romeo. Art thou so bare and full of wretchedness
　　And fearest to die? Famine is in thy cheeks,
　　Need and oppression starveth[18] in thy eyes,　　　　70
　　Contempt and beggary hangs upon thy back,
　　The world is not thy friend, nor the world's law;
　　The world affords no law to make thee rich;
　　Then be not poor, but break it and take this.

Apothecary. My poverty but not my will
　　consents.　　　　75

Romeo. I pay thy poverty and not thy will.

Apothecary. Put this in any liquid thing you
　　will
　　And drink it off; and if you had the strength
　　Of twenty men, it would dispatch you straight.

Romeo. There is thy gold—worse poison to men's　　　　80
　　souls,
　　Doing more murder in this loathsome world
　　Than these poor compounds that thou mayst
　　　　not sell.
　　I sell thee poison: thou hast sold me none.
　　Farewell; buy food, and get thyself in flesh.[19]
　　Come, cordial[20] and not poison, go with me　　　　85
　　To Juliet's grave; for there must I use thee.

　　　　　　　　　　　　　　　　　　[*Exeunt.*]

---

[18] *starveth*: stand starving.
[19] *get thyself in flesh*: I.e., he is now wasting away from hunger to skin and bones.
[20] *cordial*: stimulating medicine, restorative.

Scene 2. *Friar Lawrence's cell.*

Enter Friar John.

Friar John. Holy Franciscan friar! Brother, ho!

Enter Friar Lawrence.

Friar Lawrence. This same should be the voice
    of Friar John.
  Welcome from Mantua! What says Romeo?
  Or, if his mind be writ, give me his letter.

Friar John. Going to find a barefoot brother out,   5
  One of our order, to associate[21] me,
  Here in this city visiting the sick,
  And finding him, the searchers of the town,[22]
  Suspecting that we both were in a house
  Where the infectious pestilence did reign,   10
  Seal'd up the doors, and would not let us forth,
  So that my speed to Mantua there was stay'd.

Friar Lawrence. Who bare my letter, then, to
    Romeo?

Friar John. I could not send it—here it is again—
  Nor get a messenger to bring it thee,   15
  So fearful were they of infection.

Friar Lawrence. Unhappy fortune! By my
    brotherhood,
  The letter was not nice,[23] but full of charge[24]
  Of dear import; and the neglecting it
  May do much danger. Friar John, go hence;   20

---

[21] *associate*: accompany.
[22] *searchers of the town*: health officers who would identify the cause of a body's death.
[23] *nice*: trivial.
[24] *charge*: important matters.

Get me an iron crow,[25] and bring it straight
Unto my cell.

Friar John. Brother, I'll go and bring it thee.

[*Exit.*]

Friar Lawrence. Now must I to the monument
~~alone.~~
Within this three hours will fair Juliet wake;   25
She will beshrew[26] me much that Romeo
Hath had no notice of these accidents.[27]
~~But I will write again to Mantua,~~
And keep her at my cell till Romeo come—
Poor living corse, clos'd in a dead man's tomb!

[*Exit.*]

Scene 3. *Verona. A churchyard;*
in it the tomb of the Capulets.

Enter Paris, and his Page bearing flowers and a torch.

Paris. Give me thy torch, boy; hence, and stand
    aloof;
Yet put it out, for I would not be seen.
Under yond yew trees lay thee all along,[28]
Holding thy ear close to the hollow ground;
So shall no foot upon the churchyard tread—   5
Being loose, unfirm, with digging up of graves—
But thou shalt hear it. Whistle then to me,
As signal that thou hearest something approach.
Give me those flowers. Do as I bid thee, go.

---

[25] *crow*: crowbar.
[26] *beshrew*: blame, curse.
[27] *accidents*: happenings.
[28] *all along*: at full length.

Page. [*Aside.*] I am almost afraid to stand alone   10
    Here in the churchyard; yet I will adventure.[29]

                          [*Retires.*]

Paris. Sweet flower, with flowers thy bridal bed
    I strew—
    O woe, thy canopy is dust and stones!—
    Which with sweet[30] water nightly I will dew;
    Or, wanting that, with tears distill'd by moans.   15
    The obsequies[31] that I for thee will keep,
    Nightly shall be to strew thy grave and weep.

                   [*The Page whistles.*]

The boy gives warning something doth
    approach.
What cursed foot wanders this way to-night
To cross[32] my obsequies and true love's rite?   20
What, with a torch! Muffle[33] me, night, awhile.

                          [*Retires.*]

*Enter Romeo and Balthasar, with a torch, a
mattock, and a crow of iron.*

Romeo. Give me that mattock[34] and the wrenching
    iron.
    Hold, take this letter; early in the morning
    See thou deliver it to my lord and father.
    Give me the light; upon thy life I charge thee,   25
    Whate'er thou hearest or seest, stand all aloof
    And do not interrupt me in my course.
    Why I descend into this bed of death

---

[29] *adventure*: take the risk.
[30] *sweet*: perfumed.
[31] *obsequies*: funeral rites.
[32] *cross*: interrupt, thwart.
[33] *Muffle*: hide.
[34] *mattock*: pickaxe-like tool used to loosen soil.

Is partly to behold my lady's face,
But chiefly to take thence from her dead finger   30
A precious ring—a ring that I must use
In dear employment;[35] therefore hence, be gone.
But if thou, jealous,[36] dost return to pry
In what I farther shall intend to do,
By heaven, I will tear thee joint by joint,   35
And strew this hungry churchyard with thy
     limbs.
The time and my intents are savage-wild,
More fierce and more inexorable far
Than empty tigers or the roaring sea.

Balthasar. I will be gone, sir, and not trouble
     ye.   40

Romeo. So shalt thou show me friendship.
     Take thou that;
Live and be prosperous; and farewell, good
     fellow.

Balthasar. [*Aside.*] For all this same, I'll hide me
     hereabout;

His looks I fear, and his intents I doubt.[37]

                              [*Retires.*]

Romeo. Thou detestable maw,[38] thou womb of
     death,   45
Gorg'd with the dearest morsel of the earth,
Thus I enforce thy rotten jaws to open,

                    [*Breaking open the tomb.*]

And, in despite,[39] I'll cram thee with more food.

---

[35] *In dear employment*: for an important purpose.
[36] *jealous*: curious, suspicious.
[37] *doubt*: suspect.
[38] *maw*: stomach.
[39] *in despite*: to spite you.

Paris. This is that banish'd haughty Montague
That murd'red my love's cousin—with which
    grief   50
It is supposed the fair creature died—
And here is come to do some villainous shame
To the dead bodies. I will apprehend him.
Stop thy unhallowed toil, vile Montague.
Can vengeance be pursued further than death?   55
Condemned villain, I do apprehend thee.
Obey, and go with me; for thou must die.

Romeo. I must indeed; and therefore came I
    hither.

R came to die

Good gentle youth, tempt not a desp'rate man;
Fly hence, and leave me. Think upon these
    gone;   60
Let them affright thee. I beseech thee, youth,
Put not another sin upon my head
By urging me to fury; O, be gone!
By heaven, I love thee better than myself,
For I come hither arm'd against myself.   65
Stay not, be gone; live, and hereafter say
A madman's mercy bid thee run away.

Paris. I do defy thy conjuration,[40]
And apprehend thee for a felon here.

Romeo. Wilt thou provoke me? Then have at
    thee, boy!   [*They fight.*]   70

Page. O lord, they fight! I will go call the watch.

                          [*Exit. Paris falls.*]

Paris. O, I am slain! If thou be merciful,
Open the tomb, lay me with Juliet.   [*Dies.*]

---

[40] *conjuration*: solemn entreaty.

Romeo. In faith, I will. Let me peruse this face.
   Mercutio's kinsman, noble County Paris!   *75*
   What said my man, when my betossed soul
   Did not attend[41] him as we rode? I think
   He told me Paris should have married Juliet.
   Said he not so, or did I dream it so?
   Or am I mad, hearing him talk of Juliet,   *80*
   To think it was so? O, give me thy hand,
   One writ with me in sour misfortune's book!
   I'll bury thee in a triumphant grave.
   A grave? O no! A lantern, slaught'red youth;
   For here lies Juliet, and her beauty makes   *85*
   This vault a feasting presence[42] full of light.
   Death, lie thou there, by a dead man interr'd.

                      [Laying Paris in the tomb.]

   How oft when men are at the point of death
   Have they been merry! Which their keepers[43] call
   A lightning before death. O, how may I   *90*
   Call this a lightning? O my love! my wife!
   Death, that hath suck'd the honey of thy breath,
   Hath had no power yet upon thy beauty.
   Thou art not conquer'd; beauty's ensign[44] yet
   Is crimson in thy lips and in thy cheeks,   *95*
   And death's pale flag is not advanced there.
   Tybalt, liest thou there in thy bloody sheet?
   O, what more favour can I do to thee
   Than with that hand that cut thy youth in twain
   To sunder his that was thine enemy?   *100*

---

[41] *attend*: give attention to.
[42] *feasting presence*: festive chamber where a person of rank would receive guests.
[43] *keepers*: guards, jailers.
[44] *ensign*: banner.

Forgive me, cousin. Ah, dear Juliet,
Why art thou yet so fair? Shall I believe
That unsubstantial Death is amorous,
And that the lean abhorred monster keeps
Thee here in dark to be his paramour?   105
For fear of that I still will stay with thee,
And never from this palace of dim night
Depart again. Here, here will I remain
With worms that are thy chambermaids. O,
     here
Will I set up my everlasting rest,   110
And shake the yoke of inauspicious stars
From this world-wearied flesh. Eyes, look your
     last.
Arms, take your last embrace. And, lips, O you
The doors of breath, seal with a righteous kiss
A dateless[45] bargain to engrossing[46] death!   115
Come, bitter conduct,[47] come, unsavoury guide.
Thou desperate pilot,[48] now at once run on
The dashing rocks thy sea-sick weary bark.[49]
Here's to my love! [*Drinks.*] O true apothecary!
Thy drugs are quick. Thus with a kiss I die.   120

                                        [*Falls.*]

Enter Friar Lawrence, with lantern, crow, and spade.

Friar Lawrence. Saint Francis be my speed![50]
     How oft to-night
Have my old feet stumbled at graves!
     Who's there?

---

[45] *dateless*: eternal.
[46] *engrossing*: all-encompassing.
[47] *conduct*: guide, i.e., the poison.
[48] *pilot*: steersman of a ship.
[49] *bark*: ship, boat.
[50] *speed*: help, protection.

Balthasar. Here's one, a friend, and one that
    knows you well.

Friar Lawrence. Bliss be upon you! Tell me,
    good my friend,
  What torch is yond that vainly lends his light   *125*
  To grubs and eyeless skulls? As I discern,
  It burneth in the Capels' monument.

Balthasar. It doth so, holy sir; and there's my
    master,
  One that you love.

Friar Lawrence. Who is it?

Balthasar.   Romeo.

Friar Lawrence. How long hath he been there?

Balthasar.   Full half an hour. *130*

Friar Lawrence. Go with me to the vault.

Balthasar.   I dare not, sir.
  My master knows not but I am gone hence,
  And fearfully did menace me with death,
  If I did stay to look on his intents.

Friar Lawrence. Stay, then, I'll go alone; fear
    comes upon me;   *135*
  O, much I fear some ill unthrifty[51] thing.

Balthasar. As I did sleep under this yew tree
    here,
  I dreamt my master and another fought,
  And that my master slew him.

Friar Lawrence.   Romeo!
  Alack, alack, what blood is this which stains   *140*

---

[51] *unthrifty*: unlucky.

The stony entrance of this sepulchre?
What mean these masterless and gory swords
To lie discolour'd by this place of peace?

                              [*Enters the tomb.*]

Romeo! O, pale! Who else? What, Paris too?
And steep'd in blood? Ah, what an unkind[52]
   hour   145
Is guilty of this lamentable chance!
The lady stirs.   [*Juliet wakes.*]

Juliet. O comfortable[53] friar! Where is my lord?
I do remember well where I should be,
And there I am. Where is my Romeo?   150

                              [*Noise within.*]

Friar Lawrence. I hear some noise. Lady, come
      from that nest
Of death, contagion, and unnatural sleep;
A greater power than we can contradict
Hath thwarted our intents. Come, come away;
Thy husband in thy bosom there lies dead;   155
And Paris too. Come, I'll dispose of thee
Among a sisterhood of holy nuns.
Stay not to question, for the watch is coming;
Come, go, good Juliet. I dare no longer stay.

Juliet. Go, get thee hence, for I will not away.   160

                    [*Exit Friar Lawrence.*]

What's here? A cup, clos'd in my true love's
   hand?
Poison, I see, hath been his timeless[54] end.

---

[52] *unkind:* unnatural, unlucky.
[53] *comfortable:* comforting.
[54] *timeless:* untimely.

O churl![55] drunk all, and left no friendly drop
To help me after? I will kiss thy lips;
Haply some poison yet doth hang on them,   165
To make me die with a restorative.

> [*Kisses him.*]

Thy lips are warm.

1 Watch. [*Within.*] Lead, boy. Which way?

Juliet. Yea, noise? Then I'll be brief. O happy[56]
    dagger!

> [*Snatching Romeo's dagger.*]

This is thy sheath; there rust, and let me die.

> [*She stabs herself and falls on Romeo's body.*]

Enter Watch, with Paris's Page.

Page. This is the place; there, where the torch
    doth burn.   170

1 Watch. The ground is bloody; search about the
    churchyard.
Go, some of you, whoe'er you find attach.

> [*Exeunt some of the Watch.*]

Pitiful sight! here lies the County slain;
And Juliet bleeding, warm, and newly dead,
Who here hath lain this two days buried.
Go, tell the Prince; run to the Capulets;
Raise up the Montagues; some others search.

> [*Exeunt others of the Watch.*]

---

[55] *churl*: rude or miserly man.
[56] *happy*: opportune.

We see the ground whereon these woes do lie;
But the true ground of all these piteous woes   *179*
We cannot without circumstance[57] descry.[58]

Re-enter some of the Watch with Balthasar.

2 *Watch.* Here's Romeo's man; we found him in
    the churchyard.

1 *Watch.* Hold him in safety till the Prince come
    hither.

Re-enter Friar Lawrence and another Watchman.

3 *Watch.* Here is a friar that trembles, sighs, and
    weeps;
  We took this mattock and this spade from him,
  As he was coming from this churchyard's side.   *185*

1 *Watch.* A great suspicion; stay the friar too.

Enter the Prince and Attendants.

Prince. What misadventure is so early up,
  That calls our person from our morning rest?

Enter Capulet, Lady Capulet, and Others.

Capulet. What should it be that is so shriek'd
    abroad?

Lady Capulet. The people in the street cry
    'Romeo',   *190*
  Some 'Juliet' and some 'Paris'; and all run,
  With open outcry, toward our monument.

Prince. What fear is this which startles in our
    ears?

---

[57] *circumstance*: details.
[58] *descry*: detect, discover.

1 Watch. Sovereign, here lies the County Paris
    slain;
  And Romeo dead; and Juliet, dead before, 195
  Warm and new kill'd.

Prince. Search, seek, and know how this foul
    murder comes.

1 Watch. Here is a friar, and slaughter'd Romeo's
    man,
  With instruments upon them fit to open
  These dead men's tombs. 200

Capulet. O heavens! O wife, look how our
    daughter bleeds!
  This dagger hath mista'en, for, lo, his house[59]
  Is empty on the back of Montague,
  And it mis-sheathed in my daughter's bosom.

Lady Capulet. O me! this sight of death is as a
    bell 205
  That warns my old age to a sepulchre.

Enter Montague and Others.

Prince. Come, Montague, for thou art early up
  To see thy son and heir more early down.

Montague. Alas, my liege, my wife is dead to-
    night;
  Grief of my son's exile hath stopp'd her breath. 210
  What further woe conspires against mine age?

Prince. Look, and thou shalt see.

Montague. O thou untaught! what manners is
    in this,
  To press before thy father to a grave?

---

[59] *house*: i.e., sheath.

Prince. Seal up the mouth of outrage[60] for a while,　215
　　Till we can clear these ambiguities,
　　And know their spring, their head, their true
　　　　descent;
　　And then will I be general[61] of your woes,
　　And lead you even to death. Meantime forbear,
　　And let mischance be slave to patience.　220
　　Bring forth the parties of suspicion.

Friar Lawrence. I am the greatest, able to do
　　　　least,
　　Yet most suspected, as the time and place
　　Doth make against me, of this direful murder;
　　And here I stand, both to impeach and purge[62]　225
　　Myself condemned and myself excus'd.

Prince. Then say at once what thou dost know in
　　　　this.

Friar Lawrence. I will be brief, for my short
　　　　date of breath[63]
　　Is not so long as is a tedious tale.
　　Romeo, there dead, was husband to that Juliet;　230
　　And she, there dead, that Romeo's faithful wife.
　　I married them; and their stol'n marriage day
　　Was Tybalt's doomsday, whose untimely death
　　Banish'd the new-made bridegroom from this
　　　　city;
　　For whom, and not for Tybalt, Juliet pin'd.　235
　　You, to remove that siege of grief from her,
　　Betroth'd, and would have married her perforce,
　　To County Paris. Then comes she to me,
　　And with wild looks bid me devise some mean
　　To rid her from this second marriage,　240
　　Or in my cell there would she kill herself.

---

[60] *the mouth of outrage*: violent cries of grief and horror.
[61] *general*: ruler, leader, superintendent.
[62] *purge*: exonerate.
[63] *date of breath*: term of life.

Then gave I her, so tutor'd by my art,
A sleeping potion; which so took effect
As I intended, for it wrought on her
The form of death. Meantime I writ to Romeo   245
That he should hither come as[64] this dire night
To help to take her from her borrowed grave,
Being the time the potion's force should cease.
But he which bore my letter, Friar John,
Was stay'd by accident, and yesternight   250
Return'd my letter back. Then all alone
At the prefixed hour of her waking
Came I to take her from her kindred's vault;
Meaning to keep her closely[65] at my cell
Till I conveniently could send to Romeo.   255
But when I came, some minute ere the time
Of her awakening, here untimely lay
The noble Paris and true Romeo dead.
She wakes; and I entreated her come forth,
And bear this work of heaven with patience.   260
But then a noise did scare me from the tomb,
And she, too desperate, would not go with me,
But, as it seems, did violence on herself.
All this I know, and to the marriage
Her nurse is privy;[66] and if aught in this   265
Miscarried by my fault, let my old life
Be sacrific'd, some hour before his time,
Unto the rigour of severest law.

Prince. We still[67] have known thee for a holy man.
Where's Romeo's man? What can he say to this?   270

Balthasar. I brought my master news of Juliet's
          death;
And then in post he came from Mantua

---

[64] *as*: on.
[65] *closely*: hidden.
[66] *privy*: an accessory, privy to (the secret marriage).
[67] *still*: always.

To this same place, to this same monument.
This letter he early bid me give his father;
And threat'ned me with death, going in the
    vault,   275
If I departed not and left him there.

Prince. Give me the letter, I will look on it.
    Where is the County's page that rais'd the
      watch?
    Sirrah, what made[68] your master in this place?

Page. He came with flowers to strew his lady's
    grave;   280
    And bid me stand aloof, and so I did.
    Anon comes one with light to ope the tomb;
    And by and by my master drew on him;
    And then I ran away to call the watch.

Prince. This letter doth make good the friar's
    words,   285
    Their course of love, the tidings of her death;
    And here he writes that he did buy a poison
    Of a poor pothecary, and therewithal[69]
    Came to this vault to die, and lie with Juliet.
    Where be these enemies? Capulet, Montague,   290
    See what a scourge is laid upon your hate,
    That heaven finds means to kill your joys with
      love!
    And I, for winking at[70] your discords too,
    Have lost a brace[71] of kinsmen. All are punish'd.

Capulet. O brother Montague, give me thy hand.   295
    This is my daughter's jointure,[72] for no more
    Can I demand.

---

[68] *what made*: why or for what reason was.
[69] *therewithal*: with that (poison).
[70] *winking at*: turning a blind eye to.
[71] *brace*: pair (i.e., Mercutio and Paris).
[72] *jointure*: marriage settlement.

Montague.   But I can give thee more;
  For I will raise her statue in pure gold,
  That whiles Verona by that name is known,
  There shall no figure at such rate[73] be set   300
  As that of true and faithful Juliet.

Capulet. As rich shall Romeo's by his lady's lie—
  Poor sacrifices of our enmity!

Prince. A glooming[74] peace this morning with it
      brings;
  The sun for sorrow will not show his head.   305
  Go hence, to have more talk of these sad things;
  Some shall be pardon'd and some punished;
  For never was a story of more woe
  Than this of Juliet and her Romeo.   [*Exeunt.*] 309

---

[73] *rate*: price, value.
[74] *glooming*: gloomy, clouded.

Contemporary Criticism

Romeo and Juliet on Film

James Bemis
California Political Review

William Shakespeare's *Romeo and Juliet* may be the Bard's most beloved and frequently read play. Its story of doomed lovers has inspired countless plays, novels, films, pieces of music, and other works of art. In fact, the names of the title characters have themselves become part of the lexicon, perhaps the ultimate sign of cultural acceptance. Further, the play contains what is unquestionably some of the world's greatest love poetry.

While crowds adore the brilliant romantic surface of *Romeo and Juliet*, it is worth considering whether Shakespeare created a deeper, more profound drama, the substance of which is missed by today's audiences, so enthralled by the play's sensational pathos and sentiment. It is worth considering whether the familiar love story is only part of this tragedy's richness and whether another element of the play is nowadays overlooked. This other element can be summarized as follows: when people—adults in particular—shirk their responsibilities, then disorder, confusion, and tragedy inevitably follow. As Ulysses says in Shakespeare's *Troilus and Cressida*, "Take but degree away, untune that string, and hark what discord follows!" (1.2.113–14).[1]

The Characters of Romeo and Juliet

While Verona's social disorder is an important backdrop, the love story of Romeo and Juliet is the play's primary focus. In developing the story "of Juliet and her Romeo" (5.3.309),[2]

---

[1] William Shakespeare, *Troilus and Cressida*, Folger Library edition (New York: Pocket Books, 1966).

[2] All quotations from *Romeo and Juliet* are from the edition published by Ignatius Press: *Romeo and Juliet*, ed. Joseph Pearce, Ignatius Critical Editions (San Francisco: Ignatius Press, 2011).

Shakespeare has created two of the most unforgettable characters in all literature.

Romeo

Romeo undergoes the greatest change of any character over the play's course. From moonstruck youth to "world-wearied" husband ready for eternal rest beside his spouse, the actor playing this role must make this transformation credible, not an easy task for even the most skilled and accomplished performer.

Juliet

Juliet is one of Shakespeare's greatest creations. The Bard produced a veritable army of interesting, lively, and well-rounded young female characters. *Hamlet*'s Ophelia, *Twelfth Night*'s Viola, *As You Like It*'s Rosalind, *The Merchant of Venice*'s Portia, and *King Lear*'s Cordelia are among literature's most delightful creatures. But none exceed Juliet in brilliance and charm.

Because of the many facets of Juliet's character and her wisdom beyond her age, playing this role poses a major problem for most. Actresses of substance generally are too old to be credible, and those who are young enough have difficulty portraying the character's wisdom, grit, and determination.

Verona's Social Disorder

Shakespeare's view of the social chaos gripping Verona is revealed in the folly and weakness of four characters: the Prince (representing the state); Capulet and Montague (representing the family); and Friar Lawrence (representing the Church).

The Prince

Prince Escalus appears in the play at three key moments: in the opening scene; after Mercutio and Tybalt are killed in Act 3, scene 1; and in the finale, in Act 5, scene 3. While the Prince's words are always stern, his appeals are ignored as the disorder and street violence intensify.

The role of the Prince is larger than his few words would indicate. As the representative of the state, he is responsible for maintaining order in Verona, which has completely broken down. The brawls continue throughout the play, as if no one (except perhaps Benvolio) worries much about the long arm of the law restraining them. Thus, the Prince is responsible for much of this chaos and destruction of life.

Capulet and Montague

If the Prince represents the head of the state, then Capulet and Montague are the heads of the two hostile families. Likewise, these two fathers bear part of the blame for Verona's unruly streets. Capulet is a more fully drawn character than Montague, who has only a few lines. But with aristocrats like the mercurial Capulet, we can easily see why the Prince has so much trouble keeping order in his city.

Our last view of Capulet is in the final mourning scene, when he, along with Montague, is solemn and chastened. His final words about the young couple—"Poor sacrifices of our enmity!" (5.3.303)—indicate he has learned at last the drama's terrible lesson: when proper authority is absent, civil disorder results, and it is the weakest and most innocent that suffer most.

Friar Lawrence

Another character in which the terrible consequences of failed authority are made evident is Friar Lawrence. While beloved by the young couple and, by all accounts, a holy man, the priest displays a tendency toward connivance and Gnosticism, with fatal consequences.

Our first glimpse of the Friar comes in Act 2, scene 3, when he is absorbed in tending to his herbs and weeds:

> O, mickle is the powerful grace that lies
> In plants, herbs, stones, and their true qualities;
> For nought so vile that on the earth doth live
> But to the earth some special good doth give.
>
> (2.3.15–18)

Romeo then appears and tells the Friar of his new love. Despite knowing how quickly Romeo's emotions change, the Friar agrees to wed the couple that very day, as the priest fosters the grandiose hope that the marriage will bring peace between the two warring families:

> In one respect I'll thy assistant be;
> For this alliance may so happy prove
> To turn your households' rancour to pure love.
>   (2.3.90–92)

This hasty action by Friar Lawrence defies common sense. Neither the Catholic Church nor any adult of sound judgment would counsel any such thing of a young couple who had just met, especially knowing their families are at odds. Rather, they likely would advise that the two get to know each other and bring their relationship along slowly. Granted, the Friar's acquiescence is a plot device to keep the story moving at its fast pace; however, Shakespeare nevertheless shows yet one more adult in Verona neglecting his duty for expediency's sake.

Friar Lawrence compounds his error by making another mistake in judgment, that of concocting the "deathlike" drug plot to reconnect the two lovers. As if marrying the barely acquainted couple was not enough, he concocts this harebrained reunion scheme that is so dependent on secret potions, prompt notification, and exact timing that it seems doomed to fail. A sounder voice of authority would have counseled the couple to meet with their parents, express their love for each other, and hope to turn their household's "rancour to pure love" in that manner. Thus did this representative of the Catholic Church betray both his Church's teachings and the young couple that had depended on him for guidance. Further, his reliance on a "magic" drug to solve the couple's problem reeks of the alchemist and is unbecoming of a holy priest.

With adult leadership like the Prince, Capulet, Montague, and Friar Lawrence, it is no wonder Verona was in such an unruly state!

Romeo and Juliet on Film: Five Performances

Romeo and Juliet is frequently performed, and a wide variety of film versions are available. Let us look at how the characters are developed in five films. The results are summarized in table 1.

Metro-Goldwyn-Mayer (MGM) (1936)

This must have seemed like a great idea on paper: assemble a first-class crew of Hollywood's finest, including a very successful director (George Cukor), and have the popular, refined Leslie Howard play Romeo, and the beautiful "First Lady of MGM", Norma Shearer, portray Juliet. Have old pros like John Barrymore, Edna May Oliver, Basil Rathbone, C. Aubry Smith, and Andy Devine in key supporting roles, and—voilà—you have an instant classic.

Unfortunately, the result here is like an all-star sports team that falls flat on its face in real competition. The production is overly fussy and almost stifling. There is little chemistry among the cast, and the film floats aimlessly like a rudderless boat.

What is worse, the frequent complaint about the ancient cast is only too accurate. Selecting the forty-three-year-old Howard and the thirty-four-year-old Shearer for the title roles doomed this effort. Accentuating the problem was casting a bunch of old veterans in the supporting roles. One must restrain from chuckling when fifty-four-year-old John Barrymore appears as the fiery and energetic Mercutio, foppishly clad in ruffles and tights.

In keeping with this restrained production, the social disorder shown in the opening scene is muted. The Capulets' party in Act 1, scene 5, is more like a grand Victorian ball than a medieval Italian dance, and the first meeting between Romeo and Juliet is stiff and formal. No one would imagine that these two would be willing to die for each other just four acts later. The same holds true for Juliet's balcony scene in Act 2, scene 2.

Table 1: Summary of Five Film Productions of *Romeo and Juliet*

Year Produced	1936	1968	1976	1978	1996
Director	George Cukor	Franco Zeffirelli	Joan Kemp-Welsh	BBC	Baz Luhrmann
Casting:					
Romeo	Leslie Howard	Leonard Whiting	Christopher Neame	Patrick Ryecart	Leonardo Di Caprio
Juliet	Norma Shearer	Olivia Hussey	Ann Hasson	Rebecca Saire	Clare Danes
Prince	Conway Tearle	Robert Stephens	Peter Dynely	Laurence Naismith	Vondie Curtis-Hall
Capulet	Aubrey Smith	Paul Hardwick	Laurence Payne	Michael Hordern	Paul Sorvino
Friar Lawrence	Henry Kolker	Milo O'Shea	Clive Swift	Joseph O'Conor	Peter Postlethwaite
Act 1, Scene 1: Verona's Social Disorder	Disorder muted, like rest of production	Beautiful introduction, excellent opening	Does not show corrosive effects of disorder	Portrayal of social chaos stunning	Whacked-out youths vividly show social chaos
Act 1, Scene 5: The Capulets' Party	Party like Victorian ball; Romeo and Juliet stiff and formal	Fully realized scene, magnificent ball; Zeffirelli's gamble on casting Romeo and Juliet pays off	Party rather too tame and fussy; Romeo too old for Juliet, but Juliet winningly winsome	Party scene made memorable by Hordern's excellence as Capulet; Romeo bland, but Juliet charming	Romeo better than expected; Juliet homely and lifeless
Act 2, Scene 2: Juliet's Balcony	Too sanitized and proper; fire and passion missing	Rings with youthful passion and exuberance	Works fine, accomplished in earnest fashion	Juliet fine, but Romeo out of his element	Wooing scene touching and romantic
Act 2, Scene 3: Friar Lawrence's Cell	Forgettable, nondescript Friar	Friar just about right, earthy with romantic streak	Friar has strange, unsavory air; not credible as counselor	Friar sincere and believable	Friar is modern priest obsessed with potions
Act 3, Scene 1: Fights between Tybalt, Mercutio, and Romeo	Disappointing; fights seem implausible	A high point: McEnery's Mercutio unexcelled; Romeo's transformation credible	Film's highlight; Mercutio particularly good; death scene moving	Sword fights are embarrassment; Romeo not credible as man of action	Violent; all testosterone and no tact
Act 5, Scene 3: The Capulets' Crypt	Film's highlight; older actors better reflect matured lovers	Evocative without becoming maudlin	Horribly inept; supporting actors stiff and amateurish	Death scenes marred by poor acting	Appropriately shocking—director nails ending
Overall Grade	F	A-	D+	C+	B

Cukor's version is so sanitized and proper that the fire and passion between the lovers is completely missing.

Friar Lawrence (Henry Kolker) is a rather forgettable character here. While he enunciates his lines competently, we never get the impression that he is focused on solving the lovers' problems and bringing the families together. It is hard to imagine anyone following the catastrophic advice of such a nondescript character.

Perhaps the film's greatest disappointment is the fight scenes in Act 3, scene 1. Barrymore and Rathbone make such an unlikely Mercutio and Tybalt that their fight comes off as implausible. Further, Howard's Romeo lacks the requisite anger and passion that would have caused Romeo to attack the stronger, more experienced Tybalt.

The climatic action in the damp, dark crypt in Act 5, scene 3, works well, perhaps because the older actors better reflect the now more mature lovers. But the final scene in the tomb again reminds us of the age incongruity as we see the dead lovers mourned by parents who appear of almost equal age. Closing the film to the strains of Tchaikovsky's *Romeo and Juliet* only adds a touch of kitsch to this listless production.

Paramount Pictures (1968)

In 1968 Franco Zeffirelli directed a version of *Romeo and Juliet* that was a tremendous box office triumph. Grossing over forty-eight million dollars, it remains the biggest Shakespeare movie success to date. Starring newcomers Leonard Whiting (then seventeen) and Olivia Hussey (then fifteen), Zeffirelli's film was controversial for using two unknowns in the title roles and for a brief scene of nudity. It was royally panned by some major reviewers like Pauline Kael and John Simon, but was extremely popular with audiences, especially the young.

In Act 1, scene 1, after a beautiful introduction and setup by the director, we quickly see the social chaos that is devastating Verona. First knives, then swords, flash; women scream; and the daily business of trade and commerce become impossible.

The Prince in this production (Robert Stephens) is a tall, angular figure of authority, stern but without the gravity one might expect. His words are harsh, but one senses this is not the end of the disorder but only the beginning. The scene is effective in capturing the dramatist's intent.

The Capulets' party in Act 1, scene 5, is one of the film's two most fully realized scenes (the other is the fights between Mercutio, Tybalt, and Romeo in Act 3, scene 1). After earlier meeting the handsome, likable Romeo and his boisterous friends, we are swept inside a magnificent ball already under way. The scene is a visual delight, a rich treasure of light and shadow, music and dance, color and fabric, wine and food, and attractive men and women. But once the Moresca dance begins, there is one person from whom we cannot remove our eyes—and her name is Juliet.

Zeffirelli decided early on that he was going to make a movie, not a filmed stage production of *Romeo and Juliet*. This dictated his choice of leads—two absolutely gorgeous youngsters with virtually no experience. He never looked back. The payoff of this casting decision comes when Romeo first steals a word with Juliet. Hussey's Juliet is just the right age—part girl, part woman, all female. She is astonishingly beautiful in this scene, inno-cent and sweet with a charmingly husky laugh. You can under-stand why Romeo would rather die than live without her.

The jury is still out on whether Hussey and Whiting acted well in this movie, but in some ways that is to miss the point. Zeffirelli's aim was to capture the beauty and intensity in the couples' love, and he did this brilliantly.

The scene on Juliet's balcony in Act 2, scene 2, also rings with youthful passion and exuberance. Was there ever a more eager and endearing lover than Whiting's Romeo in this scene? Yet Juliet here shows the requisite maturity and level-headedness. When Romeo asks if she will leave him so unsatisfied, her indig-nant "What satisfaction canst thou have to-night?" (2.2.126) shows a virtuous wisdom beyond her years.

When Romeo finds Friar Lawrence (Milo O'Shea) in Act 2, scene 3, the priest is tending his herbal garden and ruminating about nature's power. O'Shea's Friar Lawrence, combining earthiness with a clear romantic streak, gets the character nearly right. His abrupt approval of Romeo's marriage seems fitting for the Friar, although it would have been astonishing in real life.

The fight between the tempestuous Tybalt and the mocking Mercutio in Act 3, scene 1, is one of the film's high points. John McEnery's portrayal of Mercutio is unexcelled. Further, Zeffirelli brilliantly captures Romeo's rage ("fire-ey'd fury be my conduct now!" [3.1.121]), switching to a handheld camera during Romeo and Tybalt's fight to show the blood, sweat, and spittle of their *mano a mano* duel. Romeo's transformation from a man of peace into a man of action seems logical and credible.

The final scene in the crypt in Act 5, scene 3, is suitably evocative without becoming maudlin, as occurs in some productions. Hussey is particularly fine here, casting off her girlish emotions and becoming a woman determined to finish what her husband has started. No convent for her, despite Friar Lawrence's suggestion—she will lie for eternity next to her beloved.

More than most productions, Zeffirelli's version ends with appropriate sadness but also a sense of peace in the belief that the families' feud is ended and order restored, albeit at great cost. Thus, though many will disagree, Zeffirelli created a cinematic masterpiece and a film that will educate and ennoble for generations. It is hard to imagine a better introduction to Shakespeare.

Thames Television (1976)

In 1976 Thames Television released a filmed performance of their production of *Romeo and Juliet*, directed by Joan Kemp-Welch. The cast features Christopher Neame and Ann Hasson in the title roles, Laurence Payne as Capulet, Clive Swift as Friar Lawrence, and Peter Dynely as the Prince.

Overall, the production lacks energy and vitality. The opening scene misses its opportunity to show the corrosive social effects of the existing disorder and instead seems to show simply a group of young men with too much spirit. Peter Dynely's Prince is elderly and weak, giving a different twist to why the social chaos persists. This carries over into a rather too-tame and fussy party scene at the Capulets' in Act 1, scene 5. Payne's performance as Capulet is far too calm and restrained to be credible. Further, Neame's Romeo appears too old for this Juliet. On the other hand, while Hasson is not a beautiful Juliet, she is winningly winsome.

Juliet's balcony scene in Act 2, scene 2, works fine and is accomplished in a straightforward and earnest fashion. Both Neame and Hasson handle themselves well, and director Kemp-Welsh resists the urge to "liven things up" with pratfalls or athletic surges by the male lead, which are the bane of many other productions.

In the action in Friar Lawrence's cell in Act 2, scene 3, Swift has a strange, unsavory air, making it hard to believe that the young couple would trust their future to such a man, undercutting a key element of the plot. Further, Swift has a tendency to rush his lines, making him sound more like a salesman than a clergyman.

In Act 3, scene 1, the brawl between Mercutio and Tybalt is a highlight, with Robin Nedwell being a particularly good Mercutio. The fight scene with Tybalt is credible, and Mercutio's death scene is particularly moving. Unfortunately, Romeo's clumsy battle with Tybalt is much less credible, and Romeo's transformation into a man of action does not work in Neame's hands.

Sadly, this production is horribly inept at portraying the action in the Capulet crypt in Act 5, scene 3. What should be the dramatic high point of the tragedy is completely undone by stiff and amateurish acting by the minor players. Simon McCorkindale's Paris is awful, and both Paris' page (Mark Rogers) and Balthasar (Robin Halstead) perform as if in a high school production. Friar Lawrence overacts dreadfully in his big scene. Competent performances by Neame and Hasson cannot raise this scene above the level of camp.

BBC (1978)

As part of its generally excellent Complete Dramatic Works of William Shakespeare, the BBC released a 1978 production of *Romeo and Juliet*, starring Patrick Ryecart and Rebecca Saire in the title roles and a veteran cast, including Michael Hordern as Capulet, Celia Johnson as the Nurse, Joseph O'Connor as Friar Lawrence, a very young Alan Rickman as Tybalt, and the venerable John Gielgud as the Chorus.

The BBC Shakespeare productions are nothing if not solid and steady, and its version of *Romeo and Juliet* is no exception. Ryecart and Saire make a passable couple, but they seem so intent on enunciating correctly that the passion and chemistry in their relationship is missing. This is primarily due to Ryecart's inadequacy as an actor. He is simply bland and shows no development throughout the play's course, quite contrary to the fascinating character Shakespeare created.

The portrayal of the existing social disorder in Act 1, scene 1, is fine and even stunning as it affects innocent bystanders, including a baby that is wounded in the swordplay. In the scene at the Capulets' soiree, the old warhorse Michael Hordern makes a memorable Capulet, lovable but with a fiery temper. The party scene is well executed; Saire's coquettishness is appealing and her flirtation with Romeo charming.

Saire is also fine in the balcony scene in Act 2, scene 2, but Ryecart seems out of his element. The direction fails also: the scene is marred by two slapstick falls by Romeo, who attempts first to climb the trellis and then the wall.

Joseph O'Connor makes an earnest and believable Friar Lawrence. In his cell in Act 2, scene 3, he exudes sincerity even as he dispenses bad advice.

It must be said that the sword fights in this production are an embarrassment, with the fight between Mercutio and Tybalt in Act 3, scene 1, being particularly awful. The actors are as clumsy as two horses on ice, undercutting the scene's importance. Likewise, Ryecart's Romeo is not credible as a man of action.

The lovers' death scenes in Act 5, scene 3, do not work well either: Saire emotes for the only time, while Ryecart underacts in his part. The excessive blood on Juliet's breast adds a jarring note in an otherwise overly sanitized production. The final reconciliation scene, however, works well, primarily due to the affection built for Capulet, whom Hordern makes likable despite the old man's flaws.

Twentieth Century Fox Film Corporation (1996)

In 1996 Baz Luhrmann directed what amounts to a rock 'n' roll version of *Romeo and Juliet*, starring Leonardo Di Caprio and Clare Danes in the title roles. Luhrmann took a great degree of risk with this production, as he kept Shakespeare's language but melded it with modern displays of violence and production values. The risk was that the language might be too foreign for youthful audiences, while the gore and flashiness might alienate older ones.

Luhrmann's production seemed to have succeeded with the former type of audience and failed with the latter. The film was widely panned, but the movie was popular with the market segment that buys most movie tickets. Receipts were enhanced by the presence of teen heartthrob Di Caprio, who was at his peak as a matinee idol.

Overall, the production certainly has its faults, but it displays surprising strengths as well. Shakespeare's message of the social chaos that results when adults abandon their responsibilities is clearly evident. The drama opens with the Prologue being said by a television news anchor, informing her audience of the double suicide of the young lovers. The brawl featured in Act 1, scene 1, is enacted by groups of whacked-out youths carrying heavy weaponry and terrorizing innocent citizens. While Shakespeare could not have foreseen the extent of social disorder in modern American society, he certainly knew what would happen to any civilization once those in authority abdicated their duty. Luhrmann's film succeeds brilliantly in showing this logical consequence in very vivid terms.

That said, the production does have some major problems. While, given the film's context, Di Caprio makes a better-than-expected Romeo, Clare Danes is a homely and lifeless Juliet. The only explanation for Romeo's attraction to her is that she stands out from the other females in having a measure of purity and innocence.

The Capulets' party in Act 1, scene 5, is a weird affair with obvious drug use and other strange goings-on. Nevertheless, the wooing scene between Romeo and Juliet—taking place on opposite sides of a fish tank—is touching and romantic. Likewise, the scene at Juliet's balcony (and swimming pool) retains much of the charm Shakespeare intended, mostly because of Di Caprio's believability as the eager Romeo.

Friar Lawrence is a revelation, as Pete Postlethwaite portrays him as a very modern priest, a Gnostic obsessed with chemicals and potions. This is an aspect of the Friar's character that Shakespeare intended to be prominent but that tends to be downplayed. However, much to Luhrmann's credit, this element of the Friar's character is given full flower.

The fight between Mercutio and Tybalt in Act 3, scene 1, is staged with the predictability of a violent modern movie—all testosterone and no tact. One surprising element added by Luhrmann is that his Romeo is cowardly in his confrontation with Tybalt, which is not what Shakespeare intended and conflicts with the boldness and determination Romeo later displays.

The play's final scene in the crypt is, surprisingly, one of the film's highlights. Juliet's end—taking her life with a single, incredibly loud gunshot to her head—is shocking to us in the way Elizabethans must have been shocked by the lovers' double suicide. Modern audiences have become so familiar with the story that they forget how astonishing it is for the couple both to commit suicide. It is especially astonishing that Christians—as Romeo and Juliet obviously are—would do such a thing, for by their act they are condemning their souls to Hell. Luhrmann deserves praise for recapturing the play's shocking ending in a way most contemporary productions miss.

Conclusion

Shakespeare's exceptional talents as a poet and dramatist can blind us to the fact that he was also an astute social commentator and had extraordinary insight into the human mind. In fact, it is the display of these talents—perhaps even more than his poetry—that rewards multiple readings of his plays and ensures him an audience in future generations. Thus it greatly profits the wise student to dig beneath the glorious surface of the Bard's plays and discover the less visible aspects of the dramas that others miss. *Romeo and Juliet*, with its dual sides of youthful love trying—but failing—to live amid social disorder and chaos, is an excellent illustration of Shakespeare's multi-faceted genius.

A Rose by Any Other Name:
The Plague of Language in *Romeo and Juliet*

Crystal Downing
Messiah College

Romeo: the Shakespearean character who risks everything for love. So goes the cliché about *Romeo and Juliet*—a bit ironic since Shakespeare's play is as much about clichés as it is about love. In fact, to judge *Romeo and Juliet* by its plot is to miss its substance. Shakespeare stole the plot, as he did with most of his plays. Scholars have long noted that plot merely serves as the canvas upon which Shakespeare paints his art.[1] The medium of his art is language, and an informed reading of *Romeo and Juliet* reveals that language functions not just as the medium of Shakespeare's art but also as its message.

Shakespeare hints at his message from the very start. Of his thirty-eight plays, only *Romeo and Juliet* begins with a sonnet, forcing us to assess his unusual tactic. Of course, since the sonnet was considered the preeminent form for love poetry in Shakespeare's day, it seems only natural that Shakespeare would use it to begin *Romeo and Juliet*. However, because he wrote many other plays about love without appending sonnets, we realize that something else must have been on Shakespeare's mind. Fortunately, *Romeo and Juliet* makes quite clear what it is: the power of clichés to control behavior.

I

By beginning *Romeo and Juliet* with a sonnet, Shakespeare alludes to the poet who made the form famous: Francesco Petrarch

---

[1] In his Bristol Lectures on Shakespeare (1813), Coleridge states, "The plot interests us on account of the characters, not vice versa; it is the canvas only." Quoted in Leo Salingar, *Shakespeare and the Traditions of Comedy* (Cambridge: Cambridge University Press, 1976), p. 19.

(1304–1374). Using the fourteen-line structure developed by a thirteenth-century Sicilian named Giacomo da Lentini, Petrarch wrote over three hundred poems idealizing—from afar—a beautiful woman named Laura. Though Chaucer had translated works by Petrarch, it was an ambassador for Henry VIII, Sir Thomas Wyatt (c. 1503–1542), who made Petrarch popular in England. Wyatt's translations of the Laura sonnets profoundly influenced poetic style during the Elizabethan era, so much so that around twelve hundred English sonnets have survived in print from the 1590s alone.[2] Significantly, Shakespeare wrote *Romeo and Juliet* at the height of the 1590s sonnet fad.[3]

In his sonnets, Petrarch describes the sublimely lovely Laura as beyond his reach, expressing the agony of unrequited love through the use of oxymorons: phrases in which an adjective contradicts the noun it modifies, as in the word "oxymoron", which literally means "sharp dullness". Romeo employs oxymorons in his very first multiline speech of the play, doing so to communicate "despair" over his own Laura: a beautiful woman named Rosaline who has "sworn that she will ... live chaste" (1.1.220, 215).[4] However, Romeo goes overboard with the oxymorons, piling them one on top of the other, as though a reiteration of the Petrarchan convention will reify his agony: "O loving hate! ... O heavy lightness! ... Feather of lead, bright smoke, cold fire, sick health! / Still-waking sleep" (1.1.174, 176, 178–79). Romeo's excess reduces Petrarchan convention—and himself—to cliché.

This is precisely Shakespeare's point, demonstrated when he has Romeo's friend Mercutio mock Romeo for his Petrarchan agonies:

---

[2] Hallett Smith, "Sonnets", in *The Riverside Shakespeare*, ed. G. Blakemore Evans (Boston: Houghton Mifflin, 1974), p. 1746. Smith notes that most scholars believe Shakespeare wrote his sonnets during the 1590s (p. 1745).

[3] Most scholars agree—if even disputing the exact year—that Shakespeare wrote *Romeo and Juliet* during the 1590s. See G. Blakemore Evans, "Chronology and Sources", in *Riverside Shakespeare*, p. 51.

[4] All quotations from *Romeo and Juliet* are from the edition published by Ignatius Press: *Romeo and Juliet*, ed. Joseph Pearce, Ignatius Critical Editions (San Francisco: Ignatius Press, 2011).

Romeo! humours! madman! passion! lover!
Appear thou in the likeness of a sigh;
Speak but one rhyme and I am satisfied;
Cry but "Ay me!" pronounce but "love" and "dove".
(2.1.7–10)

And lest we fail to see references to Petrarchan poetry here, Shakespeare makes the allusion explicit three scenes later through Mercutio's mockery of Romeo: "Now is he for the numbers that Petrarch flow'd in; Laura, to his lady, was a kitchen-wench" (2.4.38–39).

Shakespeare, like Mercutio, quite clearly means to make fun of Romeo. This is apparent in Romeo's Petrarchan effusions during his first sight of Juliet: "O, she doth teach the torches to burn bright! . . . Beauty too rich for use, for earth too dear! . . . Did my heart love till now? Forswear it, sight;/For I ne'er saw true beauty till this night" (1.5.42, 45, 50, 51). We cannot help wondering about all the nights he said similar things about Rosaline. In fact, Romeo's line "Beauty too rich for use, for earth too dear!" directly echoes his earlier description of Rosaline: "O, she is rich in beauty; only poor/That, when she dies, with beauty dies her store" (1.1.213–14). In other words, Rosaline's beauty is also "too rich for use".

Ironically, before Romeo ever lays eyes on Juliet, Benvolio prophetically suggests that Romeo might "forget" Rosaline if he were to "[e]xamine other beauties" (1.5.223, 226). But the Petrarchan lover considers it an impossibility:

Show me a mistress that is passing fair,
What doth her beauty serve but as a note
Where I may read who pass'd that passing fair?
Farewell; thou canst not teach me to forget.
(232–35)

How soon Romeo forgets not to forget! Why? Because he is in love with the idea of Petrarchan love more than with a flesh-and-blood person. Indeed, Rosaline is so unattainable that she never appears in the flesh onstage; she is merely a projection of Romeo's desire: a construction of language.[5] Romeo's reference to "a note / Where I may read" confirms our growing sense that he is a reader more than a lover.

II

Shakespeare draws attention to Romeo as reader when a Capulet servant stops him on the street: "I pray, sir, can you read?" Romeo's answer foregrounds his Petrarchan suffering: "Ay, mine own fortune in my misery." The servant's response, "Perhaps you have learned it without book", hints at just the opposite: perhaps Romeo's understanding of love comes from books. When the servant asks again, "[C]an you read anything you see?" Romeo insouciantly qualifies his reading abilities with "Ay, if I know the letters and the language", but when the servant turns to go, Romeo stops him: "Stay, fellow; I can read" (1.2.57–61, 63). Romeo then proceeds to read aloud the invitation list for a Capulet party, where he discovers Rosaline's name: an important plot device that gets him to the party where he will meet Juliet.

But Shakespeare did not need such a device to get Romeo to the party. He could have had someone inform Romeo—in one brief line—that Rosaline would be there. We therefore need to pay attention to the fact that Shakespeare not only repeats the word "read" three times in only seven lines but also visualizes Romeo in the act of reading—not just Rosaline's name but a nine-item list (64–70). Doing so, Shakespeare confirms that Romeo's actions and attitudes are based on what he reads, implying that what he reads is Petrarchan love poetry. Indeed, when the Friar hears that Romeo did "bury [his] love" for Rosaline as soon as he saw Juliet, the holy man impatiently tells the young lover, "O, she knew well / Thy love did read by rote that could not spell" (2.3.84, 87–88).

---

[5] I make this same point in Crystal Downing, "'Misshapen Chaos of Well-Seeming Form': Baz Luhrmann's *Romeo and Juliet*", *Literature/Film Quarterly* 28, no. 2 (2000): 126.

Shakespeare reinforces the idea of love by rote through his description of Paris, a suitor who talks to Capulet—but not to Juliet—about marrying the young girl. Lady Capulet asks her thirteen-year-old daughter about Paris—"Can you love the gentleman?"—and then explains how to assess his worth:

> Read o'er the volume of young Paris' face,
> And find delight writ there with beauty's pen;
>
> . . . .
> And what obscur'd in this fair volume lies
> Find written in the margent of his eyes.
>
> (1.3.80, 82–83, 86–87)

She thus advises Juliet to judge by surface appearances, to read Paris the same way Romeo reads the beautiful women he meets: according to conventions gleaned from "book[s] of love" (88). In fact, Romeo and Juliet both attend the Capulet party in order to connect with a conventional lover: Romeo will attempt to engage with Rosaline, while Juliet may become engaged to Paris.

But then something happens: Romeo and Juliet engage in conversation. And not just any conversation. Shakespeare has the two share a sonnet between them (1.5.91–105). As in all his sonnets, Shakespeare uses the style invented by Wyatt's friend the Earl of Surrey (c. 1517–1547). Unlike Petrarch, who divided each of his sonnets into an octave (eight lines) and a sestet (six lines), Surrey divided his fourteen lines into three quatrains (a rhyme scheme of ABAB, CDCD, EFEF) with a culminating couplet (GG).

Romeo delivers the first quatrain of his Surrey-like sonnet as he touches Juliet's hand:

> If I profane with my unworthiest hand
>   This holy shrine, the gentle sin is this:
> My lips, two blushing pilgrims, ready stand
>   To smooth that rough touch with a tender kiss.
>
> (91–94)

Juliet then takes over for the second quatrain, challenging Romeo's hand metaphor:

Good pilgrim, you do wrong your hand too much,
   Which mannerly devotion shows in this;
For saints have hands that pilgrims' hands do touch,
   And palm to palm is holy palmers' kiss.

                                 (95–98)

Rather than reject Romeo's sexually charged analogy, where touched hands elicit thoughts of touching lips, Juliet transforms it into a religious metaphor: palms kiss when they are pressed together in prayer. Shakespeare thus signals an effective conversation, in which a listener acknowledges what she has just heard and then develops something new in response to it.

Juliet's connection and change are reinforced by her rhyme. Romeo employs a traditional ABAB scheme in his quatrain; but rather than a CDCD response, Juliet employs a CBCB scheme, using the exact same words that Romeo employed at the end of his second and fourth lines—"this", "kiss"—a repetition that anticipates the kiss soon to follow.

Juliet's ability to engage with Romeo, using some of his words while maintaining her own metaphor, subverts the traditional sonnet not only in form but also in content. Petrarch's idealized, unattainable Laura was always the desirable object of the sonnet and hence was completely outside of it. In contrast, Shakespeare has Juliet enter into Romeo's sonnet, giving her control over its subject matter and hence over her own subjectivity.

Romeo and Juliet get even closer in the sonnet's third quatrain, zinging lines back and forth as they embellish their metaphors, Romeo with sexual connotations, Juliet with sacred. These connotations anticipate what will follow less than twenty-four hours later: the sacred and sexual become one as the lovers become one in the sacrament of marriage.

How significant, then, that the shared sonnet is consummated by its closing heroic couplet, two lines—each spoken by a different person—becoming one couplet. This time Juliet begins: "Saints do not move, though grant for prayers' sake." Romeo follows by playing with her words: "Then move not while my prayer's effect I take." Shakespeare quite obviously intended a kiss to happen at this point. Not only has the sonnet just finished, but Romeo's next line, with its starting word "Thus", makes sense only after a kiss has occurred: "Thus from my lips by thine my sin is purg'd" (103–5). Nevertheless, many editors insert "[Kisses her]" *after* Romeo's "thus" statement. The first person to do so was Nicholas Rowe (1674–1718), an English playwright who edited Shakespeare's plays in 1709. Rowe, in fact, inserted many of the stage directions we still find marked by brackets in Shakespeare plays.

Rowe reflects a tradition begun in the late seventeenth century when neoclassical poets and editors sought to clean up Shakespeare: John Dryden (1631–1700) was adulated for rewriting Shakespeare's "pester'd" and "obscure" works, one admirer commenting on a play, "You found it dirt and made it gold." When Alexander Pope (1688–1744) edited the plays for a 1725 edition, he "discarded passages he thought unworthy ... and constantly altered phrasing and meter to suit his own unyieldingly discerning tastes". As for *Romeo and Juliet*, Samuel Pepys (1633–1703) declared the play to be "the worst that ever I heard in my life", an assessment that may have inspired actor and theater manager David Garrick (1717–1779) to make changes to the script for his 1748 production, as when he has Juliet awaken in the tomb in order to have a sixty-line chat with Romeo before he dies.[6]

Significantly, the same neoclassical scholars who disdained Shakespeare's untidy writing also scorned the sonnet form. Considering the highest literary efforts to be those employed by Greek and Roman poets, the aptly named neoclassical critics dismissed the sonnet as upstart crowing. Samuel Johnson (1709–1784), though appreciative of Shakespeare's plays, described the sonnet in his famous 1755 dictionary as "a short poem consisting of fourteen lines ... not very suitable to the English

---

[6] See Bill Bryson, *Shakespeare: The World as a Stage* (London: HarperPress, 2007), pp. 169–71, and George C. D. Odell, *Shakespeare: From Betterton to Irving* (New York: Blom, 1963), 1:343–44.

language".[7] And in his edition of *Romeo and Juliet* published ten years later, Johnson says of the Chorus at the end of Act 1, "The use of this chorus is not easily discovered, it conduces nothing to the progress of the play, but relates what is already known, or what the next scene will show; and relates it without adding the improvement of any moral sentiment."[8] He has missed the fact that the Chorus is a sonnet, to be likened to the sonnet beginning the play, creating a pair of bookends that encases Romeo and Juliet's shared sonnet between them.[9] It is therefore quite likely that neoclassical editors of *Romeo and Juliet* failed to notice that Romeo and Juliet's first conversation took the form of a sonnet, and hence perpetuated Rowe's misplaced kiss. Problematic clichés have power over editors as well.

More important than the placement of the kiss, however, is the sense of agency that Shakespeare gives Juliet. When we first meet her in the play (1.3), her brief lines almost always express obedience to her mother or nurse. In fact, when Lady Capulet asks if she can "like" Paris, Juliet responds with the singsong liquid sounds we associate with children: "I'll look to like, if looking liking move" (1.3.98). We do not hear from her again until she trumps Romeo's sonnet quatrain with her own. In the midst of a sonnet, then, Juliet finally has been allowed to have a say about her life. Better yet, unlike Paris, who talks to Capulet *about* Juliet—much as Petrarch talked *about* Laura but never *to* her—Romeo responds to Juliet's words. Rather than merely echoing the language he reads, Romeo now builds upon the language of a flesh-and-blood woman. Shakespeare thus establishes why Juliet finds him attractive.

---

[7] Quoted in Alan Jacobs, "Bran Flakes and Harmless Drudges: Dr. Johnson and His Dictionary", *Books and Culture* (January/February 2006): 24.

[8] Samuel Johnson, *The Plays of William Shakespeare* (1765; repr., New York: AMS, 1968), 8:35.

[9] Johnson quotes Pope's notation that the Chorus was "added since the first edition", by which he means since the First Quarto, so it is possible that Shakespeare added the sonnet to subsequent quartos (ibid.). Even if the Chorus was added by another hand, it was a hand that understood sonnet convention.

As for Romeo, once he discovers that he has fallen for a forbidden Capulet (1.5.115–16), he revels in his Petrarchan dilemma: pining, once again, for an unattainable beauty. Romeo still loves by rote, demonstrated by the clichés he spouts as he enters the Capulet orchard, where he seeks Juliet the same way he sought Rosaline at the Capulet party.

III

The rote of Shakespeare's day, influenced by courtly love poetry, idealized the perfect woman by describing her various body parts with intense metaphors: eyes like burning coals, hair like spun gold, skin like purely driven snow, teeth like pearls, lips like rosebuds. Thomas Campion (1567–1620), for example, employs multiple clichés in a 1617 poem:

> There is a garden in her face
> Where roses and white lilies grow,
>
> . . . .
>
> There cherries grow, which none may buy
> Till "Cherry-ripe" themselves do cry.
>
> Those cherries fairly do enclose
> Of orient pearl a double row;
> Which when her lovely laughter shows,
> They look like rose-buds filled with snow.[10]

Like Campion, Romeo idealizes white skin the first time he sees Juliet: "So shows a snowy dove trooping with crows/As yonder lady o'er her fellows shows" (1.5.46–47). Not surprisingly, Mercutio mocks Romeo's desire for clichéd beauty: "I conjure thee by Rosaline's bright eyes,/By her high forehead and her scarlet lip" (2.1.17–18).

In contrast, Shakespeare challenges the use of such clichés in one of his most famous sonnets:

[10] Thomas Campion, "There Is a Garden in Her Face", in *The Norton Anthology of English Literature*, ed. M. H. Abrams et al. (New York: Norton, 1968), 1:842.

My mistress' eyes are nothing like the sun;
Coral is far more red than her lips' red;
If snow be white, why then her breasts are dun;
If hairs be wires, black wires grow on her head.
I have seen roses damask'd, red and white,
But no such roses see I in her cheeks.[11]

Shakespeare ends the sonnet asserting that the beauty of his mistress depends on qualities far exceeding the superficial conventions of the day: "And yet, by heaven, I think my love as rare / As any she belied with false compare."

Assuming this sonnet was written around the same time as *Romeo and Juliet*, we might conclude that Shakespeare means Romeo's words in the Capulet orchard to illustrate the "false compare" of poetic convention:

But, soft! What light through yonder window breaks?
It is the east, and Juliet is the sun.

. . . .

Two of the fairest stars in all the heaven,
Having some business, do entreat her eyes
To twinkle in their spheres till they return.
                                        (2.2.2–3, 15–17)

Unlike Shakespeare, Romeo asserts that his mistress' eyes are everything like the sun!

While Romeo allows conventional poetic language to mold his perception, Juliet grapples with the problem of language itself, signaled by her repetition and repudiation of the word "name"—along with related words like "title" and "called"—ten times in only fourteen lines (2.2.34–48). She implies that language—that which names our thoughts—often skims the surface of truth, not illuminating the heart underneath: "That which we call a rose / By any other name would smell as sweet" (2.2.43–44). Her point, of course, is that the name Montague conventionally means "enemy" to her people, but she sees

---

[11] William Shakespeare, Sonnet 130, lines 1–6, in *Riverside Shakespeare*, p. 1773.

something different under the surface of a young man called Montague. Like Shakespeare, she thinks her love as rare as any Romeo belied with false compare. After all, he allowed her to enter into his sonnet, giving her agency over its content.

When Romeo overhears Juliet's effusions, he comes out of hiding, proclaiming, "Call me but love, and I'll be new baptiz'd;/ Henceforth I never will be Romeo" (50–51). Doing so, he entirely misses her point. Whereas Juliet longs to engage the authentic self that lurks underneath names, Romeo simply offers to switch names. Worse, he ends up echoing what he said in despair over Rosaline: "This is not Romeo, he's some other where" (1.1.196). Both times he sounds like the Petrarchan lover whose entire identity becomes obliterated in his agony. Indeed, Romeo responds to Rosaline's vow of chastity with, "[A]nd in that vow/Do I live dead that live to tell it now" (1.1.221–22), invoking a cliché that Mercutio later mocks: "Alas, poor Romeo, he is already dead: stabb'd with a white wench's black eye; run through the ear with a love-song" (2.4.13–15).

In contrast, when Juliet ascertains that the voice in the orchard is Romeo's, she thinks not of Romeo's metaphoric death but of his literal demise: "[T]he place [is] death, considering who thou art,/If any of my kinsmen find thee here" (2.2.64–65). And when Romeo responds that love is strong enough to conquer danger, she puts things quite baldly: "If they do see thee, they will murder thee" (70). Rather than indulging the tender "names" of romantic love, Juliet shows concern for the person underneath the language.

In this scene, then, we see Juliet repeatedly countering Romeo's poetic excesses with pragmatic considerations: "How cam'st thou hither?" "I would not for the world they saw thee here", "By whose direction found'st thou out this place?" (62, 74, 79). Unfortunately, Romeo is so molded by his reading that he trumps her every statement with a more outrageous conceit, at one point invoking the pièce de résistance of Petrarchan clichés: "Alack, there lies more peril in thine eye/ Than twenty of their swords" (71–72).

Juliet realizes that she needs to take a different tack to get at the man underneath the names. First she delivers her longest speech of the play so far, blatantly proclaiming her love without metaphoric excess. She alludes to the love convention— the "form"—that required a woman of her day to play coy, but she sacrifices form for honesty: "Fain would I dwell on form, fain, fain deny / What I have spoke; but farewell compliment! / Dost thou love me?" (88–90). She then challenges Romeo's language: "If thou dost love, pronounce it faithfully" (94).

Nevertheless, and despite the fact that Juliet warns against the swearing of love (91–92), Romeo starts to swear by the moon: "Lady, by yonder blessed moon I vow, / That tips with silver all these fruit-tree tops—" (107–8). This time Juliet cuts him off midcliché in order to challenge his language: "O, swear not by the moon, th' inconstant moon, / That monthly changes in her circled orb, / Lest that thy love prove likewise variable" (109–11). Doing so, she foregrounds the problem with clichés, reminding us of what Shakespeare does in Sonnet 18:

> Shall I compare thee to a summer's day?
> Thou art more lovely and more temperate:
> Rough winds do shake the darling buds of May
> And summer's lease hath all too short a date.[12]

To compare someone to summer is to forget all the negative aspects of the season: its destructive winds, its changefulness. This, of course, is Juliet's point about swearing by the moon, a celestial body with characteristics inimical to authentic love. Juliet, like Shakespeare, challenges any love based only on the names of things.

When Juliet takes away his conventional name for love, Romeo is at a loss, asking, "What shall I swear by?" Her reply, "[S]wear by thy gracious self", reiterates her earlier distinction between language ("a rose") and authentic identity underneath it. Romeo tries again, this time saying, "If my heart's dear love—", at which point Juliet curtly cuts him off with,

---

[12] Shakespeare, Sonnet 18, lines 1–4, ibid., p. 1752.

"Well, do not swear" (2.2.112–13, 115–16). As Gayle Whittier notes, Juliet operates as "a disperser of poetic convention and 'form' itself", while "Romeo does not forego, but rather surpasses, even Petrarchan hyperbole." [13]

So what makes Romeo worthy of Juliet's love? The answer lies in the question he directs toward her: "What shall I swear by?" Romeo deserves Juliet because he listens to her, allowing her to invade his metaphors just as she had invaded his sonnet. And, in the process, he allows her to change him. Shakespeare makes Romeo's transformation clear two scenes later. When he runs into his friends, who have been mocking him for his poetic clichés, Romeo acts in such a way that Mercutio notices a difference: "Why, is not this better now than groaning for love? Now art thou sociable, now art thou Romeo; now art thou what thou art by art as well as by nature" (2.4.85–87). Mercutio, in other words, notices the return of Romeo's authentic self.

The real hero of this play, then, is Juliet. As the mouthpiece for Shakespeare's animus against cliché, Juliet lives her love in the flesh rather than merely naming it from a script. While Romeo, under the influence of Petrarch, uses the words "I live dead" (1.1.222), Juliet actually does live dead, taking a potion that makes her flesh appear dead so that she might someday be reunited with the banished Romeo. Thus, instead of merely speaking love-sick oxymorons, Juliet turns her flesh into an oxymoron, becoming what Friar Lawrence calls a "[p]oor *living corse*, clos'd in a dead man's tomb" (5.2.30, emphasis mine). And she would have survived her time in the tomb if poetic convention were all she had to battle. Unfortunately, a more insidious cliché ends up destroying Juliet and her Romeo.

IV

A feud, by its very definition, is based on clichéd thinking: individuals fight not because of a particular insult or injury

---

[13] Gayle Whittier, "The Sonnet's Body and the Body Sonnetized in *Romeo and Juliet*", *Shakespeare Quarterly* 40 (1989): 35.

but because that is the way their clans have treated each other for generations. Their belligerence has become conventional. This explains the start of the play. After the Chorus delivers the poetic form most associated with Petrarchan convention, servants fulfill the conventions of a feud, antagonizing each other only because of the "ancient quarrel" between Capulet and Montague (1.1.102).

Shakespeare repeats the juxtaposition of conventional hatred with conventional love at the Capulet party. Immediately after Romeo spouts clichés upon first seeing Juliet, Tybalt reacts with his own clichés:

> This, by his voice, should be a Montague.
> Fetch me my rapier, boy.
>
> .   .   .   .
>
> Now, by the stock and honour of my kin,
> To strike him dead I hold it not a sin.
>   (1.5.52–53, 56–57)

Tybalt's perception is so molded by the discourse of the feud that he loses touch with his context: a party meant for "comfort" and "delight" (1.2.26, 28). Capulet must therefore talk Tybalt out of acting on his clichéd understanding of hate, just as Capulet's daughter must later talk Romeo out of his clichéd understanding of love.

Furthermore, despite his high social standing as a relative of Lord Capulet, Tybalt's clichéd response makes him sound like a servant from the first scene: "Draw thy tool; here comes two of the house of Montagues" (1.1.31–32). Thus, just as Romeo's statement about Juliet's beauty echoes what he said earlier about Rosaline, so Tybalt's invocation of violence echoes the crass behavior of the lower classes. Clichéd thinking is like a plague that infects all levels of society.

This might explain why Shakespeare puts the word "plague" at the center of the play: Mercutio shouts, "A plague a both your houses" three times after he has been stabbed by Tybalt (3.1.88, 96, 103). Significantly, conventional love and conventional hatred work hand in hand to cause the fatal wound.

Having just married Juliet, Romeo encounters an escalating argument between Tybalt and Mercutio. Loving them both—Mercutio as his friend, Tybalt as his in-law (3.1.60, 67)—Romeo attempts to stop the fight, but the distraction he causes enables Tybalt to deliver his lethal blow.

Romeo thus fails to conquer the conventions of the feud. He starts out practicing Juliet's lessons about love and naming, telling Tybalt, "[G]ood Capulet, which *name* I tender / As dearly as mine own—be satisfied" (3.1.69–70, emphasis mine). But distress soon causes him to forget his lessons, even to the point of blaming Juliet for Mercutio's injury: "O sweet Juliet, / Thy beauty hath made me effeminate, / And in my temper soft'ned valour's steel!" (3.1.110–12). Then, when Mercutio dies, Romeo kills Tybalt in a conventional expression of anger and violence.

When Juliet hears that her husband has killed her cousin, her agony takes the form of oxymorons—with a difference. While Petrarchan oxymorons capture the turmoil of a speaker who loves from afar, Juliet's oxymorons describe not herself but Romeo, who juxtaposes love and hate in one body, like an oxymoron:

> Beautiful tyrant! fiend angelical!
> Dove-feather'd raven! wolfish-ravening lamb!
> Despised substance of divinest show!
> Just opposite to what thou justly seem'st,
> A damned saint, an honourable villain!
> (3.2.75–79).

However, once the Nurse responds with "Shame come to Romeo!" Juliet regrets her harsh words (90–95) and returns to a position in which she controls language rather than in which language controls her.

Shakespeare demonstrates Juliet's control when Lady Capulet comes to tell her that a marriage has been arranged with Paris. Juliet has so much power over language that she can simultaneously speak the truth while telling her mother what the woman wants to hear. When Lady Capulet says of Romeo, "[T]he traitor murderer lives", Juliet truthfully responds, "Ay, madam, from the reach of these my hands" (3.5.84–85). The mother, of course, assumes Juliet refers to hands that might do violence, while the daughter means hands extended in love. When Lady Capulet delivers a convention of the feud—"We will have vengeance" (87)—Juliet deftly develops double meanings:

> Indeed I never shall be satisfied
> With Romeo till I behold him—dead—
> Is my poor heart so for a kinsman vex'd.
>
> .   .   .   .
>
>   O, how my heart abhors
> To hear him nam'd, and cannot come to him,
> To wreak the love I bore my cousin Tybalt
> Upon his body that hath slaughter'd him!
>   (93–95, 99–102)

Shakespeare puts the word "dead" at the end of line 94 so that it can look both ways: the mother hears, "I never shall be satisfied with Romeo till I behold him dead", while the daughter means she will never be satisfied until she beholds Romeo, aligning "dead" with the next line so that it reads, "Dead is my poor heart." And the love Juliet plans to "wreak" on Romeo's "body" is far different from what her mother imagines.

Juliet's power over language aligns her, once again, with Shakespeare, who repeatedly exercised power over language to indict the cliché-driven poetry of his day. He therefore maintains Juliet's control for the remainder of the play: she takes a dangerous potion in order to live with Romeo, and she takes her life rather than live without him. Meanwhile, Romeo tends to react rather than act. Infected by the conventions of his day, both in love and hate, Romeo cannot escape the plague. Significantly, Shakespeare establishes that Romeo fails to get the message about Juliet's false death because the messenger was "[s]eal'd up" in "a house / Where the infectious pestilence did reign" (5.2.11, 9–10).

Shakespeare offers Juliet as an inoculation against the pestilent clichés of conventional thinking. Thanks to Juliet, Capulet and Montague renounce their feud, causing the Prince to reference Juliet's healing influence. He could have easily said, "And now we see the sun doth set / On Romeo and Juliet." But instead, Shakespeare has him end the play by asserting that the tragedy is hers: "For never was a story of more woe / Than this *of Juliet* and *her* Romeo" (5.3.308–9, emphasis mine). Though she dies in the process, Juliet's response to the plague of language demonstrates the substance under her name. No rose could smell as sweet.

Why Juliet Makes the Torches to Burn Bright:
The Luminous Quality of Beauty

Richard Harp
University of Nevada, Las Vegas

Why, is not this a lamentable thing ... that we should be thus
afflicted with these strange flies, these fashion-mongers, these
pardon-me's, who stand so much on the new form that they cannot sit at ease on the old bench?
      —Mercutio in *Romeo and Juliet* (2.4.31–35)[1]

Romeo and Juliet is a play about its heroes putting the new
wine of young love into new wineskins, about (some) old forms
and rituals giving way to new ideas and behaviors. It is also
about one of the most familiar of human attitudes, the being
quick to react to perceived enemies in aggressive and threat-
ening ways simply because of the perception itself, quite
divorced from reality and fact. In one of the Bible's most famous
passages, Saint Paul talks of how when he was a child he acted
in childish ways but that as an adult he put away childish things
(1 Cor 13:11). In Shakespeare's play we see mature and even
elderly men so addicted to childish actions that none of the
institutions of society seems able to save them—not their families, the law, or the wisdom of Friar Lawrence. Only the sac-
rificial love of their children can move them to put away their
foolish toys.

Both the antiquity and the senselessness of the feud between
Montague and Capulet are demonstrated in the play's opening scene. The biblical names of two of the rival families' servants, Sampson and Abraham, suggest the ancient standing
of their masters, and Sampson (Samson) is also the name of

---

[1] All quotations from *Romeo and Juliet* are from the edition published by Ignatius Press: *Romeo and Juliet*, ed. Joseph Pearce, Ignatius Critical Editions (San
Francisco: Ignatius Press, 2011).

one of the fiercest and most destructive of Old Testament heroes. There is irony to Sampson's name here, though, for his dialogue with his fellow servant Gregory shows he has no great strength or courage. For example, rather than pulling down the great city doors of the Philistines or slaying a thousand of his enemies with the jawbone of an ass, as did the Hebrew hero, he shows contempt to the servants of the Montagues by biting his thumb, which will be a "disgrace to them if they bear it" (1.1.42). This absurd action, thought ludicrously to be the epitome of defiance by Sampson, is still sufficient to reignite the quarrel between other, more pugnacious members of the two families.

Useless feuds with forgotten origins, their fires stoked by meaningless gestures and insults—such is the Verona of the star-crossed lovers. The play as a whole frequently challenges this exalting of form over substance, of the (sometimes violent) gesture or word smothering the deeper movements of mind and heart. "A word and [then] a blow": this old proverb, spoken defiantly by Mercutio to Tybalt (3.1.39), reveals the colors these Veronese madmen live by. Romeo and Juliet are two of Shakespeare's greatest heroes not because they are singularly unlucky and victims of a malign fate but principally because they act older than their years in marshaling what are their most human qualities, their intellects and wills, to attack rigid and lethal conventions in love and family honor.

Romantic dialogue in the Renaissance was rooted in the Petrarchan love lyric, typically taking the form of sonnets from a distant lover to an unreachable and sometimes heartless lady. Petrarch, the medieval poet who inaugurated this fashion by writing hundreds of sonnets to his beloved Laura (whose very existence is questionable), was ultimately responsible for the sonnet sequences of Shakespeare's era—groups of poems celebrating in elaborate and excruciating detail a lady's charms. It was an astonishingly fertile convention, even though it often only tangentially discussed real human experience in love. Perhaps the intricacies of the sonnet form were useful to aspiring writers in trying to master the craft of poetry writing.

Shakespeare himself wrote 154 sonnets, although some of them contradict Petrarchan convention, such as the famous Sonnet 130:

> My mistress' eyes are nothing like the sun;
> Coral is far more red than her lips' red;
> If snow be white, why then her breasts are dun;
> If hairs be wires, black wires grow on her head.[2]

Here all clichéd comparisons about appearance or about a mistress' likeness to a divinity are rejected for her own concrete individuality:

> I grant I never saw a goddess go;
> My mistress, when she walks, treads on the ground:
> And yet, by heaven, I think my love as rare
> As any she belied with false compare.[3]

She is "rare" because she is his, and there is no one else in that category.

At the beginning of the play, Romeo is the Petrarchan lover pining away during long nighttime walks for the heartless Rosaline, who "hath forsworn to love, and in that vow/Do I live dead that live to tell it now" (1.1.221–22). When he goes to the Capulet ball, he continues to follow convention by falling completely in love at first sight with another woman, Juliet, despite earlier protestations that such fickleness on his part would be impossible (1.2.88–93). Showing how shallow and fatuous his previous love for Rosaline was, Romeo declares, "Did my heart love till now? Forswear it, sight;/For I ne'er saw true beauty till this night" (1.5.50–51). And if convention were to be followed, there is no reason to expect that this love for Juliet would be any more firmly based.

---

[2] William Shakespeare, Sonnet 130, line 1, in *The Necessary Shakespeare*, ed. David Bevington (New York: Longman, 2002), p. 883. Quotations from works of Shakespeare other than *Romeo and Juliet* are taken from Bevington's edition.

[3] Ibid., lines 11–14.

That things are changed, however, is apparent the first time Romeo and Juliet are together. Upon seeing her from a distance, Romeo exclaims that "she hangs upon the cheek of night/As a rich jewel in an Ethiop's ear—/Beauty too rich for use, for earth too dear!" (1.5.43–45). Their initial words to each other are in the form of a sonnet (1.5.91–105)—no surprise here—but what is surprising is that they each compose individual parts of the sonnet: Romeo eight lines, Juliet six. The sonnet form had been almost exclusively a man speaking to a passive woman, but now Juliet shows herself as adept as Romeo in extemporaneously developing the sonnet's theme of a pilgrim (Romeo) approaching a "holy shrine" (Juliet) in order to kiss her hands and lips. And when the sonnet is concluded, Juliet gets in the last words of their exchange by telling Romeo, "You kiss by th' book" (108). By this statement, she both acknowledges that Romeo has made a conventional approach to her and gives a not-so-subtle hint that something more natural would be welcome in the future.

It is indeed Juliet who is the quicker of the two lovers to dispense with formalities. In this, she is like many of Shakespeare's great heroines of the comedies and romances—Rosalind in *As You Like It*, for example, or Miranda in *The Tempest*—who do not stand on ceremony in taking the lead in matters of the heart. Romeo surely realizes every young man's dream later that same night when in the orchard beneath Juliet's window he hears her declare to the darkness that she has fallen in love with him: "[B]e but sworn my love,/And I'll no longer be a Capulet" (2.2.35–36). After Romeo identifies himself, Juliet forthrightly tells him that she is blushing "[f]or that which thou hast heard me speak to-night./Fain would I dwell on form, fain, fain deny/What I have spoke; but farewell compliment!" (87–89). She realizes that he "mayst think [her] haviour light" (99) for the speed with which she has fallen in love with him but avows: "[T]rust me, gentleman, I'll prove more true/Than those that have more cunning to be strange" (100–101).

But even in the face of this astonishing honesty from Juliet— she could, after all, have found many coy excuses to modify or even deny what Romeo had overheard her confess—Romeo still does not abandon Petrarchan convention, so infatuated are male lovers with their own words. He makes trite romantic statements: "Lady, by yonder blessed moon I vow" (107), to which Juliet admonishes him not to swear by the inconstant moon. To his question "What shall I swear by?" (112), she responds that he should swear by nothing at all unless it is "by [his] gracious self,/Which is the god of [her] idolatry" (113–14). Juliet is interested in neither heavenly bodies nor mythological gods but rather in the concrete individual. For she sees in Romeo love itself, quite divorced from the accidental associations of names and family ties and histories: "O Romeo, Romeo! wherefore art thou Romeo?/Deny thy father and refuse thy name" (33–34). To come into contact with the essence of human nature—this is where Shakespeare over and again brings his characters. King Lear, to take an example from another of Shakespeare's tragedies, says to a mad, naked beggar that he meets on a stormy heath, "Thou art the thing itself; unaccomodated man" (*King Lear*, 3.4.108–9), meaning that this is what human nature really is when stripped of all of the finery of a corrupt civilization. In extreme existential situations such as the forbidden love of Romeo and Juliet or the abandonment of the aged Lear by most of his kingdom, individual names, while of course always having important connections to family, country, and traditions, cannot compellingly signify the even more profound reality that has been glimpsed.

Juliet has often been accused of the philosophical error of nominalism, the view that universal concepts such as honor or virtue exist in name only and not in reality. The content with which we invest such concepts, so the argument goes, is dependent on subjective opinion or preference. There is no space here for a formal refutation of the nominalist position; let us say only that Juliet is not a nominalist. One of Shakespeare's true nominalists, Falstaff in *Henry IV*, did indeed claim that honor was only a word, not a thing, and gave proofs that many have found persuasive; that Shakespeare himself did not find them convincing, however, is clear in that he has Prince

Hal perform a number of obviously honorable acts immediately after Falstaff's speech. Hal is not as concerned about what names his noble acts are given as he is about doing the acts themselves—fighting bravely against Hotspur, for example. That he is concerned with things, not words, is also shown by his willingness to go along with Falstaff's lie that it was he that killed the valiant Percy: "If a lie may do thee grace, I'll gild it with the noblest terms I have" (*Henry IV, Part I*, 5.4.155–56). (Falstaff's claiming to have killed Percy shows in fact that he really *does* believe in the traditional concept of honor: he expects public credit for the "deed". His argument against honor derives from his cowardice.)

Juliet, though, is not a nominalist; she is not denying that there is such a person as Romeo when she invites him to "refuse [his] name"—how could she, when she has just been smitten by him?—any more than she is denying that there is such a thing as a rose when she famously says, "[A] rose / By any other name would smell as sweet" (2.2.43–44). She is clearly right—the world's languages have all manner of different words for that same rose. And she is certainly not saying that a real rose is only a word; rather, she is saying that no word, ultimately, can be adequate to the thing that is a rose—a very different matter. Her love for Romeo is of the same kind, as evidenced by what she says to him when she comes to Friar Lawrence's cell to be wed: "[M]y true love is grown to such excess / I cannot sum up ... half my wealth" (2.6.33–34). As there are graces beyond the reach of art, so there are things beyond the reach of words.

The discarding of worn-out forms and rituals when their connection to any important substance had been forgotten—or worse, ignored—was a characteristic of Jesus' message in the New Testament. The days are coming, he told the Samaritan woman at the well, when those who worship God will neither do so at the Temple in Jerusalem nor at any of the other holy sites in Israel but will rather worship him in "spirit and truth", wherever they may happen to be (Jn 4:24). He also taught that the hundreds of legalistic observances and laws that had come to encumber Old Testament religion could be reduced to two: to love God and to love neighbor. On the secular plane, Shakespeare's plays, too, typically fight through literary artifice and human convention to reveal a deeper level of spirit than was customary to writers of his time—or of any time. The women in his comedies and in some tragedies (Juliet, of course, and perhaps Cleopatra as well) practice a humane, womanly assertiveness as they teach their often-distracted male counterparts about love. The custom of the arranged marriage is another social convention that finds little support in Shakespeare, fathers in particular having little success in telling their daughters whom to marry. In *Romeo and Juliet* old Capulet initially displays wisdom in telling Paris that he is welcome to marry Juliet *if* he can first gain her consent (1.2.16–19), a wisdom that the speed of subsequent events after the death of Tybalt causes him to forget. Human society has broken down in the play; Prince Escalus, for example, understands that the Montague-Capulet quarrel is bred of nothing more than "airy word[s]" (1.1.87), but he is powerless to change the bloody course of events.

Friar Lawrence is much more active in trying to resolve the lovers' dilemma. When we first meet him, he is in his cell experimenting with herbs to find which are healthful and which are poisonous, and he is struck by the fact that the same plant may have both beneficent and maleficent effects, much like human nature, which is divided between "grace and rude will" (2.3.28). He also has insight into love and shows Romeo the folly of loving passionately Rosaline and then Juliet in the same day. When Romeo speaks obscurely to him about the help he desires, the Friar responds, "Be plain, good son . . ./Riddling confession finds but riddling shrift" (2.3.55–56), and he tells him candidly that Rosaline rejected his Petrarchan advances because his "love did read by rote that could not spell" (2.3.88); that is, "he repeated conventional expressions without understanding them." [4] After the Friar is convinced of the genuineness of

---

[4] Bevington, *Necessary Shakespeare*, p. 462.

Romeo's love for Juliet, he is the one person who can quickly see the greater good the marriage of the two can bring about: the ending of the ancient quarrel. But because of the caprices of fortune, his practical attempts to do this badly misfire. Only the lovers themselves, by their deaths, can manage to end the feud.

Another literary convention given new life in the play is that of the aubade, a morning song typically sung by lovers protesting the too-early arrival of the dawn after a night of lovemaking. The tradition goes back at least to the Roman poet Ovid and has many famous Christian representatives as well, such as the complaints against the morning sun by Chaucer's doomed lovers Troilus and Cressida. It is easy to see how the aubade would be especially favored by tragic lovers, who see in the all-too-brief night an image of endangered love. In Shakespeare's time the love poet John Donne wittily had the woman challenge, not the sun for daring to arise in the east, but rather the man for leaving her side because he had business to attend to; he that has business, says the lady, "and makes love, doth do/Such wrong, as when a married man doth woo".[5] Sometimes the man is eager simply to return to a masculine environment, as in Robert Browning's brief but pointed aubade "Parting at Morning":

> Round the cape of a sudden came the sea,
> And the sun looked over the mountain's rim:
> And straight was a path of gold for him,
> And the need of a world of men for me.[6]

Romeo and Juliet's morning love song at the beginning of Act 3, scene 5, is different from all of these. For one thing, it is spoken by married lovers. Shakespeare goes to sometimes great lengths in his plays to ensure that his protagonists marry, a

---

[5] John Donne, "Break of Day", lines 17–18, in *John Donne's Poetry*, ed. Arthur L. Clements (New York: Norton, 1992), p. 14.

[6] Robert Browning, *My Last Duchess, and Other Poems* (New York: Dover, 1993), p. 26.

sign that he does not despise convention per se but rather wishes to see it revivified so that it is not routine. So his aubade here is no conventional complaint about the daytime's responsibilities as opposed to the nighttime's relaxation and merriment, which underlies Ovid's very witty and charming song in his *Amores* (1.13), nor is it as generalized a denunciation of the night as is Troilus and Cressida's, which shows the influence of rhetorical exercises comparing day and night and in which there are hints that the lovers will ultimately not remain faithful. Lack of mutual passion is apparent in the poems of Browning and Donne cited above—the woman in the latter poem cleverly says, "Why should we rise because 'tis light?/Did we lie down because 'twas night?" [7] But Romeo and Juliet breathe new life into the old lyric form by weaving their heartfelt mutual love into the conventional setting. Juliet, noticing Romeo's preparation to leave, asks, "Wilt thou be gone? It is not yet near day" (3.5.1), the traditional context for complaints about the lover's fickleness or the sun's (or dawn's) envy of the happy lovers. Juliet tells her new husband that he has mistaken the nightingale for the lark, dawn's harbinger; Romeo replies that it was indeed the lark he heard, for the "envious streaks" of daylight are piercing the clouds in the east, and he must be "gone and live, or stay and die" (11). Juliet replies that the light is merely "some meteor that the sun exhales/To be to thee this night a torch-bearer/And light thee on thy way to Mantua" (13–15). It is clear at this point that this is no academic debate between playacting lovers remembering their grammar school composition assignments but that important issues are at stake: like the lovers, meteors give off brilliant but transient light, and the fact that Juliet at the Capulets' masked ball did "teach the torches to burn bright" (1.5.42), as Romeo beautifully says, suggests—to those who know the end of the story—that Juliet's life will be all the briefer by virtue of its very intensity.

[7] Donne, "Break of Day", lines 17–18, p. 14.

But then there is a sharp turn in the lovers' gentle debate: Romeo no longer insists that he must leave for his own security but says, "Let me be ta'en, let me be put to death;/I am content, so thou wilt have it so" (3.5.17–18). The rhythm of day and night, which in the typical aubade is fundamental and determinative, is subordinated to Romeo's desire to stay with his wife: "I have more care to stay than will to go" (23). But then it is Juliet who insists that Romeo leave, a most unconventional role for the woman to assume in these duets, as her concern for his safety overcomes her desire for him to stay: "O, now be gone! More light and light it grows" (35).

It is appropriate that the lovers should not ultimately curse the light. It is true that much of the play's most passionate life takes place at night—Romeo and Juliet meet at night at the Capulets'; they declare their love for each other that same night when Juliet is at her bedroom window; they consummate their marriage the evening after Romeo kills Tybalt; they die at night in the graveyard. Still, there is a running current of imagery throughout the play insisting that the lovers themselves make luminous this darkness and each other. Romeo imagines what would happen if Juliet's eyes were placed in the heavens, replacing two of its finest stars; they would, he says, "through the airy region stream so bright/That birds would sing, and think it were not night" (2.2.22–23). And Juliet declares, "Lovers can see to do their amorous rites/By their own beauties" (3.2.8–9), without needing the aid of any heavenly body. When Romeo sees Juliet apparently dead in the burial vault, he says, "[H]er beauty makes/This vault a feasting presence full of light" (5.3.85–86). All this is, of course, pleasure at each other's physical beauty, but there is also more to it: the ecstatic nature of their responses suggests an apprehension of who the other truly is in his innermost nature. This is what makes them impatient with exhausted superficial conventions and the irrational rites of antiquated feuds.

For the physical and spiritual senses of beauty are closely connected in traditional philosophical thought. "Radiance of the inner being", says Thomas Dubay, "is the chief element in the beautiful."[8] One of the essential elements of beauty in the philosophy of Saint Thomas Aquinas, whose thought was still vital in England in the sixteenth century, is that of *claritas*, "radiance" or "splendor".[9] This is not the clarity of mathematical proof or textbook diagrams but rather a mysterious seeing of the inner form of the beloved as "luminous in itself".[10] This is what Romeo and Juliet are talking about in their declarations that "[l]overs can see . . . [b]y their own beauties" and that Juliet makes of a grave "a feasting presence full of light". Despite his slowness to shed the traditional clichés of love poetry, Romeo has been in the embrace of this beauty from his first sight of Juliet, when he saw flowing from her luminous form the light that made the torches burn bright at the Capulets' masquerade ball.

[8] Thomas Dubay, *The Evidential Power of Beauty* (San Francisco: Ignatius Press, 1999), p. 35.

[9] See Thomas Aquinas, *Summa theologica* I, q. 39, art. 8, where the elements of beauty are discussed, in *The "Summa theologica" of St. Thomas Aquinas*, trans. Fathers of the English Dominican Province, 2nd rev. ed. (1920), available online from New Advent, http://www.newadvent.org/summa/1039.htm#article8.

[10] Dubay, *Evidential Power of Beauty*, p. 36.

The Crossing of Love: Shakespeare's Chiastic Wit in *Romeo and Juliet*

Andrew J. Harvey
Grove City College

Mercury, the god of rhetoric, has a special place in *Romeo and Juliet* if for no other reason than that his namesake, Mercutio, is Romeo's closest companion. Early on in the play, the rhetorically gifted Mercutio advises Romeo, in a bit of ironic foreshadowing given the violent ends both of them meet, "[I]f love be rough with you, be rough with love" (1.4.27).[1] The inversion of "love" and "rough" here is known by the rhetorical term *chiasmus*. And though the play is done with silver-tongued Mercutio rather quickly, Mercutio is not done with the play. Even the jargon of rhetorical manuals is employed as a metaphor for true love. Juliet explains how the experience of love opens the lover's understanding: "Conceit, more rich in matter than in words,/Brags of his substance, not of ornament" (2.6.30–31). Juliet is asserting that Romeo's love must requite her own in being substantial and capable of action and must not consist merely of words. Her own love and the love she inspires in Romeo indeed make his former flame Rosaline insubstantial and immaterial to Romeo. But the word "conceit", the distinctions between matter and words, substance and ornament—these are all of Mercury's lexicon: terms and distinctions traditionally taught to every Renaissance schoolboy in order that he may learn the proper use of rhetorical figures. Shakespeare's mastery of language, especially as seen in the arguments he invents for his characters as well as the way they present them, did not come out of nowhere but arose

[1] All quotations from *Romeo and Juliet* are from the edition published by Ignatius Press: *Romeo and Juliet*, ed. Joseph Pearce, Ignatius Critical Editions (San Francisco: Ignatius Press, 2011).

195

from a conventional and well-documented curriculum in rhetoric.[2] This training in rhetoric, along with his ready wit, is brilliantly on display with Shakespeare's virtuoso development of one rhetorical device—chiasmus. It is my "conceit", or understanding, that chiasmus in *Romeo and Juliet* is not mere ornament but is "rich in matter". I wish to brag of its substance.

Chiasmus takes its name from the Greek letter *chi* (χ) and is a crisscross, an X, of language that may invert diction, ideas, grammar, or syntax; this inversion might span a phrase, a line, a speech, a whole scene, or even an entire narrative. Implying both symmetry and inversion, chiasmus often conveys themes of reciprocity, cyclical flux, transformation, circularity, and exchange. In over forty instances in *Romeo and Juliet*, Shakespeare uses it to create punch lines, to convey the reciprocity of true love, and to trace the turns of fortune. The primary focus of this essay, however, is to see how chiasmus helps dramatize the conflicts between appearance and reality and between, as Friar Lawrence says, "grace and rude will" (2.3.28). Additionally, a conceptual chiasmus emerges as the religious imagery that is used early on to convey romantic love subsumes the lovers themselves so that their tragic fate is most properly understood in religious terms.

The conflict between perception and reality and their relation to language pervades the entire play, but in Act 3, the central crux of the play, two scenes with Juliet employ chiasmus to highlight this theme for us. Juliet's immediate response upon hearing from her nurse of Romeo's banishment for the killing of her cousin Tybalt demonstrates the power of love to invert the perception of reality. Juliet and Romeo at this point in the play have already been secretly wed by Friar Lawrence, and she is awaiting Romeo's arrival to consummate their marriage

---

[2] Many excellent "rhetorical" readings of Shakespeare have been done in the past twenty years. See especially R. McDonald, *Shakespeare and the Arts of Language* (Oxford: Oxford University Press, 2001). The definitive scholarship on Renaissance curriculum with reference to Shakespeare's education in Stratford, of course, remains T. W. Baldwin, *William Shakspere's Small Latine and Lesse Greeke* (Urbana: University of Illinois Press, 1956).

when their fragile plans take a disastrous turn. Juliet cannot believe that her beautiful Romeo is capable of such ugly violence and that they both now must suffer his banishment:

> O serpent heart, hid with a flow'ring face!
> Did ever dragon keep so fair a cave?
> **Beautiful tyrant**! **fiend angelical**!
> **Dove-feather'd raven**! **wolfish-ravening lamb**!
> Despised substance of divinest show!
> Just opposite to what thou justly seem'st,
> A **damned saint**, an **honourable villain**!
> O nature, what hadst thou to do in hell,
> When thou didst bower the spirit of a fiend
> In mortal paradise of such sweet flesh?
> (3.2.73–82, emphasis mine)

I have emphasized Juliet's oxymorons that occur in three sets of chiastic pairs. In each of the first two sets, the negative noun or adjective is in the inner position, while the positive term takes the outer position—e.g., "tyrant" and "fiend" are framed by "beautiful" and "angelical" (75). She had hoped (as did Romeo) that their love would enable them to transcend their families' vicious feud, and it seemed possible. Romeo's slaying of Tybalt, however, reveals the work of a "serpent heart" that only appeared to be a "[d]ove-feather'd" "lamb" (76). The "wolfish" reality of Romeo's "substance" has belied his outward "show" (77). Juliet now realizes that he is quite the "opposite" of the gentle and peaceable man who wooed her. And so she reverses the pattern in the third set of chiastic oxymorons: his "damned" villainy is now on the outside and hides the appearance of an "honourable" "saint" (79). Juliet's three sets of chiastic oxymorons or oxymoronic chiasmi mirror her realization that even a lover as well intentioned as Romeo cannot escape from the violence of Verona.

But when the Nurse, quite logically and sympathetically, echoes this displeasure and says, "Shame come to Romeo!" (90), Juliet changes her tune. Her love cannot allow Romeo to be shamed, and she repents of her judgment of him: "O what a beast was I to chide at him!" (95). The Nurse does not expect Juliet's attempt to exculpate Romeo. Juliet counters: "Shall I speak ill of him that is my husband?" (97). She sums up her "joy" with this bit of chiastic reasoning: "My husband lives that Tybalt would have slain, / And Tybalt's dead that would have slain my husband. / All this is comfort" (105–7). Not only does Juliet justify Romeo's actions as self-defense, but she rhetorically crosses out Tybalt by making Romeo the beginning and end of her consideration. She prefers to rejoice as a new wife rather than to grieve as a bereaved kinswoman.

The use of chiasmus here, moreover, emphasizes Juliet's optimism in coping with misfortune. Juliet successfully reframes the bitter reality and dismay of a banished Romeo and converts it into the comforting knowledge that her Romeo is *only* banished. In this way Juliet does not ignore the unpleasant truth; she accounts for even the unfortunate phenomena of her circumstances and lovingly chooses to accentuate the positive.

In Act 3, the second chiastic moment—a moment of poetic and rhetorical brilliance—sees Juliet in her optimism yield to wishful thinking. As she argues to the brink of denial concerning Romeo's and her hard circumstances, Romeo successfully turns Juliet back to their vexed reality. Chiasmus, once again, negotiates the rhetorical turn. Juliet and Romeo perform a rhetorical exercise known as *disputatio in utrumque partem*, a disputation over an arbitrary topic where both sides are argued equally. In Act 3, scene 5, the question is whether it is day or night:

> *Juliet.* Wilt thou be gone? It is not yet near day;
>   It was the **nightingale**, and not the **lark**,
>   That pierc'd the fearful hollow of thine ear;
>   A [Juliet claims it is night.]
>   Nightly she sings on yond pomegranate tree.
>   Believe me, love, it was the nightingale.
> *Romeo.* It was the **lark**, the herald of the morn,
>   No **nightingale**. Look, love, what envious streaks
>   Do lace the severing clouds in yonder east;
>   B [Romeo claims it is day and that he must leave.]

Night's candles are burnt out, and jocund **day**
Stands tiptoe on the misty mountain tops.
I must **be gone** and live, or **stay** and die.
Juliet. Yond light is not **daylight**; I know it, I:
It is some meteor that the sun exhales
To be to thee this **night** a torch-bearer
             X [Turning point—Juliet insists that he stay.]
And light thee on thy way to Mantua;
Therefore **stay yet**; thou need'st **not** to **be gone**.
Romeo. Let me be ta'en, let me be put to death;
I am content, so thou wilt have it so.
I'll say yon gray is not the morning's eye,
'Tis but the pale reflex of Cynthia's brow;
Nor that is not the lark whose notes do beat
           B′ [Romeo pretends it is night, ironically.]
The vaulty heaven so high above our heads.
I have more care to stay than will to go.
Come death, and welcome! Juliet wills it so.
How is't, my soul? Let's talk—it is not day.
Juliet. It is, it is; hie hence, be gone, away!
It is the lark that sings so out of tune,
Straining harsh discords and unpleasing sharps.
Some say the lark makes sweet division;
This doth not so, for she divideth us.
           A′ [Juliet is persuaded, reluctantly.]
Some say the lark and loathed toad **change** eyes;
O, now I would they had **chang'd** voices too!
Since arm from arm that voice doth us affray,
Hunting thee hence with hunts-up to the day.
O, now be gone! More light and light it grows.
Romeo. More light and light—more dark and dark our woes!
             (3.5.1–36, emphasis mine)

Note Juliet's repetition of the word "change" (change—chang'd) in her last speech. One kind of chiasmus is also called antimetabole or counterchange, and three counterchanges occur in this scene: (1) nightingale, lark—lark, nightingale; (2) night, day—daylight, night; and (3) be gone, stay—stay yet, not be gone. A greater chiasmus, however, is also at work.

The five speeches here form a clear pattern around Juliet's central speech, which serves as the crux or pivot so that the sequence goes Juliet-Romeo, Romeo-Juliet, in roughly equal proportions. In this formal five-part disputation, then, Juliet first takes a sophistic approach and tries to make the weaker argument appear the greater by confusing appearances (the sun has not yet risen) and reality (it really is dawn, nevertheless). First, she makes a contrary-to-fact claim: it is the nightingale, not the lark; then Romeo refutes this claim; then she continues to persist in her claim and insists that he stay. Now she has used her fact claim to warrant action on his part. This assertion is the turning point at the center of this rhetorical chiasmus. Romeo then changes tack and agrees with both her claim to stay and her warrant that it is not day, merely adding the further consequence, "Come, death, and welcome!" He is being ironic, but it has the desired effect. Juliet then reverses her position and quickly dismisses him for fear that he shall be caught and killed. The disputation, thus, begins and ends with Juliet. Romeo effects his will on her by turning her argument against her. She can no longer safely blur appearance and reality even if only in playful jest.

The playfulness between them that has turned serious here in Act 3 begins as merely mirthful in Act 1. In a manner worthy of the metaphysical poet John Donne, who could have been in Shakespeare's original London audience at the Globe Theatre, religious imagery is innocently employed to negotiate their first kiss.

> *Romeo.* If I profane with my unworthiest hand
>   This holy shrine, the gentle sin is this:
>   My lips, two blushing pilgrims, ready stand
>   To smooth that rough touch with a tender kiss.
> *Juliet.* Good pilgrim, you do wrong your hand too much,
>   Which mannerly devotion shows in this;
>   For saints have hands that pilgrims' hands do touch,
>   And palm to palm is holy palmers' kiss.
> *Romeo.* Have not saints lips, and holy palmers too?
> *Juliet.* Ay, pilgrim, lips that they must use in pray'r.
> *Romeo.* O, then, dear saint, let lips do what hands do!
>   They pray; grant thou, lest faith turn to despair.

Juliet. Saints **do not move**, though grant for prayers' sake.
Romeo. Then **move not** while my prayer's effect I take.
    Thus from **my lips by thine** my sin is purg'd.
Juliet. Then have *my lips* the *sin* that **they** have took.
Romeo. Sin from *my lips?* O trespass sweetly urg'd!
    Give me my sin again.
Juliet.   You kiss by th' book. (1.5.91–108, emphasis mine)

One should not fail to notice this tour de force of Shakespeare's lyric poetry: the first fourteen lines of their dialogue form a sonnet. (There are two others in this play: the lines spoken by the Chorus in the Prologue to the play and in the Prologue to Act 2.) The exchange of kisses itself, though, concerns our topic now and involves three chiastic exchanges: (1) do not move—move not; (2) the purging of sin from Romeo's lips and its transfer to Juliet's lips: my lips, by thine—my lips, they; and (3) Romeo's taking back of the sin he gave her: my lips, sin—sin, my lips. This chiastic exchange of kisses or "sin" is, as the metaphors suggest, efficacious, and the scene helps cement our identification between love and grace. This exchange, however, is paralleled in the final scene in the crypt, where the couple's kisses are an attempt not to purge sin but to communicate death itself.

Shortly after Romeo has associated kissing Juliet with grace comes Friar Lawrence's discourse on herb lore: "Within . . . this weak flower/**Poison** hath residence, and **medicine power**. . . . **Two such opposed kings encamp them still**/In man as well as herbs—**grace** and **rude will**" (2.3.23–28, emphasis mine). The antithesis of the poison of man's rude will and the medicinal power of grace is rendered chiastically. The twofold potential of the apothecary's art is prominent in the final kissing scene as well. In Act 5 Romeo buys the poison from the apothecary: "Come, **cordial** and not **poison**, go with me/To Juliet's grave; for there must I use thee" (5.1.85–86, emphasis mine). And Juliet awakens to see him dead from the poison: "I will kiss thy lips;/Haply some **poison** yet doth hang on them,/To make me die with a **restorative**" (5.3.164–66, emphasis mine). They both see deadly poison as efficacious—a cordial, a restorative—because it offers a means to reunite them, albeit in death. Deeming Juliet to be dead, Romeo, unlike in the earlier disputation, is the one who mistakes appearances for reality. Juliet, one can easily imagine, pictures herself in terms of a tragic lover in Dante's *Inferno*: she is Francesca, and Romeo is her Paolo. She clearly imagines an eternal union for them, even if it may be outside a state of grace. Perhaps this is the fruit of their "extreme sweet" love that the Chorus speaks of, but it is bad theology on their part (2 Prol. 14). A suicide cannot be a cordial to them.

Borrowing the words of the Prince, we can "clear these ambiguities, / And know their spring, their head, their true descent" (5.3.216–17). If we follow the chiasmi, we can disambiguate the major cruxes of the play: divine grace is thwarted or crossed by the rude will of those who mistake appearances for reality again and again. But to whose "rude will" and to whom can grace be applied? Initially, of course, we think of Romeo and Juliet's rashness in committing their suicides and thus cutting off the grace that has been associated with their love throughout the play. But here at the end of the play, the Prince unequivocally places their tragic love within the greater context of providence: "Capulet, Montague, / See what a scourge is laid upon your hate, / That heaven finds means to kill your joys with love!" (5.3.290–92). The deaths of Romeo and Juliet, who are the joys of their respective families, are Heaven's means by which both Capulet and Montague pay for the rude will of their hateful feud. The Prince, who besides Friar Lawrence is the only character in the play who correctly discerns Heaven's will, realizes that he, as Verona's head of state and kinsman of both families, is also being punished: "And I, for winking at your discords too, / Have lost a brace of kinsmen. All are punish'd" (5.3.293–94). And here we have that word "discords", which, coming here in almost the last speech of the play, nicely recapitulates much of Shakespeare's wit throughout the play, contrasting harmony, peace, union, life, and love with discord, violence, division, and hate.

It is within this rich verbal tapestry that the deaths of Romeo and Juliet can be understood as "sacrifices", a word used twice here in the final scene. The seething violence at the play's beginning is the true nature and reality of feuding Verona, while the Prince's peacekeeping measures are merely cosmetic or apparent. But here at the end, we have true reconciliation in light of Romeo's and Juliet's violent deaths. "Reconciliation" was not a common term in early modern English; more familiar in Shakespeare's time was the Latin phrase *concordia discors*. This notion of "discordant harmony" demonstrates how grammar can reflect philosophy. The nature of things, the way things really are, takes the form of the noun which in this case is concord or harmony while the adjective conveys not reality but the apparent discord that we have to endure in this fallen world. Thus, a higher order really perseveres against forces of chaos such as mutability, the fickle human condition, and evil, which only appear to rule the cosmos. What is at stake is one's understanding of Providence in the face of suffering and evil. Which is real and which is apparent? The radical claim of the Christian tradition which Shakespeare reflects consistently insists that Providence is real and that suffering and evil only appear to be. One could summarize the state of Verona, then in a final chiasmus, an inversion of the classical phrase familiar to Renaissance ears—as initially a *discordia concors*, where chaos rules under the guise of a superficial concord (and indeed the Prince thinks he has put an end to the feud as the play opens), that ultimately changes into a *concordia discors*, where the feud has actually ended and peace obtained. The discord represented by the phenomenon of two dead lovers no longer reflects familial feud or Verona but contrasts the true harmony that now obtains. Thus the Prince aptly describes the final state of affairs with an oxymoron that is at once a paradox—a "glooming peace", but a true peace nonetheless (5.3.304).

I am not suggesting that this peace crosses out the "gloom" of this tragedy or even that Romeo's and Juliet's deaths were necessary and good to accomplish providence's ends. No, thwarted lovers who successfully contradict antagonistic powers through a fake death, a clever priest, and much chiasmus always yield a comedy; see Shakespeare's *Much Ado about Nothing*. Rather, I insist that the bad theology that kills Romeo and Juliet is not the theology of the play as a whole or the theology of Shakespeare. The collision of a tragic vision and a Christian context begs this question: Is there such a thing as Christian tragedy? That is, is there a play that presents death as completely without grace? If there is one, and *King Lear* shows perhaps Shakespeare's closest attempt to produce such a play, it is not *Romeo and Juliet*. The play is about them. They are the foregrounded protagonists, and their families are the antagonizing forces in the background, yet the portraits of their tragic deaths must be properly framed. Fittingly, the last image of Juliet Capulet is a statue rendered in gold by Montague, and the last image of Romeo Montague is a statue rendered just as richly golden by Capulet. Shakespeare asks us not to see their golden statues as idols inspired by bad theology or as graven images of impetuous love but as "sacrifices of [their families'] enmity", as symbols of forgiveness, and as the affirmation of that "pity sitting in the clouds / That sees into the bottom of . . . grief" (5.3.303; 3.5.197–98). Shakespeare emphasizes the civic and familial dimension right from the opening Chorus, which announces that "their death" will "bury their parents' strife", which "nought could remove" but "their children's end" (Prol. 8, 11). Whereas in the course of the play religious imagery consistently serves as a metaphor conveying the depths of the love between Romeo and Juliet, Shakespeare in the end inverts this conceit so that we are forced to see Romeo and Juliet's love in the context of a providential efficacy.

This shadow of grace, if not the substance of it, provides an appropriate lens through which to glance back at the chiasmus of Mercutio that started our exploration of Shakespeare's language of inversion and the crossing of love. "If love be rough with you," he said to Romeo, "be rough with love." Earlier we noticed the dramatic irony—Mercutio's casual platitude here turns out to be a bitter foreshadowing when both he and Romeo find that love is as rough as death. Both are victims of Romeo and Juliet's star-crossed love. But the chiasmus itself (love—rough, rough—love) deepens the ironic adumbration. Love in this play is both the beginning and the end of the violence.

A Case against Natural Magic:
Shakespeare's Friar Lawrence as
Romeo and Juliet's Near-Tragic Hero*

Jill Kriegel
St. Joseph's Catholic School

In the Renaissance milieu of fervent Neoplatonism, we are not surprised to find within its literature a focus on cosmology and the hierarchy of the universe as they are manifested in narratives of the period. Mankind's relationship to the divine and the responsibilities and freedoms to be found therein were questioned by the humanists, while devotion to the Church strongly persisted. With this in mind, if, as Elizabeth Spiller maintains, "early modern imaginative literature and experimental science are inventions of a startling new attention to knowledge ... [that] represents new ways of thinking, new understandings of how man could create knowledge, and new ways of writing that try to recreate those ideas",[1] the tensions inherent in the period are indeed noteworthy. In a writer like William Shakespeare, they can perform on multiple levels with purposes at once seemingly latent yet quietly revelatory. Upon a close reading of William Shakespeare's *Romeo and Juliet*, and more specifically of Friar Lawrence, we will find, under the priest's rocky trail of misguided missteps, a positive path toward ultimate salvation. Reflective of the time, Friar Lawrence is, at the outset, an image of splintered piety, a man clearly called by God but also drawn by earthly passion

*A version of this essay first appeared in "A Case Against Natural Magic: Shakespeare's Friar Laurence as *Romeo and Juliet*'s Near-Tragic Hero", *Logos: A Journal of Catholic Thought and Culture* 13, no. 1 (Winter 2010):132–45.

[1] Elizabeth Spiller, *Science, Reading, and Renaissance Literature* (Cambridge: Cambridge University Press, 2004), p. 1. Although Spiller gives only very brief mention of Shakespeare, her opening contention appropriately sets the Renaissance scene as it applies to my study.

and the charitable—though destructive—drive to manipulate nature in opposition to divine law. To examine this splintering—its evident oppositions, its unalterable ramifications, and its final, healing transformation—will not be to ignore the tragedy of Romeo and Juliet but to highlight the undeniable importance of the Friar's role and Shakespeare's view of the dangers inherent in the self-deifying nature of natural magic.

Within the works of William Shakespeare is a profound reverence for the God of Christianity. Revisiting *Romeo and Juliet*, then, with an eye on the philosophies surrounding Shakespeare will serve to elucidate the paradoxical role of Friar Lawrence. For example, in Plato's dialogue on the hierarchy of the universe, the *Timaeus*, Plato asserts that one who "has devoted himself to the love of learning and to true wisdom" has thoughts that are "immortal and divine": "constantly caring for his divine part as he does, keeping well-ordered the guiding spirit that lives within him, he must indeed be supremely happy."[2] Indeed, we will find a Friar Lawrence not singularly happy with his decisions and his actions until he at last submits to and enjoys the freedoms concomitant with divine wisdom. Before that time, he falls out of the "perfect order" of Plato's illustration. Moreover, in keeping with the thoughts of Boethian philosophy, the Friar—to actualize his priestly role—must recognize the opposing forces within his own soul and know that if he "turn[s] [his] eyes away from the light of truth above to things on a lower and dimmer level, they are soon darkened by the mists of ignorance."[3] This sound philosophical precedent resonates throughout the play, as the Friar speaks words of wisdom yet acts contrary to them.

While contrariety is to be noted among many of the play's characters, it is in Friar Lawrence most problematic, for he stands *in persona Christi* (in the person of Christ) and is thus

---

[2] Plato, *Timaeus* 90b–c, trans. Donald J. Zeyl, in *Plato: Complete Works*, ed. John M. Cooper (Indianapolis: Hackett, 1997), pp. 1224–91.
[3] Boethius, *The Consolation of Philosophy* 5.2, trans. V. E. Watts (London: Penguin, 1969).

trusted and respected by those who most need his wisdom. According to Lucy Beckett, "Shakespeare explored the dilemmas of kingship, or any exercise of great power, and of the mismatch between men and the roles they must play, the healing qualities of human simplicity, the responsibility of the soul before God." [4] Acknowledging the validity of Beckett's claim, I will apply it to Friar Lawrence as the center of just such an exploration. Beckett does not consider Romeo and Juliet as tragic characters because, "however poignant their love and their deaths, [they] are no more than adolescent victims of . . . [an] Italian city feud." [5] If Romeo and Juliet are not entirely to blame for their missteps, in whom, then—more supposedly mature and thus supposedly more reverent and rational—lies the flaw? It is Friar Lawrence's culpability—clearly owing to his embrace of natural magic—that positions him as a near-tragic hero, with his ultimate salvific repentance promoting the Christian orthodoxy so indispensable to Shakespeare.

Prior to an examination of the Friar's dramatic representation, we must discuss Shakespeare's Christian orthodoxy and its place in Renaissance England. Lucy Beckett presents Elizabethan England at the time of Shakespeare's birth (1564) as a place once again stripped of its Catholic tradition. Although during the brief reign of the Catholic queen Mary (1533–1538), the Mass, altars, crucifixes, saintly images, and prayers for the dead—which had been prohibited early in the Reformation—were all restored, under Queen Elizabeth they "were again swept out". [6] In Elizabeth's England, Catholicism and treason were synonymous, causing a prohibition of Catholicism that lasted for two hundred years. [7] Considering this legal restraint on devout Catholics, the faith-driven choices of

---

[4] Lucy Beckett, *In the Light of Christ: Writings in the Western Tradition* (San Francisco: Ignatius Press, 2006), p. 213. Beckett's discussion in this section focuses on Richard II as Shakespeare's first truly tragic character, but her arguments are appropriate as well for Friar Lawrence and serve to fortify the contention that his role is that of a near-tragic hero.

[5] Ibid., p. 218.

[6] Ibid., p. 207.

[7] Ibid., p. 209.

Shakespeare's family are quite interesting, as well as quite vital to a true appreciation of his works. Refusing to attend the established Anglican church, Shakespeare's parents were recusants and, as such, suffered fines and persecution. Shakespeare, in addition to being raised in this persistent Catholic atmosphere at home, attended a grammar school run primarily by recusants. In consequence, Beckett confidently claims the existence of "evidence everywhere in his plays [of] ... his intimate responsiveness, intellectual, emotional, and imaginative, to the tradition in which he was brought up, officially wrecked but persisting in secret corners of the country".[8]

In his work on Shakespeare's Catholicism, Joseph Pearce describes the Church of England in Shakespeare's time, "neither Catholic nor Protestant but ... an uneasy amalgam of both ... rooted in compromise between its 'catholic' and 'protestant' members".[9] Although the state church endured the differences practiced by the "Catholic", conservative "high" church and the Protestant "low" church, refusal to join the accepted Anglican communion was not tolerated. Undoubtedly, growing up in such an environment and moving toward a public career placed Shakespeare in a possibly perilous position. Scrutinizing his work, then, as part of the struggle to maintain Christian orthodoxy in a milieu of ever-expanding secular fundamentalism will mean looking for interlinear signs—signs of disapproval for heretical tendencies and signs of hope and gratitude for divine obedience.

John S. Wilks discusses the role of conscience in Renaissance tragedy. "Because the age which nurtured Shakespeare's own beliefs still inherited its doctrines and cosmology more or less unchanged from the Middle Ages, the idea of conscience manifests itself amongst a variety of religious concepts to which his characters refer, ... orthodox in [their] assumptions about

---

[8] Ibid., p. 210.
[9] Joseph Pearce, *The Quest for Shakespeare* (San Francisco: Ignatius Press, 2008). As I discuss the Catholic tenor of *Romeo and Juliet* and my interpretation of Friar Lawrence's choices, I am indebted to Joseph Pearce. By sharing his research with me, he helped me to more solidly formulate my thesis.

the moral nature of man."[10] Indeed, man's moral nature is of prime importance in *Romeo and Juliet*, as it is in Shakespeare's other plays. So closely connected to the Middle Ages, the Renaissance still portrayed a providential design, in which God created and willed the interdependence of material and spiritual nature. For Shakespeare, "the doctrine, implying as it did an infinitely recurring set of relationships connecting man with the universe, provided ... the basis for both a moral and an artistic vision: it infused one and enriched the other."[11] In Shakespeare, man's role in the interdependence differs greatly from that propounded by the Renaissance magi, whose work suggested an elevated place for man. As we examine Friar Lawrence, the difference will become clear. With this in mind, the distinction between the Friar's Catholic training, from which he strays yet to which he returns, and his interim experiments in natural magic convey sure signs of the tensions caused by the Renaissance's break from the orthodoxy of the Middle Ages. David Beauregard notes Shakespeare's sympathetic depiction of Roman Catholic religious and his accompanying inversion of anti-Catholic dramatic conventions,[12] but this sympathy comes to its full fruition only in *Romeo and Juliet* after Friar Lawrence's deviation from his vows has been fatal to others and nearly to himself. In his artistic vision for *Romeo and Juliet*, therefore, Shakespeare elucidates a recognition of the imminent danger posed by fading religious orthodoxy.

Romeo and Juliet was written in the midst of a substantial legacy of Renaissance natural philosophy. In the earlier phases

---

[10] John S. Wilks, *The Idea of Conscience in Renaissance Tragedy* (London: Routledge, 1990), p. 6. Wilks' study does not emphasize man's moral nature in *Romeo and Juliet*, or Shakespeare's own religious tendencies, but rather gives attention to the Scholastically influenced issue of conscience in many other tragedies (i.e., *Hamlet, Macbeth, King Lear, Richard III*). Still, his discussion of conscience as manifested in the works is applicable here.

[11] Ibid., pp. 15–16.

[12] David Beauregard, "Shakespeare on the Monastic Life: Nuns and Friars in *Measure for Measure*", in *Shakespeare and the Culture of Christianity in Early Modern England*, ed. Dennis Taylor and David N. Beauregard (New York: Fordham University Press, 2003), pp. 312–13.

of this philosophy, devout Christianity played a much more prominent and revered role. Although Marsilio Ficino, for example, saw magic as a contemplative means of uniting with God, he "trembled to approach heaven on paths not blessed by the church",[13] and as evidenced by his numerous translations of Plato, he held in great esteem the teachings of antiquity. In contrast, Paracelsus "fors[ook] the logic and book learning of Plato, Aristotle, and Galen",[14] choosing instead to focus on worldly observation to promote his ideas on medicine, magic, and natural philosophy as a path to perfection. In his work—chemical, alchemical, and medical—he "rejected 'organized religion and classical scholarship'".[15] Similarly, Giordano Bruno "ignored the constraints of orthodoxy" as he propounded the operative role of magic as it manifests itself in man's will.[16] The philosophical and magical practices of Paracelsus and Bruno were known to Shakespeare's educated audience, and Shakespeare's method of simultaneously incorporating them and repelling them in *Romeo and Juliet* is intriguing indeed. As these beliefs of Paracelsus and Bruno are reflected in Friar Lawrence's choices, Shakespeare's attitude toward them becomes all the more evident, and the atmosphere that gave birth to these attitudes too merits consideration.

The "misadventur'd piteous overthrows" of Romeo and Juliet (Prol. 7)[17] are not entirely of their own doing. The couple are the victims of the feudal animosity of their respective families. In the midst of this hatred, Shakespeare provides his heroine, by means of his hero, with a mentor—in the person of Friar Lawrence—one with the opportunity to offer valuable

---

[13] Brian P. Copenhaver, "Astrology and Magic", in *The Cambridge History of Renaissance Philosophy*, ed. Charles B. Schmitt and Quentin Skinner (Cambridge: Cambridge University Press), p. 279.

[14] Ibid., p. 290.

[15] Bernard I. Cohen, *Revolution in Science* (Cambridge, Mass.: Harvard University Press, 1985), p. 183.

[16] Copenhaver, "Astrology and Magic", pp. 293–94.

[17] All quotations from *Romeo and Juliet* are from the edition published by Ignatius Press: *Romeo and Juliet*, ed. Joseph Pearce, Ignatius Critical Editions (San Francisco: Ignatius Press, 2011).

moral lessons. In this role, we will find him at once honorable and dishonorable, reverent and irreverent, salvific and destructive. The unmistakably contrasting elements in his words and deeds posit him as an example of Renaissance contrariety but certainly not in a positive sense. He will escape tragic fall himself only when his heart and soul regain their proper order.

Before we meet Friar Lawrence in Act 2, we witness Romeo and Juliet's first encounter, as their immediate passion overwhelms them. Early in the balcony scene, Juliet's feminine reason still stands as she worriedly scolds Romeo for being there: "The orchard walls are high and hard to climb; / And the place death, considering who thou art" (2.2.63–64). Perhaps she can ground flighty Romeo, who with "love's light wings" (66) entered the forbidden Capulet garden, for initially she shies away from being "too quickly won" (95). But, alas, just a moment later, naming Romeo "the god of [her] idolatry" (114), Juliet's abuse of God's First Commandment foreshadows her imminent downfall. Alice Von Hildebrand reminds us, "Original sin was a sin of pride, of disobedience, of irreverence, and of metaphysical revolt that led to an inversion of the hierarchy of values."[18] This value inversion is key to Romeo and Juliet's tragedy, and it is their mentor's poor model, one overtly negligent of moral virtue, that fuels the frenzied action.

Scrutinizing this aspect of Friar Lawrence's role leads to his near-tragic status, for herein rests his tragic flaw. Arthur Kirsch, in speaking of Shakespeare's heroes, says that they "not only are obviously subject to the evanescence of human passion, but they also consciously protest against it, and that consciousness and ultimately unavailing protest constitute a substantial part of their suffering."[19] Juliet's short-lived protest, and thus her manifestly imminent suffering, has been already noted, but we rightfully expect and hope that Friar Lawrence's protests will be more steadfast. Instead, we watch

---

[18] Alice Von Hildebrand, *The Privilege of Being a Woman* (Ann Arbor: Sapientia Press, 2005), p. 21.

[19] Arthur Kirsch, *The Passions of Shakespeare's Tragic Heroes* (Charlottesville: University Press of Virginia, 1990), p. 11.

him veer more and more toward a reliance on self and nature that mirrors Renaissance philosophy and science as they increasingly distanced themselves from the Church. His path is a profound downward spiral, which is righted only by a return to the cosmic order that his vocation professes.

Since Friar Lawrence begins as Romeo's friend, priest, and confessor, each decision he makes will inevitably affect Juliet as much as it does Romeo. At the Capulet masquerade, Romeo momentarily recognized Juliet as a "holy shrine" (1.5.92), but haste prevails over humility, and true reverence soon disappears. Wisely, Friar Lawrence initially chastises Romeo "for doting, not for loving" (2.3.82), but no sooner does he say this than he agrees to secretly marry the two impetuous lovers. Peter Milward claims that Shakespeare "goes out of his way to multiply testimonials to the honesty and sanctity of Friar Lawrence",[20] with textual references such as "reverend holy friar" (4.2.31). Even so, I maintain that while, indeed, the Friar's intentions are always honorable—hoping "[t]o turn [the] households' rancour to pure love" (2.3.92), for example—he is nonetheless a weak guide for our hero and heroine. His plan to heal the evil of the feud using deception is unsound, and his words are at variance with his actions.

Looking back to the Friar's first speech, we see Shakespeare's very purposeful introduction of this vital character. It is his avocation, rather than his vocation, that takes center stage, as he soliloquizes over his mystical garden. Here, Friar Lawrence's losing game of tug-of-war begins. His philosophy, at face value, is sound and pious. He knows that anything "so good but, strain'd from that fair use,/Revolts from true birth, stumbling on abuse" (2.3.19–20). Yet, only a day later, he abuses his priestly vocation and his medical art in just such a way by hastily concocting a potion with so many innate risks. As he joins Romeo in his "sudden haste" (93) toward the altar, he warns, "Wisely and slow; they stumble that run fast" (94);

---

[20] Peter Milward, S.J., *Shakespeare the Papist* (Naples, Fla.: Sapientia Press, 2005), p. 73.

yet on their heels, Juliet too will fall. Sensing even that "[t]hese violent delights have violent ends" (2.6.9), he nonetheless "make[s] short work" (35)—and Romeo and Juliet are wed. If he understands that when "rude will ... is predominant, / Full soon the canker death eats up that plant" (2.3.28–30), what, then, of his actions? He rightly sees Romeo as an "ill-beseeming beast" (3.3.113) in his suicidal agony over his banishment, yet he devises a clandestine plan, relegating respect for the minors' parents and for the law to secondary importance, as he assumes the irreverent and, as the plot soon reveals, unwise role of a magus.

Friar Lawrence sends Romeo to Mantua and remains as Juliet's mentor. Having already wed Juliet to Romeo, thus aiding in her deception of her parents, he now leads her yet closer to doom as he concocts his plan to fake her death, avoid her arranged marriage to County Paris, and again deceive her parents. He becomes overconfident, and his actions become all the more dangerous as time progresses. What happened to his intention, stated to Romeo, to "blaze [his] marriage, reconcile [his] friends, / Beg pardon of the Prince, and call [him] back / With twenty hundred thousand times more joy / Than [he went] forth in lamentation" (3.3.151–54)? Why such haste to acquiesce to Romeo and Juliet's impetuous passion but not to save them from self-destruction? Ensuring the tragic conclusion, Juliet accepts the Friar as her guide with filial and reverent trust. His well-intentioned yet ill-conceived scheme only heightens her immature hubris. As she grabs his potion and exclaims, "O, tell me not of fear!" (4.1.121), she yields to a temptation that will mean death. Such convoluted plans as Friar Lawrence's—so distanced from Truth—are doomed to fail.

Scenes from Franco Zeffirelli's 1968 film adaptation illustrate perfectly the Friar's splintered nature. Akin to the garden scene, where the Friar first acted poorly in his role as moral mentor to Romeo, is the scene in his cell, which is outfitted much more like a Renaissance alchemist's laboratory than a monastic cell. It is in this setting, and not in the church, that Juliet pleads for his assistance. After Romeo's banishment for

Tybalt's murder, she is prepared to "leap . . . / From off the battlements of any tower" (4.1.77–78) rather than commit bigamy and acquiesce to her arranged marriage to Paris. At this height of deep inner struggle and emotional despair, Juliet seeks guidance from the one who has thus far granted her wishes, no matter how foolish. As she moans and weeps profusely, Friar Lawrence "sp[ies] a kind of hope" (4.1.68). Juliet's terrestrial desires lure her to the Friar's vial, although her practical wisdom leads her to question the ramifications. But, remembering that Friar Lawrence "hath still been tried a holy man" (4.3.29), she places her life in his hands.

In the Friar's actions, "so tutored by [his] art" (5.3.242), we see reflections of Bruno, whose "disenchantment with Aristotle made him receptive to Neoplatonic and Hermetic authorities even friendlier to a magical worldview".[21] In addition, the Friar assumes a Paracelsian character, in that "Paracelsus transferred to the plane of natural philosophy or natural magic the mystic's direct, inward vision of God."[22] So steeped in the Friar's ill-chosen devotion to magical devices, Juliet's desires are doomed. Misinformation and ill timing lead to the demise of both Paris and Romeo, each of whom is misled by Juliet's apparent death. Far too late, Friar Lawrence "fear[s] some ill unthrifty thing" (5.3.136) and has not even the strength or courage to lure Juliet away. He "dare[s] no longer stay" (159), and Juliet, left alone, takes her life.

Discussing the play's tragic ending, Milward argues that Shakespeare illuminates "an element of personal responsibility in Romeo's fate".[23] This may be true, but the same is true for Juliet, and moreover, Friar Lawrence's responsibility is the greatest. In his self-appointed role as a philosopher of nature, he strays, like Bruno, from the Platonists' "emphasis on the supernatural and on the soul's ascent to God", leaning instead toward

---

[21] Copenhaver, "Astrology and Magic", p. 293.

[22] Ibid., p. 290.

[23] Peter Milward, S.J., *Christian Themes in English Literature* (Tokyo: Kenkyusha, 1967), p. 55.

the belief in "nature itself . . . as a self-sufficient system".[24] While he is for Romeo and Juliet a poor mentor, for us he provides—through his negative example—a vital Catholic lesson, one which, I believe, Shakespeare intended. It is true, as Milward maintains, that through Friar Laurence, Shakespeare instills the play with "a deep Christian wisdom that is aptly related . . . to [the Friar's] religious profession",[25] but through him we also see the weakness of every man—weakness that is healed only by admission, confession, and atonement. Friar Lawrence relinquishes control, admitting that "[a] greater power than we can contradict/Hath thwarted our intents" (5.3.153–54), confessing all that was "[m]iscarried by [his] fault" (266), and atoning with an offering of his life for his sins. Thus we can agree with the Prince's absolving decree: "We still have known thee for a holy man" (269) and know that Friar Lawrence's newly regained humility, faith, and reason—if realized earlier—could have saved Juliet, and thus her Romeo.

---

[24] Frederick Copleston, S.J. *Late Medieval and Renaissance Philosophy* (New York: Doubleday, 1993), p. 248.

[25] Milward, *Shakespeare the Papist*, p. 74.

Fools for Love? Shakespeare's Qualified Defense of *Romeo and Juliet*

Jonathan Marks
Ursinus College

When I teach *Romeo and Juliet*, most of my students fall into one of two camps. The debunkers of young love think that Romeo and Juliet are deluded. Since Romeo and Juliet know almost nothing about each other, they cannot possibly be in love. They must be mistaking physical attraction for real love. The romantics, however, believe in love at first sight. Perhaps they have even experienced it. They admit that the lovers know very little about each other, but they deny that falling in love is a matter of vetting available candidates. Love is mysterious, but we know it when we feel it, and it may well come—it may even be best when it comes—before lovers exchange their life stories.

I think, and try to demonstrate to my students, that each camp has something to learn from a second look at the play. The romantics miss how funny *Romeo and Juliet* is and how funny young lovers are. Romeo and Juliet are foolish, and sceptics are right to doubt, even to ridicule, them. The debunkers miss how tragic *Romeo and Juliet* is and how young love ennobles those who devote themselves to it. If Romeo and Juliet want each other's bodies and call this attraction love, then nothing very mighty falls when they do. Their deaths are sad and senseless but not tragic. But Shakespeare does not take the debunkers' side either. The most important of young love's detractors in *Romeo and Juliet* evidently think that what appear to be noble and uniquely human sentiments are at bottom neither noble nor uniquely human, or that there is no natural basis for noble and uniquely human things. But this narrow and reductionist understanding makes for misunderstanding and, in Friar Lawrence's case, disaster.

Shakespeare, at least at first, makes us laugh at the outrageous professions of love. Romeo thinks his love unique, but Mercutio thinks all lovers are alike: "Speak but one rhyme and I am satisfied;/Cry but 'Ay me!' pronounce but 'love' and 'dove'" (2.1.9–10).[1] Mercutio is right. When Romeo first sees Juliet, he pronounces both "love" and "dove" in his rhyming praise of her beauty (1.5.46, 50). In the celebrated speech that follows Mercutio's burlesque, Juliet's first words are "Ay me!" (2.2.26).

We are also made to laugh at the lover's promise of eternal faith. In Act 1, when Romeo is infatuated with Rosaline, Benvolio wounds him by suggesting he can easily be made to drop her in favor of someone else: "Compare her face with some that I shall show,/And I will make thee think thy swan a crow" (1.2.86–87). Of course, Romeo's vehement denial notwithstanding, Benvolio is right. At the Capulets' feast, with Rosaline in attendance, Juliet seems to Romeo "a snowy dove trooping with crows" (1.5.46).

Mercutio mocks the lover's high-mindedness by reducing love to sex: "O that she were/An open et cetera, thou a pop'rin pear!" (2.1.37–38). He is funny in part because he is right. Romeo protests to himself: "He jests at scars that never felt a wound" (2.2.1). But if Romeo's heart is pure, why does he hate chastity so much? In his famous speech below Juliet's window, his first concern is to strip Juliet of her virginity: "[V]estal livery is but sick and green,/And none but fools do wear it; cast it off" (2.2.8–9). In this context, Romeo's plea, "O wilt thou leave me so unsatisfied?" (2.2.125), hardly passes muster, as he hopes it will, as a request for "[t]h' exchange of thy love's faithful vow for mine" (2.2.127) rather than as a request for an invite upstairs. That exchange has, after all, taken place. It is Juliet who has to introduce, shortly thereafter, the subject of marriage, a vow, that, unlike those that Romeo has given so far, will guarantee that his "bent of love be honourable" (2.2.143). If Mercutio

---

[1] All quotations from *Romeo and Juliet* are from the edition published by Ignatius Press: *Romeo and Juliet*, ed. Joseph Pearce, Ignatius Critical Editions (San Francisco: Ignatius Press, 2011).

overstates the case when he compares love to "a great natural that runs lolling up and down to hide his bauble in a hole" (2.4.88–89), Juliet knows there is something to it.[2]

That the love of Romeo and Juliet has a strong connection to bodies is also suggested by the language the lovers use. Looks figure prominently. The religion of Romeo's love is "the devout religion of [his] eye" (1.2.88); "Did my heart love till now? Forswear it, *sight*" (1.5.50, my emphasis). Even the Chorus thinks Romeo and Juliet "alike bewitched by the charm of looks" (2 Prol. 6). The lovers praise cheeks, eyes, faces, hands; they are worshippers of form, so much so that each compares the beauty of the other to that of the stars, which are otherwise thought to mark out human fate (Prol. 6; 1.4.107): "The brightness of her cheek would shame those stars" (2.2.19), says Romeo. And as for Juliet:

> Give me my Romeo; and, when he shall die,
> Take him and cut him out in little stars,
> And he will make the face of heaven so fine
> That all the world will be in love with night,
> And pay no worship to the garish sun.
>
> (3.2.21–25)

Romeo and Juliet raise up their beloveds to rival the immortal beings who mark off the beginning and end of life. Yet their new religion, being a religion of the eye that worships the beauty of perishable bodies, is an illusion that is shattered by the death of the lovers. One commentator has observed that "the play literally culminates in the tomb. . . . The illusion of eternal life and beauty, the delicious, fleshy

---

[2] For a delightfully subversive reading of this scene, according to which Juliet deliberately baits Romeo by offering and withdrawing her body, see Carolyn E. Brown, "Juliet's Taming of Romeo", *Studies in English Literature 1500–1900* 36 (1996): 339–49. I think Brown is right that Romeo deserves to be mocked more than the more realistic Juliet, but she overstates the extent to which Juliet is master of rather than mastered by love. As Brown depicts Juliet, she would be equally capable of carving out her freedom with the County Paris; if she is not carried away by her love for Romeo, her suicide is inexplicable.

bodies that embrace and will never decay, is the opposite of the skeletons in the tomb."[3]

Death is only the most striking reason that the passion of Romeo and Juliet cannot last. The beauty to which that passion is devoted will fade with age. Passion itself will cool and lose ground to other adult concerns. Romeo and Juliet are surrounded by older men and women who cannot feel the kind of love they feel, which is not to say that the older people do not miss it. Juliet's bawdy nurse obviously delights in her part in Juliet's affair and willingly risks her job and betrays her employers in order to arrange the consummation of Juliet's marriage. Nonetheless, she, unlike Juliet, has learned the fine, adult art of compromise and urges Juliet to marry Paris, although Juliet is secretly already married to Romeo: "Your first is dead, or 'twere as good he were/As living here and you no use of him" (3.5.225–26). But in my view, the best words on the fond but resigned perspective of age on the fleetingness of young love belong to old Capulet.

> Welcome, gentlemen! I have seen the day
> That I have worn a visor and could tell
> A whispering tale in a fair lady's ear,
> Such as would please. 'Tis gone, 'tis gone, 'tis gone!
> (1.5.19–22)

Romeo and Juliet's love is founded on the illusion that bodies and their passions will retain their beauty and strength forever. No wonder it thrives on darkness. Romeo and Juliet have more reasons than most lovers for avoiding daylight, but Romeo, even before he finds himself in danger, is a lover of privacy and night.

> But all so soon as the all-cheering sun
> Should in the farthest east begin to draw
> The shady curtains from Aurora's bed,
> Away from light steals home my heavy son,

---

[3] Allan Bloom, *Love and Friendship* (New York: Simon and Schuster, 1993), pp. 281–82.

> And private in his chamber pens himself,
> Shuts up his windows, locks fair daylight out,
> And makes himself an artificial night.
>
> (1.1.132–38)

Love sees by its own light. The beloved is light in darkness: "Come, night; come, Romeo; come thou day in night" (3.2.17). But those who live solely by this light live in willful ignorance. Young love is blind to all that is not love, and it is impatient with reasoned attempts to oppose it or place it in perspective: "Hang up philosophy;/Unless philosophy can make a Juliet, ... [i]t helps not" (3.3.57–58, 60). Romeo seeks the darkness not because he is depressed but because he wants to be in love without the nagging distractions of friends, fathers, and friars who want him to love moderately.

While Romeo still pines for Rosaline, Montague worries that his son's lovesickness will kill him before he grows up. Romeo is like "the bud bit with an envious worm,/Ere he can spread his sweet leaves to the air" (1.1.149–50). But young lovers run this risk willingly; to them, mature love is diluted love, and that is not the thing they crave. Better that young love should perish before it matures. It is fitting for Romeo and Juliet to die young. The darkness that is a friend to their kind of love can be preserved only when they are both closed in the darkness of the tomb. This perfection of Romeo and Juliet's love is also the play's salient criticism of it. This type of love wants to avoid learning the truth.

Obviously, however, Shakespeare does not simply debunk young love. Our sympathies remain entirely with Romeo and Juliet. One reason the couple is able to hold on to our sympathy is that the alternatives to their outlook are themselves defective. Mercutio and Friar Lawrence, the most important critics of Romeo and Juliet, do not understand the lovers.

Mercutio is the patron saint of debunkers. While his barbs often stick, he understands only the filthy and ridiculous in love. His Queen Mab speech masterfully asserts that love is sheer vanity, indistinct in kind or source from any other desire.

Mab's chariot, which stimulates the dreams of lovers, is flimsy and disgusting, built of insect parts, spiders' webs, and an empty nut (1.4.53–95). Love, which speaks of itself in such a lofty and serious way, can be reduced to the low and the light. If Shakespeare fully shared Mercutio's view, of course, we would have to laugh at the Montagues and Capulets for raising statues to their children, as they promise to do in the final scene, since the only thing that makes Romeo and Juliet worth immortalizing, in pure gold or in poetry, is their love. Their heroism consists entirely in what they do for love.

Shakespeare comes to the aid of the lovers by showing that Mercutio contradicts himself. In the Mab speech, Mercutio criticizes not only love but other dreams, including the soldier's dream:

> Sometime she driveth o'er a soldier's neck,
> And then dreams he of cutting foreign throats,
> Of breaches, ambuscadoes, Spanish blades.
>
> (1.4.82–84)

Mercutio, surprisingly, devotes more of his speech to the soldier's dream than to any other, including the lover's. And that is, of course, far from the only interest he shows in fighting. His hatred of Tybalt centers less on Tybalt's passionate hatred of his friends than on Tybalt's newfangled, artificial dueling style:

> The pox on such antic, lisping, affecting fantasticoes; these new tuners of accent!
>   … Why, is this not a lamentable thing, grandsire, that we should be thus afflicted with these strange flies, these fashion-mongers, these pardon-me's? (2.4.28–33)

Tybalt is too fancy for Mercutio: "O calm, dishonourable, vile submission! / Alla stoccata carries it away" (3.1.71–72); "Come, sir, your passado" (3.1.82). Mercutio itches to fight Tybalt not only to protect his friend but also to defend his idea of what is noble and ignoble, real and artificial, in combat. Even insofar as he acts to protect Romeo, it is Romeo's honor he wants to protect. The Mab speech notwithstanding, he is himself a dreamer of the soldier's dream.[4]

Mercutio's understanding of the world does not support his own activity in it. There is no basis in the view he advances in the Queen Mab speech for the distinction he makes and cares about between real and artificial ways of conducting oneself in combat, between real nobility and fashionable pretense. Much of what we admire in Mercutio, his courage and his loyalty, falls completely outside of his reductionist perspective. Given the choice between thinking that Shakespeare meant for us to despise Mercutio's bravery and thinking that Shakespeare meant for us to doubt Mercutio's intellectual premises, it is hard to avoid choosing the latter. When Mercutio reduces what seem to be distinctly human phenomena to nonhuman components, he fails to take into account what is most important in his own life—nobility, the thing he is ready to die for. This error diminishes his standing as a critic of lovers, since he dismisses the lover's dream for the same unlikely reason that he dismisses the soldier's: namely, he believes that there is no foundation in nature for high sentiments or the high deeds that they inspire. Yet no one, not even Mercutio, acts or speaks as if he really believes that.

Friar Lawrence sides with reason against the foolish excesses of love. He dispenses "[a]dversity's sweet milk, philosophy" (3.3.55) to young people who are not thirsty for milk. His religious office and the sententious advice he offers to the lovers make him seem almost the opposite of the obscene Mercutio, but his understanding of human things is at least as reductionist as Mercutio's. He first appears with a basket, collecting plants, presumably ingredients for his potions. The Friar, a skilled alchemist, is a manipulator of nature; his art does not, by itself, say anything about his understanding of nature or of human beings, but his speech does:

---

[4] In Franco Zeffirelli's 1968 film production of the play, Mercutio is brought nearly to tears by the Mab speech, so much so that Romeo's lines "Peace, peace, Mercutio, peace! / Thou talk'st of nothing" (1.4.95–96) are delivered not to chide but to reassure Mercutio.

O, mickle is the powerful grace that lies
In plants, herbs, stones, and their true qualities.
For nought so vile that on the earth doth live
But to the earth some special good doth give;
Nor aught so good but, strain'd from that fair use,
Revolts from true birth, stumbling on abuse:
Virtue itself turns vice, being misapplied.
And vice sometime's by action dignified.

(2.3.15–22)

Friar Lawrence reads virtue and vice, grace and rebellion, into nature. But he thinks that the virtue or vice of things depends on their right or wrong use and that he is capable of distinguishing between right and wrong use, and even of transforming vice into virtue, through his knowledge. Virtue and vice, grace and rebellion, are objects to be manipulated by the knower of nature.[5]

The Friar's activities suggest that he thinks he can use human beings just as he uses herbs. He attempts to use Romeo and Juliet to make peace between the Montagues and Capulets, concerning himself more with this objective than with the souls of the young lovers. Indeed, he marries Romeo and Juliet in haste, despite his misgivings about Romeo's sudden change of loyalty from Rosaline to Juliet. Although the Friar thinks Romeo's love is fleeting and fickle, he gives in to what, from his perspective, is a foolish whim, in order to secure his political objective. The Friar thinks he can turn Romeo's vice of inconstancy into a virtue by using it to perform another work of alchemy, namely, turning the hate of the warring families into love:

---

[5] For a reading of Friar Lawrence's opening speech that sees it as a "hymn to power", see Gerry Brenner, "Shakespeare's Politically Ambitious Friar", *Shakespeare Studies* 13 (1980): 51. For another reading of the Friar as a politically ambitious manipulator, see Jerry Weinberger, "Pious Princes and Red Hot Lovers: The Politics of Shakespeare's *Romeo and Juliet*", *Journal of Politics* 65 (May 2003): 350–75. I think both readings overestimate the Friar's mastery of politics; as I will argue in a moment, his inability to understand human passions makes him a bumbler.

> But come, young waverer, come, go with me,
> In one respect I'll thy assistant be;
> For this alliance may so happy prove
> To turn your households' rancour to pure love.
>
> (2.3.89–92)

In the Friar's defense, we can say that he has confidence in his ability to talk sense to his charge and consequently does not imagine he is putting anyone's soul or happiness at risk. Perhaps he intends to school Romeo and Juliet about love after he marries them. But that defense, while it saves the Friar's decency, merely underscores the extent to which he thinks he can shape people according to his needs.

At the Friar's core, then, we find not a priest's humility but a scientist's confidence in his knowledge.[6] The speech in which the Friar consoles the Capulets for Juliet's apparent death is thick with irony, for while it professes to be about the wisdom of submitting to the will of God, the actual source of the Friar's equanimity is not his trust in the promise of eternal life but his trust in the power of pharmaceuticals.

The Friar, like Mercutio, does not fully acknowledge a distinction between the human and nonhuman. While the plants the Friar manipulates have their tendencies (some may be woody, while others may be succulent), even their attractions and repulsions (some may like cold weather, while others may like hot), none of them loves as Romeo loves Juliet or hates as Tybalt hates the Montagues. The Friar is lost in the realm of unbending love and implacable hatred, and his plan is foiled in large part by actions that originate in that realm. Tybalt, who hates peace and Montagues (1.1.68–69), is the cause of Romeo's banishment. And the Friar is so ignorant of the character of Romeo's longing that it does not occur to him that Romeo, in banishment, might ask someone in Verona to give him news of Juliet. This mistake causes the Friar to arrive at

---

[6] Brenner compares the Friar to a "scientific meddler" who "tampers with God's natural order and uses nature's secret powers to serve his own purposes" ("Shakespeare's Politically Ambitious Friar", p. 55).

the tomb too late to prevent Romeo's suicide. The Friar's impotence is summed up in his reaction to Juliet's death. He is found trembling and weeping (5.3.183), having abandoned Juliet, unforgivably, because he is afraid he will get caught.

Mercutio's and Friar Lawrence's failure to understand Romeo and Juliet, though it does not by itself vindicate young lovers, prepares us to reevaluate young love. Suppose Romeo and Juliet's love is, as even some of their advocates will agree, love at first sight; suppose too that such love, being founded on a hope that no first sight can justify, deserves ridicule. Even so, one need not consider it altogether ridiculous. One may even, as Allan Bloom does, think it good: "Love at first sight, tapping the most generous sentiments and focusing the whole of two persons' energies on each other, bringing out the best in each, suppressing the petty and ugly passions, seems to be good manifestly."[7] In each other, Romeo and Juliet sense a beauty and a goodness that transcend the familial and political struggle that occupies the other characters in the play. Insofar as they mistake their beloved for the whole of beauty and goodness, or even see each other as perfectly beautiful and good, they are deluded. But their sensitivity to and willingness to stake all on beauty and goodness is admirable and distinguishes them from others. Insofar as they, in their enthusiasm, sometimes forget that their love has something to do with wanting each other's bodies, they are perfect subjects for Mercutio's comedy. But if their professions of love are sometimes too pious, then their sense that their desires are noble, that there is a harmony between their bodily and spiritual longings, is not simply an error. The harmony is temporary— Romeo's and Juliet's beautiful souls will not always inhabit desirable bodies—but its existence for the time being makes it easy to understand why the lovers get so carried away.

Moreover, Romeo and Juliet do not precisely love at first sight. Romeo, admittedly, announces his love the moment he sees Juliet, but we know from his professed devotion to Rosaline that Romeo's declarations of love are not always trustworthy.

[7] Bloom, *Love and Friendship*, p. 273.

We begin to be persuaded that Juliet suits Romeo only when they first speak to each other and Romeo, himself a superb verbal duelist capable of matching even Mercutio in a battle of obscene wit (2.4.37–96), finds Juliet his equal or better in the more subtle battle of wits that surrounds their first two kisses (1.5.91–108). Soon enough, Romeo matches words with deeds by risking his life even to speak to Juliet, and Juliet, while at first in no position to risk her life, shows that she is prepared to abandon everything to marry him. Although love at first sight can be defended, one need not defend love at first sight to defend Romeo and Juliet. They learn more about each other in the short course of the play than others learn about each other from a long courtship. Most important, they quickly learn that each is capable of being moved by love to speak beautifully and act courageously.

That praise does not mean that Romeo and Juliet are wise. Our defense of the lovers concedes that they are deeply attached to false beliefs about each other and that they prefer these beliefs to knowledge. But they are also very young, and there is no reason to believe that they are permanent enemies to moderation. Unfortunately, neither has a decent guide. The play, whose perspective comprises the most serious and most ridiculous in young love, indicates the kind of perspective that such a guide would have to have and that no individual character in it actually has. When reasonable and observant people are not constrained, as Mercutio and Friar Lawrence are, by a narrow vision of nature, they are capable of giving love its due without deferring to its excesses and delusions.

Romeo and Juliet and the Petrarchan
Love Poetry Tradition

Rebecca Munro
Belmont Abbey College

One of my former students, a devout Roman Catholic, said of Shakespeare's *Romeo and Juliet*, "I hate this play; it's about two people who fall in love, act totally irresponsibly, commit suicide, and go to Hell. What's so great about that?" She raises an age-old question: How should we respond to imaginative literature from the standpoint of our ethical and religious principles? Sir Philip Sidney in the sixteenth century addressed the question when he defended "poesy" (imaginative verbal art) from the charge of immorality.[1] Such art, Sidney argued, crowns all others in its ability to "teach and delight", to move a reader or hearer toward right action through the delightfulness of storytelling, "with a tale which holdeth children from play, and old men from the chimney corner",[2] a tale that includes both good and evil. The moral effects of verbal art come to us indirectly, argued Sidney, not by overt moral or religious instruction.

In response to my student's summary condemnation of Shakespeare's play, approaching the work from an aesthetic perspective will yield more fruitful exposition and analysis. *Romeo and Juliet* is among Shakespeare's most poetic plays, 90 percent in verse, thus a work of poetic art. It is also a tragedy, the dramatic genre in which death in some terrible way overtakes the tragic hero or heroine. Because the play *is* a work of literary art, to recognize and examine it as such will also yield better access to its moral and religious implications. The

---

[1] Sir Philip Sidney, "The Defense of Poesy", in *Sir Philip Sidney: A Critical Edition of the Major Works*, ed. Katherine Duncan-Jones (Oxford: Oxford University Press, 1989), pp. 212–50.

[2] Ibid., pp. 217, 227.

Petrarchan love poetry tradition provides an appropriate vehicle for such an approach. Everywhere in the play, Shakespeare utilizes Petrarchan conventions to tell Romeo and Juliet's story and create the atmosphere of their world. To get to the core of this particular tragedy, we need to examine the way in which Shakespeare utilizes and exploits the poetic conventions of Petrarchan love poetry so that he might transcend and transform them and, as the love poetry tradition prescribes, sublimate passion into unforgettable verse.

Some knowledge of the Petrarchan tradition will help us. What came to fruition as Petrarchan love poetry in the fourteenth century began with the Provençal troubadours of eleventh-century France. Their courtly love songs were precursors of the great European Arthurian chivalric romances. The ancient Roman Ovid's *Ars amatoria* (Art of love) contributed to these medieval stories and poems of courtly romance with Ovid's tongue-in-cheek rules for the courtly lover, often taken with great seriousness by medieval translators and readers. Ovid's *Ars amatoria* set up a kind of rival to Christianity: the religion of love. In *The Allegory of Love*, C. S. Lewis demonstrates the development of the courtly love ideal in the Western world: the notion of the idealized lady deferred to by her courteous chivalric lover and the idea of "falling in love" as a transformative and exalting experience. These notions, Lewis tells us, evolved out of the complicated interplay between literature and the realities of medieval life. Lewis writes, "[A]n unmistakable continuity connects the Provençal love song with the love poetry of the later Middle Ages, and thence, through Petrarch and many others, with that of the present day."[3] In thirteenth-century Italy, Dante introduced the sweet new style of love poetry in his *La vita nuova*, a series of love poems addressed to a woman named Beatrice. With Dante and Petrarch, the Neoplatonic "ladder of love" came into the mix: if one loves what is beautiful in this world—the lady—one

---

[3] C. S. Lewis, *The Allegory of Love* (1936; London: Oxford University Press, 1981), p. 3.

may ascend by steps to love the ultimate beauty and reality, God. But it was Petrarch in his fourteenth-century love poems to a woman named Laura who established the final form and conventions of the sonnet, those attributes we call "Petrarchan".

The classic Petrarchan form demands fourteen iambic pentameter lines and a rhyme scheme dividing the poem into octave and sestet. Characteristically, the Petrarchan sonnet expresses a *psychomachia*, an intense emotional, psychological, and spiritual struggle—love as warfare—captured within the sonnet's formal limitations. In the traditional Petrarchan sonnet, an agonized lover tends to seek the favor of an unimaginably virtuous, chaste, beautiful, and unapproachable woman. Petrarchan love poetry also expresses an unresolved tension between the sensual and the divine, between physical desire and an idealized Platonic love leading to virtue and salvation. Imagery in this poetry demonstrates love's contradictory nature: its destructive potential—love as sickness, love as poison, love as danger, the lover as "enemy"—as well as its elevating and transformational aspects. The "blazon", a catalogue of the lady's attributes, is characteristically found in the sonnet: her eyes like stars, her cheeks like roses, her hair like spun gold. Finally, the sonnet in the Petrarchan tradition tends to be obsessed with the relationship between love and death, the two life-problems that cause human beings the greatest difficulty and elicit the most chaotic emotional responses. Subsuming other attributes of this poetry, one ultimately stands out above the rest: paradox. Petrarchan poetry takes on and attempts to express the contradictory and paradoxical nature of passionate romantic love. Exemplifying Robert Frost's description of poetry as "a momentary stay against confusion",[4] the Petrarchan sonnet endeavors to impose poetic order on the chaos of intense human emotion and experience.

Petrarchan love poetry made its way to England in the sixteenth century through translation and imitation. The British

[4] Robert Frost, "The Figure a Poem Makes", introduction to *Complete Poems of Robert Frost* (New York: Holt, Rinehart, and Winston, 1964), p. vi.

poets, Shakespeare greatest among them, took up the genre, ridiculed what had become hackneyed and clichéd, modified the form, and expanded its expression. In Elizabethan England, the sonnet, working within and from its Petrarchan, courtly love, Ovidian conventions and origins, took up the great themes of life and literature: passionate romantic love, the ravages of time, the immortality of beauty, death, the cycle of existence, salvation. *Romeo and Juliet* follows firmly in this tradition.

From the very beginning of the play, we are meant to recognize the conventions of Petrarchan love poetry. The play begins with an actual sonnet introducing the themes of conflict, love, fate, and death. Before we even meet Romeo, we find he is afflicted with the characteristic malady of the Petrarchan lover: romantic melancholy. Romeo lurks about at night "[w]ith tears augmenting the fresh morning's dew", his "deep sighs" making the cloudy sky more cloudy, and steals home at sunrise, where he "[s]huts up his windows, locks fair daylight out, / And makes himself an artificial night" (1.1.130–31, 137–38).[5] The word "artificial" should alert us to Romeo's affected Petrarchan pose. In his conversation with Benvolio, Romeo trots out a litany of conventional and hackneyed Petrarchan conceits as he affects the love-sick courtly lover:

> O brawling love! O loving hate!
> O anything, of nothing first create!
> O heavy lightness! serious vanity!
> Mis-shapen chaos of well-seeming forms!
> Feather of lead, bright smoke, cold fire, sick health!
> Still-waking sleep, that is not what it is!
> This love feel I.
>
> (1.1.174–80)

Romeo defines love as "a smoke rais'd with the fume of sighs … a sea nourish'd with loving tears … [a] madness … [a]

---

[5] All quotations from *Romeo and Juliet* are from the edition published by Ignatius Press: *Romeo and Juliet*, ed. Joseph Pearce, Ignatius Critical Editions (San Francisco: Ignatius Press, 2011).

choking gall, and a preserving sweet" (1.1.188, 190–92). He describes his idealized lady, Rosaline, in traditional Petrarchan terms. "[S]he'll not be hit/With Cupid's arrow", Romeo tells Benvolio,

> And in strong proof of chastity well arm'd,
> From Love's weak childish bow she lives unharm'd.
> . . . .
> She hath forsworn to love, and in that vow
> Do I live dead that live to tell it now.
>   (1.1.206–9, 221–22)

The exaggerated Petrarchan conventions reveal Romeo's affectation; he is not in love, but in love with being in love. Like Orlando in Shakespeare's *As You Like It*, who also affects the courtly Petrarchan lover, Romeo is a bad poet.

County Paris, whose "love" for Juliet is mainly confined within the practical conventions of an arranged marriage, is also described with a nod to Petrarch. In a sonnetlike fourteen lines of verse, Lady Capulet delivers to Juliet an ironic (and bookish) blazon—the County's beauties are finally summed up in his material wealth, with a bawdy pun on his connected sexual potency. "Read o'er the volume of young Paris' face," says Lady Capulet,

> And find delight writ there with beauty's pen;
> Examine every married lineament,
> And see how one another lends content;
> . . . .
> That book in many's eyes doth share the glory
> That in gold clasps locks in the golden story;
> So shall you share all that he doth possess,
> By having him making yourself no less.
>   (1.3.82–85, 92–95)

Another sonnet is created by the first words Romeo and Juliet say to one another when they meet at Capulet's feast:

> *Romeo.* If I profane with my unworthiest hand
>   This holy shrine, the gentle sin is this:

> My lips, two blushing pilgrims, ready stand
> To smooth that rough touch with a tender kiss.
> *Juliet.* Good pilgrim, you do wrong your hand too much,
>   Which mannerly devotion shows in this;
>   For saints have hands that pilgrims' hands do touch,
>   And palm to palm is holy palmers' kiss.
> *Romeo.* Have not saints lips, and holy palmers too?
> *Juliet.* Ay, pilgrim, lips that they must use in pray'r.
> *Romeo.* O, then, dear saint, let lips do what hands do!
>   They pray; grant thou, lest faith turn to despair.
> *Juliet.* Saints do not move, though grant for prayers' sake.
> *Romeo.* Then move not while my prayer's effect I take.
>   (1.5.91–104)

Marjorie Garber writes, "This is love at first sonnet."[6] Although Juliet differs from the unapproachable lady of Petrarchan love poetry, of which contrast more will be said, the elevated emotions of the lovers are captured in the sonnet form, and the sonnet's themes come directly from the courtly love tradition. The conventional personifications of the god of love, Venus, and of her wayward son, Cupid or Eros, bearing his arrows, are absent, but the lovers themselves have become part of the machinery of the religion of love. Juliet has become a saint, and the reward of the pilgrim's prayer is a kiss.

One last sonnet makes the Petrarchan associations in the play formally explicit. Before the lovers' balcony scene, the Chorus steps in to tell us of Romeo's new passion, sprung up on the deathbed of his love for Rosaline: "Now old desire doth on his death-bed lie,/ And young affection gapes to be his heir" (2 Prol. 1–2). The plot summary, which the Chorus goes on to give here, is usually left out of productions of the play. Nevertheless, overtly invoking the Petrarchan love poetry tradition, the sonnet ends with a couplet celebrating romantic passion ratcheted up to the highest degree: "But passion lends them power, time means, to meet,/ Temp'ring extremities with extreme sweet" (2 Prol. 13–14).

---

[6] Marjorie Garber, *Shakespeare after All* (New York: Anchor, 2005), p. 194.

As form and content are held in tense relationship in the sonnet tradition, so they are in the art of the play as well. Intensity is achieved in the Petrarchan sonnet by the attempt to confine a psychomachia, a fierce psychological and emotional struggle characterized by paradox and contradiction, within the poem's formulaic limitations. *Romeo and Juliet* vibrates with this kind of tension. Though the elements of the play derive from the Petrarchan tradition, they also vie with it. Much of the tension and explosive energy of the play results from the placement of characters and events in overt relationship with and in contrast to Petrarchan conventions. Maynard Mack comments on this artistic strategy: "As a high-bred horse shows his truest fire when curbed, so the artifices of the play's style and structure create a condition of containment from which its energies break out with double force."[7] For instance, the sonnet of the Prologue summarizes the story in fourteen poetically ordered iambic lines, but the street scene immediately following explodes into violence provoked by a rude hand gesture. Garber writes of this contrast, "[T]he 'civil hands' of the sonnet have already become very uncivil. . . . Obviously, pretty poetry and formal sonnets cannot contain this kind of psychic energy and disorder. Reality and loss overtake literary artifice, and the play is forced ... to acknowledge its own tragic shape, which stylized language cannot contain."[8]

However, in its use of and contrast with Petrarchan conventions, the play achieves this very thing: it contains in its art the tensions and contradictions of Romeo and Juliet's fictional world. Romeo spouts hackneyed Petrarchan conceits at the beginning of the play, but when he meets Juliet, the empty poetry changes. Romeo's object is no longer the literary "idea" of the Petrarchan lady but a real person, the "real thing". Romeo exclaims,

---

[7] Maynard Mack, *Everybody's Shakespeare: Reflections Chiefly on the Tragedies* (Lincoln: University of Nebraska Press, 1993), p. 85.

[8] Garber, *Shakespeare after All*, p. 190.

> O, she doth teach the torches to burn bright!
> It seems she hangs upon the cheek of night
> As a rich jewel in an Ethiop's ear—
> Beauty too rich for use, for earth too dear!
>   (1.5.42–45)

He cries, "Did my heart love till now?" (1.5.50). This is love at its most impetuous, impulsive, and idealistic, but a very different thing from the love-sick Petrarchan pose of the Romeo we first meet, who, playing the part of the melancholy courtly lover, speaks in clichés and shuns the daylight ("makes himself an artificial night"). As Romeo's empty clichés become "real" poetry, the "artificial" darkness also becomes "real", a matter of necessity, not of solipsistic emotional self-indulgence. Because of their families' enmity, Romeo and Juliet have no choice but to meet secretly, at night, in the darkness. "Come, gentle night, come, loving, black-brow'd night," says Juliet in unforgettable poetry as she waits for Romeo after their secret marriage,

> Give me my Romeo; and, when he shall die,
> Take him and cut him out in little stars,
> And he will make the face of heaven so fine
> That all the world will be in love with night,
> And pay no worship to the garish sun.
>   (3.2.20–25)

The chilly and unapproachable lady of Romeo's bad Petrarchan poetry also becomes in Juliet his heavenly lady, "bright angel", and "dear saint", all Petrarchan tropes, but she is a warm, approachable living woman who desires to give herself fully to her beloved:

> My bounty is as boundless as the sea,
> My love as deep: the more I give to thee,
> The more I have, for both are infinite.
>   (2.2.133–35)

Once married, in contrast to the icily chaste ideal Petrarchan lady, Juliet ardently acknowledges her sexuality:

> [L]earn me how to lose a winning match,
> Play'd for a pair of stainless maidenhoods;
>
> .   .   .   .
>
> O, I have bought the mansion of a love,
> But not possess'd it; and though I am sold,
> Not yet enjoy'd.
>
> $\qquad\qquad\qquad\qquad$ (3.2.12–13, 26–28)

In addition to the tension created by juxtaposition of the artificial with the "real", conflict, tension, contradiction, and paradox pervade the very atmosphere of the play and drive the drama on every level. Love and hate, youth and age, materialism and spirituality, the public and the private, darkness and light, lust and love—the play is built on polarities—are only some of the many diametrically opposed but intricately related dichotomies of the play. In the conflict between the warring families, hate and love are set in opposition. "My only love sprung from my only hate!" cries Juliet when she realizes Romeo is a Montague. "Prodigious birth of love it is to me,/ That I must love a loathed enemy" (1.5.136, 138–39). This line between love and hatred in the play is finely drawn. Thus Romeo, motivated by love for Juliet, gets between the dueling Mercutio and Tybalt, Juliet's cousin, and causes Mercutio to be slain in the confusion. Romeo immediately explodes in a paroxysm of blind rage and violently accosts and kills Tybalt, to whom a moment before Romeo was offering his love and friendship. "O, I am fortune's fool!" he cries when he comes to himself (3.1.133).

> Doth not she think me an old murderer,
> Now I have stain'd the childhood of our joy
> With blood remov'd but little from her own?
> $\qquad\qquad\qquad\qquad$ (3.3.94–96)

Conflict also rages between the youth and adults of the play—law, parental authority, and social convention are pitted against the immediacy and intensity of youthful passion, in love and in war. "Let me dispute with thee of thy estate", the Friar placates a distraught Romeo, who retorts, "Thou canst not speak of that thou dost not feel" (3.3.63–64). The imposition of the law by Verona's prince proves futile to control or mitigate the family feud, perpetuated by the young. Legal ultimatums fail to bring order and instead only exacerbate the conflict, leading to more violence and final tragedy.

Materiality and spirituality, the practical economics of the arranged marriage and the lovers' passionate devotion to one another, are also at odds. When her nurse advises Juliet to forget Romeo and accept the "second marriage" to Paris, Juliet, barely fourteen, becomes a suffering woman. She parts company with her nurse, the adult closest to her in whom she has till now been fully able to confide, and demonstrates the resolve to face her difficulties and make her decisions alone. "Go, counsellor", Juliet says after coldly sending the Nurse away,

> Thou and my bosom henceforth shall be twain.
> I'll to the friar to know his remedy;
> If all else fail, myself have power to die.
>
> (3.5.240–43)

From the beginning of the play, tension also grows between the public world and its pressures and the private world of dream and romantic intensity. As the conflicts and contingencies of the public daylight world encroach upon Romeo and Juliet, the couple will meet only at night in increasingly isolated and confined spaces: the enclosed garden, the Friar's cell, Juliet's bedroom, the Capulet tomb. Also pitted against one another are lust and a sexuality that demonstrates genuine appreciation for the person of the beloved. Mercutio, a realist about physical sexuality and cynical of its idealization, exposes the falseness of Romeo's poetic Petrarchan pose but also, by contrast, the superiority of Romeo and Juliet's secret and genuine love. As the Montague boys leave the feast and call Romeo to join them, Mercutio reveals his opinion of romantic love in an anti-Petrarchan blazon of Rosaline's "beauties":

I conjure thee by Rosaline's bright eyes,
By her high forehead and her scarlet lip,
By her fine foot, straight leg, and quivering thigh,
And the demesnes that there adjacent lie,
That in thy likeness thou appear to us.

                                                  (2.1.17–21)

Mack comments on the striking contrast made evident by Mercutio's banter at this point in the play: "Shakespeare places this washroom chatter in immediate juxtaposition with the luminous beauty of Juliet and the exalted feelings she has stirred in Romeo—both of which we have just witnessed."[9] Oxymoronic, endemic, and irresolvable tensions dominate the world of the play. As Friar Lawrence gathers his volatile herbs with their dual medicinal and poisonous properties, he gives a voice to these contradictions:

The earth that's nature's mother is her tomb;
What is her burying grave, that is her womb.
And from her womb children of divers kind
We sucking on her natural bosom find. . . .

. . . .

Within the infant rind of this weak flower
Poison hath residence, and medicine power. . . .

. . . .

Two such opposed kings encamp them still
In man as well as herbs—grace and rude will.

                          (2.3.9–12, 23–24, 27–28)

The nature of tragedy is in itself paradoxical. Tragedy results not only from the actions of others but also from the actions and choices of the tragic hero himself. The hero of tragedy is always implicated in his own destruction, but this destruction is paradoxically brought about through exercise of the hero's greatest virtue.[10] Romeo and Juliet's paradoxical tragic flaw is

[9] Mack, *Everybody's Shakespeare*, p. 78.
[10] See A.C. Bradley, *Shakespearean Tragedy: Lectures on "Hamlet", "Othello", "King Lear", and "Macbeth"* (Cleveland: Meridian, 1961), pp. 26–28. "In the

firmly tied to the Petrarchan tradition. What constitutes their fatal flaw is their greatest virtue: the purity and devotion of their idealized romantic love and their capacity to choose this love in spite of the hatred that surrounds them. Romeo and Juliet's love for one another sets them above everyone else in the play, but also hurtles them toward their deaths. Clearly, other factors in the lovers' world conspire against them and help shape the tragic situation in which they must act; contingencies over which they have no control overtake them. But the choices the lovers make from the time they meet set the wheels on the track that leads to disaster—Romeo climbs the garden wall; the lovers secretly communicate and marry; Juliet deliberates in horror what she is about to do when it comes time to drink the potion, and she drinks it anyway. The lovers continue to make choices until the very end when, to them, there seems only one choice remaining that will preserve their love inviolable: death. Juliet shows her maturity and resolve when the Nurse encourages her to marry Paris. In the same way, Romeo is a far cry from his earlier childish romantic pose—he will die if Rosaline cannot love him—when he receives the (erroneous) news that Juliet is dead. "Well, Juliet," he says, "I will lie with thee to-night" (5.1.33).

In the Petrarchan, courtly love, Ovidian tradition, love and death are closely associated and opposed. Petrarch's sonnets express an exalted spiritualized love for the divine (and dead) Laura, but the language he uses is sensuous, earthly, and emotional. The idea of being "sick with love", a sickness leading to death, is built into the Petrarchan tradition. In England it became a commonplace to identify the sexual act with death. To have sexual intercourse meant to die a little death, and each sexual climax or "death" was believed to shorten one's

---

circumstances where we see the hero placed, his tragic trait, which is his greatness, is fatal to him. To meet these circumstances, something is required which a smaller man might have given, but which the hero cannot give.... [I]t is necessary that he should have so much greatness that in his error and fall, we may be vividly conscious of the possibilities of human nature" (pp. 27–28).

life. The great heroes and heroines of courtly love are death-marked: Tristan and Isolde, Lancelot and Guinevere. Eros and death are intimately related and opposed in *Romeo and Juliet.* As the play develops, we are never allowed to escape the dread of imminent death and disaster, the tragic precipice upon which the vulnerable beauty of the lovers is poised.

It is, however, at the end of the story where the plot's irresolvable contradictions meet, where Shakespeare creates a poetic and dramatic consummation, transcending and resolving the conflicts of the play. In his study of what he calls the "complementarity" of *Romeo and Juliet,* Norman Rabkin writes, "Having led us to reject wanton Petrarchanism, Shakespeare . . . brings us to affirm the existential antinomies from which Petrarch drew his true power." [11] Here, in the lowest place, the place of greatest devastation, the poetry takes flight. Petrarchan death-obsession becomes transfiguration. Death and love, death and the vitality of youthful passion meet in the Capulet tomb, a paradox brought more ironically home in that Juliet is not truly dead. "Ah, dear Juliet," Romeo exclaims,

> Why art thou yet so fair? Shall I believe
> That unsubstantial Death is amorous,
> And that the lean abhorred monster keeps
> Thee here in dark to be his paramour?
>
> (5.3.101–5)

"O my love! my wife!" he cries,

> Death, that hath suck'd the honey of thy breath,
> Hath had no power yet upon thy beauty.
> Thou art not conquer'd.
>
> (5.3.91–94)

Here darkness and light meet: to Romeo the dim tomb is transfigured into "a lantern. . . . For here lies Juliet, and her beauty

---

[11] Norman Rabkin, *Shakespeare and the Common Understanding* (Chicago: University of Chicago Press, 1984), pp. 180–81.

makes/This vault a feasting presence full of light" (5.3.84–86). In the grave, youth and age are reconciled: the bodies of Tybalt and Mercutio, the youthful perpetuators of the age-old feud, lie still at last, their weapons put to rest. Paris is slain at the entrance of the vault by a Romeo who at this point in the story is no longer a boy. "Good gentle youth, tempt not a desp'rate man", Romeo says when Paris accosts him.

> I beseech thee, youth,
> Put not another sin upon my head
> By urging me to fury.
>
> (5.3.59, 61–63)

Here in the tomb, death is joined with sexual consummation.[12] "Thus with a kiss I die", says Romeo, as he drinks the poison (5.3.120). "O happy dagger!" says Juliet, as she drives the blade into her breast. "This is thy sheath; there rust, and let me die" (5.3.168–69). Mack comments, "The most remarkable among the ancient phrases that Shakespeare regenerates by causing them to be acted out in front of us is every lover's conviction that love must conquer death: *Amor vincit omnia.*"[13] As Mack points out, Romeo vies with death for love and possession of Juliet as he chooses to be her husband even in death, and Juliet reciprocates without a moment's hesitation.[14] However, as Romeo breaks open the tomb to claim his wife, the ancient classical phrase is also paired with the Christian association. "For love is strong as death, jealousy is cruel as the grave" (Song 8:6),[15] says the lover of the biblical Song of Solomon, prefiguring the assault on the gates of death by the risen Christ himself.

---

[12] "[I]n the tomb-scene ... death and sexual consummation become indistinguishable" (Mack, Everybody's Shakespeare, p. 80).

[13] Ibid., p. 88.

[14] "When Romeo reclaims her for his own by freely choosing to be her husband in death as well as life, she gives herself in turn to be again his wife by her free choice in falling upon his dagger.... Romeo ... asserts his claim to Juliet against death's claim" (ibid.).

[15] Revised Standard Version, Second Catholic Edition.

A. C. Bradley explains another important paradoxical component of Shakespearean tragedy: the idea of tragic waste.[16] In order to set a disordered world to rights, the good, put in opposition to the disorder of that world, must also be destroyed or, through its action to set things right, must destroy itself. "See what a scourge is laid upon your hate," says the Prince to the mourning families, invoking a perfect Petrarchan contradiction, "[t]hat heaven finds means to kill your joys with love!" (5.3.292). Romeo's and Juliet's deaths do "bury their parents' strife" (Prol. 8), but it is a diminished world in which this "glooming peace" is realized because the radiant lovers are no longer in it (5.3.304). It is the poorer for their absence and even for the absence of the angry young men, so full of misdirected promise and intensity, who carried on the feud. The world of the play returns to order and safety, but also to convention: now only the empty lifeless forms of the lovers remain. "I will raise her statue in pure gold," says Montague to Capulet,

> That whiles Verona by that name is known,
> There shall no figure at such rate be set
> As that of true and faithful Juliet.
> $$(5.3.298–301)$$

Capulet replies, "As rich shall Romeo's by his lady's lie / Poor sacrifices of our enmity!" (5.3.302–3). As the artificial conventions of Petrarchan love poetry reveal the worth of the "real thing" in the world of the play, here convention makes more fully evident the value of what has been lost. Romeo and Juliet's idealized romantic love is made the more sublime

---

[16] "With Shakespeare ... the pity and fear which are stirred by the tragic story seem to unite with, and even to merge in, a profound sense of sadness and mystery, which is due to this impression of waste.... Tragedy is the typical form of this mystery, because that greatness of soul which it exhibits oppressed, conflicting and destroyed, is the highest existence in our view. It forces the mystery upon us, and it makes us realize so vividly the worth of that which is wasted that we cannot possibly seek comfort in the reflection that all is vanity" (Bradley, *Shakespearean Tragedy*, pp. 28–29).

and authentic, their loss more tragic, in contrast to the static and pathetic formality of the world they leave behind.

To all of us who have loved, loved and lost, longed to love, or regarded with amazement or perhaps alarm the love of others, *Romeo and Juliet* must speak. Literature does something other than explain or simply illustrate the proper rules or principles by which we should live. It rather seeks through its beauty, its artifice, and the pleasure it gives us to present a picture of life that we recognize as human, in which as humans we participate. Through the lens of Petrarchan love poetry, we find our way into what G. Wilson Knight calls "the burning central core"[17] of Shakespeare's play: its themes, its characters, the moral and religious implications of this particular story captured in this particular work of dramatic art. Unlike a stance of intractable moral condemnation, the aesthetic approach allows us to recognize the breathtaking artistry of *Romeo and Juliet* as worthy of our admiration and appreciation. As this approach opens up the play and its themes, it also calls us to sympathize with these fictional tragic figures, to see their greatness as they face their plight and die because, for them, any other response would deny the supreme inviolability of their love. Finally, evoking a fundamentally moral impulse,[18] the aesthetic critique permits us, as in the special province of literary art it must, to recognize the fallible, frail, and vulnerable nobility of Romeo and Juliet's humanity and acknowledge this humanity as akin to our own.

[17] G. Wilson Knight, "On the Principles of Shakespearean Interpretation", in *Modern Shakespearean Criticism: Essays on Style, Dramaturgy, and the Major Plays*, ed. Alvin B. Kernan (New York: Harcourt Brace Jovanovich, 1970), p. 9.

[18] See Nicholas Boyle, *Sacred and Secular Scriptures: A Catholic Approach to Literature* (Notre Dame, Ind.: University of Notre Dame Press, 2005). Boyle argues that secular literature is intrinsically moral: it "tells us that everything matters, even the sparrows on the rooftops" (p. 132).

Romeo and Juliet:
The "True Ground of All These Piteous Woes"

Stephen Zelnick
Temple University

Most believe that *Romeo and Juliet* is a tragedy of fate, where "star-cross'd lovers" suffer their doom and no one is to blame. The Prologue to the play tells us this, which helps explain a tragedy that lacks a tragic hero and the flaw that precipitates his fall. This explanation fits also a romantic reading of the play, in which innocent love finds perfect expression in death, where Romeo, looking at Juliet's still form, recalls the myth of Persephone, in which "unsubstantial Death is amorous,/And ... keeps/[Her] here in dark to be his paramour" (5.3.103–5).[1] The catastrophe seemingly brought on by cosmic misalignment makes the lovers' fleeting affair thrillingly emotional. The "star-cross'd" reading explains also the string of coincidences that drives the plot: the Friar's message to Mantua going awry and the brief moment separating Romeo's suicide from Juliet's awakening. There are, therefore, several good reasons for accepting this "fatalistic" account of the play. Yet the First Watchman remarks: "We see the ground whereon these woes do lie;/But the true ground of all these piteous woes/We cannot without circumstance descry" (5.3.178–80). A broader view identifies this "true ground" as the failure of social and political values in Verona and more particularly the widespread failure of people in positions of consequence to observe their civic, institutional, familial, and personal responsibilities. The perfection of natural passion—brilliantly expressed in the love of Romeo and Juliet—cannot flourish when a city fails to marshal

---

[1] All quotations from *Romeo and Juliet* are from the edition published by Ignatius Press: *Romeo and Juliet*, ed. Joseph Pearce, Ignatius Critical Editions (San Francisco: Ignatius Press, 2011).

its cultural stability, where the Prince "wink[s] at . . . discords" (5.3.293), where heads of great families behave like boys, and where churchmen fail the test of honor and of truth.

The Prologue is a sonnet, the last three lines of which describe the play's performance. Of the remaining eleven lines, only two mention the evil fate of the lovers, while the remaining nine address issues of social stability and of the "ancient grudge" that sets two families not so much in conflict with one another as in deadly mutiny against civil order (Prol. 4). The Prologue emphasizes the peace of Verona; the families and their raging feud; and how the sacrifice of perfect lovers was required to end these deadly outrages. The Prologue's full account of the play—often curtailed in performance—sustains this broader emphasis. Nature rages in human beings—the fires of youth, the bloody madness of vendetta, pride, sexual aggressions, the desire for social preeminence, parental posturing, youthful rebelliousness, cowardice, and evasions of the truth—a city unarmed against these formidable deficits of human nature can expect catastrophe.[2]

The play opens with the crude lawlessness of two servants of the Capulet household. Bored and sexually restless, they are looking for trouble. Although Sampson and Gregory know the

---

[2] Shakespeare's main source for *Romeo and Juliet* is Arthur Brooke, whose *Tragicall Historye of Romeus and Juliet* (1562) approached this popular story with an intense and disapproving moralism, aimed not only at most of the characters but also the young lovers. Brooke's summary is as follows:

> To this ende (good Reader) is this tragicall matter written, to describe unto thee a coople of unfortunate lovers, thralling themselves to unhonest desire, neglecting the authoritie and advise of parents and frendes, conferring their principall counsels with dronken gossyppes, and superstitious friers (the naturally fitte instruments of unchastitie) attemptyng all adventures of peryll, for thattaynyng of their wished lust, using auriculer confession (the kay of whoredome, and treason) for furtheraunce of theyre purpose, abusying the honorable name of lawefull marriage, the cloke the shame of stolne contractes, finallye, by all means of unhonest lyfe, hastyng to most unhappy deathe.

Shakespeare reworked these materials to produce a positive portrait of love and a touchstone for our Western heritage.

law against public brawling, they maneuver to make it seem that Montague servants initiated the fight. These are swaggering young men, rebellious against the law. Benvolio (his name means "good will"), a young Montague master, tries to control the Montague servants, but Tybalt, his Capulet counterpart, attacks him. In some film and video productions, this opening fight destroys the marketplace and scatters the citizens of Verona, imperiling women and young children.[3] The fight ends only when the Prince of Verona, speaking to the heads of both families, specifies that these "civil brawls" were "bred of an airy word / By thee, old Capulet, and Montague" (1.1.87–88). The two lords are responsible for controlling their family members and servants and for enforcing the law as being more than airy words. The Prince makes his decree brutally clear to old Capulet and Montague: at the next brawl, "Your lives shall pay the forfeit of the peace" (95). The Prince then takes both Capulet and Montague aside, one at a time, so they can know his "farther pleasure in this case" (99). There is, however, something weak in requiring discussion after the decree has been declared publicly—what is there to discuss?—and in speaking with the battling lords one at a time instead of together—what could be said to one that could not be said to both? For all the force of his warning against "airy word[s]", the Prince has weakened the majesty of the law. At the end of the play, when lawlessness has reaped its grim harvest, the Prince owns up to his responsibility "for winking at [their] discords" (5.3.293).

Shakespeare shows us the Capulets, Juliet's family, in intimate detail. Old Capulet, as a great lord of the city, exercises

---

[3] Commentators often forget how serious this opening is and try to suggest that until the death of Mercutio the play could well be a classical comedy. Film and video productions, however, show clearly that Verona's civil disorder is no joke. In Franco Zeffirelli's 1968 film, Verona's central market is all but destroyed, and local citizens are badly injured. The BBC production (1978) is even more graphic in depicting injuries to innocent bystanders, including women and babies—the commanding image shows a bloodied infant, abandoned in the middle of the road, screaming in terror. Baz Luhrmann's MTV-styled film (1996) fills the screen with the orange fireball of an exploding gas station while people run for their lives.

considerable social power in Verona.[4] However, old Capulet is unstable and lacks personal force. Affable and a bit doddering, he enjoys reminiscing about his young manhood and assuring others that he too was once a bit of a rascal and on the prowl. At his festivities, he wants his guests to enjoy themselves and not stand on ceremony. While he is an elder, with the responsibilities of an elder, old Capulet prefers to be one of the boys and to wink at youthful indiscretions.[5] He loves the revelry: "A hall, a hall! give room; and foot it, girls./More light, you knaves; and turn the tables up" (1.5.24–25). No wonder the fiery and rebellious Tybalt has the temerity to turn Capulet's ball into a brawl.

Tybalt cannot take his jolly uncle seriously. When Capulet attempts to lay down the law, Tybalt challenges him, and the two, elder and youth, engage in a growling match, leaving old Capulet to ask, "Am I the master here or you?" (76). Old Capulet talks Tybalt down, but Tybalt immediately resolves to revenge himself on Romeo for Romeo's intrusion.

Old Capulet also lacks consistency in his judgments and actions. In Act 1, Capulet is a reasonable father. Urging Paris to court Juliet, Capulet explains that he cannot compel his daughter to marry: "But woo her, gentle Paris, get her heart;/My will to her consent is but a part" (1.2.16–17). Later, Capulet denies Juliet the right to her choice and threatens to turn her out onto the streets if she does not obey him (3.5.192–95). In his rush to marry her to Paris, Capulet decides upon a small wedding, and soon after, in his characteristically excessive way, he is hiring "twenty cunning cooks" for the event (4.2.2).

---

[4] Shakespeare draws upon the images of the great clans of Renaissance Italy and their deadly feuds. The most notable of these is the confrontation between the Donati and Cherchi families that disrupted the civil order of Florence from the 1280s until well into the next century. Dante, himself caught up in these battles, later immortalized this feuding in his *Inferno*.

[5] The BBC, committed to presenting the Shakespeare plays in their entirety, cast Sir Michael Hordern as old Capulet in its 1978 production of the play. The result is a *Romeo and Juliet* in which the politics of Verona and the interior life of the Capulet family are much more central to the play.

Lady Capulet is intemperate and ineffectual but, unlike her husband, petulant and mean-spirited. Like the Prince, the Capulet parents rule but cannot command; and what fails in the state to achieve civic order fails also in the family to bring trust and stability. In early scenes with Juliet and the Nurse, Lady Capulet proves incapable of quieting her unruly servant, who in the midst of a serious discussion cannot be restrained from repeating, endlessly and mindlessly, her little lewd story. In the liberality of the Capulet household, servants say and do as they please. A second instance of Lady Capulet's instability is her intemperate outburst at the death of Tybalt. While understandably distraught, she tells an outrageous lie in response to Benvolio's balanced account of the murderous brawl. In Lady Capulet's inflammatory speech, twenty assailants set upon Tybalt and murdered him (3.1.175–76). She desires vengeance, and her story threatens to drown Verona in blood. As it is, her vehemence and selfishness mean that she cannot be an aid or ally to Juliet as her daughter struggles to manage impossible conflicts. While the lovers may seem "star-cross'd", they are in truth parent-crossed.

If the Prince and the lords fail, perhaps the clergy can uphold a civic order that seems unable to protect its children. In their extremity, Romeo and Juliet turn to Friar Lawrence to assist them. The Friar is a good man and seemingly a model of temperate judgment, ready to offer "[a]dversity's sweet milk, philosophy" to calm their desperate spirits (3.3.55). He offers the young lovers sturdy maxims and artfully dissuades both of them from suicide. His counsel is standard, sensible stuff:

> These violent delights have violent ends,
> And in their triumph die; like fire and powder,
> Which, as they kiss, consume. The sweetest honey
> Is loathsome in his own deliciousness,
> And in the taste confounds the appetite.
> Therefore love moderately.
>
> (2.6.9–14)

Not surprisingly, these calming words have little effect upon the rash lovers, and for all the Friar's counsel of moderation and thoughtfulness, his actions are themselves ill-considered and dangerous.

In 1563, at the Council of Trent, the Catholic Church adopted the public announcement of the banns of marriage as standard Church practice. The council was concerned about clandestine marriages, that is, marriages performed without public notice and without the knowledge of the couple's families. While this requirement would not have been in force in Renaissance Verona, the problem and dangers were well understood in Shakespeare's time. With Romeo and Juliet's desperate desire to be married, the Friar faces what should be a difficult choice. While the feud explains their need for secrecy, it should explain also the Friar's need to exercise caution. Instead, the Friar serves the immediate desire of the lovers while imagining that in doing so he will somehow reconcile the families and bring peace to Verona: "For this alliance may so happy prove / To turn your households' rancour to pure love" (2.3.91–92).

As the Friar's involvement deepens, his counsels become more dangerous. When Juliet, at the news of Romeo's banishment, tells the Friar that she will kill herself, the good Friar takes this cue and advises his plan to administer a drug with effects that mimic death. This desperate plan requires that several uncontrollable pieces fall into place. The Friar's plot involves also a conspiracy of lies and deceptions—this from the man who counsels moderation, caution, and the consolations of philosophy. Nor is the deception merely passive: the Friar lies to the Capulets, even as they suffer through the apparent death of their daughter (4.5.64–76). Yet the worst charge against Friar Lawrence is his cowardice. Once Romeo is banished, the Friar should step forward to announce Romeo's marriage to Juliet to the respective families and personally face their displeasure. Worse yet, when Juliet awakens in the tomb— Romeo already dead by poison, and she about to discover this devastating fact—the Friar runs off, fearful he will be discovered as a part of the plot.

Once deceptions start, where do they end? Juliet, contemplating the risks of swallowing the potion, suspects that the drug may be a ruse and that the Friar may be carrying out a plot to murder her: "What if it be a poison which the friar / Subtly hath minister'd to have me dead, / Lest in this marriage he should be dishonour'd / Because he married me before to Romeo?" (4.3.24–27). They all know that this marriage is not only clandestine but also dishonorable. In his long and self-exculpating account of events at the end of the play, Friar Lawrence confesses his involvement to the Prince: "[A]nd if aught in this / Miscarried by my fault, let my old life / Be sacrific'd . . . / Unto the rigour of severest law" (5.3.265–68). Friar Lawrence knows the fault is not in the stars but in himself, that everything miscarried by his fault, and that in his readiness to do good, by reconciling the feuding families, he had allowed his goodwill to overwhelm his duty to his community. The Nurse had been impressed by Friar Lawrence's "good counsel" (3.3.160), but the priest failed to abide by his own advice and played a critical role in the catastrophe.

As we work our way down the roster of social responsibility from the Prince, to the lords, to the priest, it may seem odd to consider the Nurse. However, the Nurse is a second mother to Juliet. While Lady Capulet considers only propriety and property, the Nurse champions emotion and the call of the flesh. It is pleasant to think of the Nurse as realistic and sweetly if lewdly human, a female Falstaff (see Shakespeare's *King Henry IV*, parts 1 and 2), but she fails the Capulets and her beloved Juliet. Like Falstaff, the Nurse is a treasured Shakespearean role. This does not, however, mean that the Nurse, so amusingly garrulous and plainspoken, does not contribute to the sequence of events that destroys the young lovers.

The Nurse's childish fascination with sex never stops: from the little dirty joke on Juliet as a toddler (1.3.42–45) to her later comments to Juliet on bearing the weight of her husband (2.5.76–77), the Nurse cannot avoid a smutty comment. Her leering materialism never ends; she cannot resist the comment to Romeo that "he that can lay hold of her / Shall have the chinks" (1.5.114–15). Her disloyalty is most painful. With Romeo banished and Juliet's parents pressuring their daughter to marry Paris, the Nurse advises Juliet to forget Romeo and make believe she is not married (3.5.213–26). This defection leaves Juliet further isolated and desperate and a good candidate for Friar Lawrence's desperate plot.

The lewdness of the Nurse is nothing, however, to that of Mercutio. Even more so than the Nurse, Mercutio is a much-prized role and also the very model for all that is wrong in Verona. In play after play, Shakespeare explores the instability of human character. In the great tradition of humanism, he celebrates the potential for human beings to behave rationally but also fears our capacity for following our lower nature. Both in his tragedies, such as *Othello*, and in his comedies, such as *Much Ado about Nothing*, the distance between angel and beast is a razor's edge. Mercutio exemplifies this frightening potential and the consequences when social barriers have not been erected against this rage and confusion.

Mercutio is as lewd as the Nurse but is far more aggressive, more dangerous, and more appealing because of his brilliance. Mercutio is an intriguing mix of low-mindedness and poetic capacity for lofty metaphysical flights. His "Queen Mab" speech is an irresistible discourse on fantasy, presenting a fabulous fabric beyond the tedious mundane. Mercutio is intoxicated with words and visions and is consequently restless in the world in which he finds himself. While he advises Romeo, quite cynically, that love pains can be relieved by sexual release (1.4.27–28), Mercutio's own wild spirit vents only by violence in word and deed. Mercutio's deadly swordplay with Tybalt is triggered by the heat of the day, by the play of words, by a game that releases the beast in Mercutio and finally in Romeo too. While Mercutio justifies himself by wishing a plague on both houses, the fact is that he brings about his own destruction and the play's catastrophe by his own mad actions.

Critics have embraced the Nurse and Mercutio for their realism, their assertion of the giddy demands of the flesh against the sober requirements of propriety and the law. Mercutio, in particular, has been identified as the artist in the play, a man of irrepressible linguistic creativity and metaphysical reach. The poet John Dryden's comment that Shakespeare was forced to kill off Mercutio in Act 3 or risk having Mercutio kill the play by his exuberance suggests that Shakespeare had fallen in love with his creation, a character supposedly most like the play-wright himself. However, Mercutio is a figure of disorder and an enemy to the sweet perfection of Romeo and Juliet. The embrace of Mercutio by the critics aligns them with the forces that pre-cipitate the catastrophe. Shakespeare cunningly invites us to embrace those forces—Mercutio, the Nurse, old Capulet—in order to instruct us about the dangers in what pleases us.

Mercutio helps us identify "the true ground of all these pite-ous woes". He is of the Prince's family, yet the Prince has no control over him, just as old Capulet has no control over Tybalt. These young men run wild because their elders are themselves still enamored of these fires of youth and have not accepted the responsibilities of adulthood. In the midst of the brawl that opens the play, old Capulet calls out, "Give me my long sword, ho!" (1.1.73)—even as his wife advises that he call instead for his crutch. Old Montague is no better, "flourish[ing] his blade" in the melee even after being warned earlier by the Prince (76). With the immature dereliction of duty by society's elders, there is nothing to temper young men enflamed by nature and by their generational ambitions. The sexual strains, the wild flow of thoughts, the rebelliousness to assert themselves against one another and against the hierarchies of power are dry pow-der waiting for a spark. Shakespeare's play argues insistently that when society fails to counterbalance these forces with the majesty of the law, with the authority of political leaders, with the affectionate embrace of families, with the cultural coun-terweight of idealism and romance, and with the spiritual force of religion, then the pure gifts of nature will be swamped by the beast within us.

And where do Romeo and Juliet themselves fit into this most lyrical of all Shakespeare's plays? The young lovers appeal to us most for their innocence and full commitment to the blessings of nature. In Juliet's orchard, we are back in the original Garden before the Fall, when lovers speak with one mind and heart, and every thought is a poetic utterance to treasure forever. They are beyond time and change and have transcended the pettiness of our tawdry world. They recall God's gifts, the mystery by which two strangers become one flesh, perfect companions in feeling and devotion. Their defeat— and what could be more tragic?—is not an accident of mis-aligned constellations but instead is grounded in man's failure to control his wayward nature and direct himself and his soci-eties to proper ends.

Shakespeare begins his account of paradise from outside the garden walls. Romeo is melodramatically in love with "fair Rosa-line" (1.2.83), a pretty young woman who, by Romeo's own account, shows little interest in his wooing. Her indifference catapults Romeo into stagey poetic suffering expressed through secondhand poetic tropes. His riot of oxymoronic figures—"O brawling love! O loving hate! … O heavy lightness! serious vanity! / Mis-shapen chaos of well-seeming forms! / Feather of lead, bright smoke, cold fire, sick health! / Still-waking sleep, that is not what it is!" (1.1.174, 176–79)—is tiresome. Romeo labors to create love poetry, which is a world away from sing-ing his heart's song directly. We see this lumbering artifice in Romeo's recourse to Ovid's tales of the gods:

> [S]he'll not be hit
> With Cupid's arrow. She hath Dian's wit,
> And in strong proof of chastity well arm'd,
> From Love's weak childish bow she lives unharm'd.
> She will not stay the siege of loving terms,
> Nor bide th' encounter of assailing eyes,
> Nor ope her lap to saint-seducing gold.
> O, she is rich in beauty; only poor
> That, when she dies, with beauty dies her store.
>   (1.1.206–14)

Shakespeare asks his audience to admire, and soon after to see the limits of, this euphuistic poetry. Romeo is already an ardent lover and a polished poet of a lower sort. He rehearses these worn figures—the beloved as votary of Diana's virginal retinue, her chastity beyond the sting of Cupid's arrows and Zeus' shower of gold—but is merely practicing what soon he will experience full force. Unlike his estimable friend Benvolio (devoted to self-control and good judgment) and Mercutio (ablaze with lust and fantasy) and Tybalt (hungry for violence and power), Romeo is already devoted to idealizing Eros through art. Even so, he as yet has no idea of the force of feeling that will enflame his thought and language into new and direct, unpremeditated and original poetry.

From the moment Romeo sees Juliet across the dance floor at the Capulet festivities, he is a changed man, and the change registers in his elevated language: "O, she doth teach the torches to burn bright! / It seems she hangs upon the cheek of night / As a rich jewel in an Ethiop's ear—/ Beauty too rich for use, for earth too dear!" (1.5.42–45). Gone are the clanging conceits and creaky references to mythology. In their place is this explosion of light, mirroring in his imagery what is happening in his mind and heart. More remarkable still is the sonnet Romeo and Juliet share on their first meeting, each completing the other's lines and thoughts (91–105) in an elegant dance of mutual recognition. Shakespeare's lovers transcend the prosaic world of family politics and property claims and enter a world of innocent delight where complex thought and ardent feeling flow together effortlessly.

Shakespeare accentuates the contrast between this elevated plane of existence and the demented crudeness of Mercutio's mockery. Mercutio mocks love poetry: "Cry but 'Ay me!' pronounce but 'love' and 'dove'; / Speak to my gossip Venus one fair word, / One nickname for her purblind son and heir, / Young Adam Cupid" (2.1.10–13). Romeo has already abandoned this self-dramatizing poetry and now speaks his mind and heart, which under the light of love is pure poetry. Mercutio, like a cynic of our own time, reduces love to raw sex: "To raise a spirit in his mistress' circle / Of some strange nature, letting it there stand / Till she had laid it and conjur'd it down. . . . O that she were / An open et cetera, thou a pop'rin pear!" (24–26, 37–38). Mercutio's roiling madness identifies him as the brilliant beast in us, the snake in the garden of love. By contrast, Romeo and Juliet, while they are together—at the Capulet ball, in the balcony scene, in the sweet aubade of their honeymoon morning—the lovers sing the sweetest songs; as soon as they part, however, they fall back into the carping world of miseries.

The balcony scene continues both tropes of love introduced in the earlier recognition scene. Seeing Juliet on her balcony, Romeo experiences again an explosion of light: "But, soft! What light through yonder window breaks?/It is the east, and Juliet is the sun" (2.2.2–3), and the praise of radiance follows through the next twenty-two lines. Soon after, the lovers, still strangers, finish one another's thoughts in a dance of two minds and hearts becoming one. Juliet delights Romeo by answering his ardent voice with her own untrammeled boldness: "Or, if thou think'st I am too quickly won,/I'll frown, and be perverse, and say thee nay.... But trust me, gentleman, I'll prove more true/Than those that have more cunning to be strange" (95–96, 100–101). The rules of courtship require that she be coy, but these rules are overthrown when love in all its innocent force rules. Juliet leaves behind all caution and the courtly politics of love when she advises Romeo to "swear by [his] gracious self,/Which is the god of [her] idolatry" (113–14). The balcony scene offers a lovers' duet of elevated thoughts and impassioned feelings and sensations, a vision of perfection rich with cosmic images and Heaven's blessings.

Romeo and Juliet enacts the familiar story where the confusion and viciousness of a fallen world demolishes perfection. The lovers are destroyed not by some clash of constellations but by the failures of Verona, our world, to provide properly for the kind of creature we are. There rages in us the beast of pride and self-aggrandizement, of sex and violence; and our failure to meet these monsters with resolve threatens our better natures. The process is subtle and tests our wits. There are no villains in this tragedy, no Iagos or Edmunds to impersonate the Devil. The Prince is a good person who wants to show mercy but winks at evils; old Capulet anticipates old Fezziwig in Charles Dickens' *A Christmas Carol*; the Friar wants only to help, to be the one who solves the riddle of the vendetta; the Nurse pleases every time she appears, as does Mercutio with his titanic wit and wild energies; even Tybalt never really means the violent results to which his feelings drive him.

Shakespeare catches us in the same net of moral discovery as Dante does in his depiction of Paolo and Francesca in his *Inferno*. We love what destroys us, and we prefer these destructive things to the difficult regimen our mixed nature requires to bring us to the good for which we hunger. Only moral leadership, the integrity of the law, the calm authority of religious institutions, and the assumption of adult responsibilities can ensure peace and honor.

Romeo and Juliet, like all great tragedies, leaves us, even after its catastrophic final moments, with an image of the perfection we desire. We will never lose the poetry of the lovers. As Juliet imagines, Romeo has become immortal, for when he dies, "Take him and cut him out in little stars, / And he will make the face of heaven so fine / That all the world will be in love with night / And pay no worship to the garish sun" (3.2.22–25). Their sweet perfection, the rich full voice of love's ardor and devotion, lives forever in our cultural heritage. The sobering and painful lesson of what blocks our way to this perfection, our continuing citizenship in Verona, is less often recognized.

CONTRIBUTORS

James Bemis is an editorial board member, weekly columnist, and film critic for *California Political Review* and is a frequent contributor to *The Latin Mass Magazine*. His five-part series "Through the Eyes of the Church", on the Vatican's list of the forty-five "Most Important Films in the Century of Cinema", was published in the *Wanderer*. His essays on film adaptations of *King Lear*, *The Merchant of Venice*, and *Macbeth* have appeared in the Ignatius Critical Editions of these three plays. He is currently writing a book on Christianity, culture, and the cinema.

Crystal Downing taught Shakespeare for several years at UCLA before taking a position at Messiah College in Pennsylvania, where she is professor of English and film studies. In addition to presentations at academic conferences, her work on Shakespeare has appeared in *College Literature* and *Literature/Film Quarterly*. Her first book, *Writing Performances: The Stages of Dorothy L. Sayers* (Palgrave), was granted the Barbara Reynolds Award for outstanding Sayers scholarship in 2009. Her second book, *How Postmodernism Serves (My) Faith* (IVP Academic) is used as a textbook in college and seminary classrooms throughout North America.

Richard Harp is chair of the Department of English at the University of Nevada, Las Vegas, and is founding coeditor of the *Ben Jonson Journal* (Edinburgh University Press). His article on Father Martin D'Arcy's unpublished literary correspondence was the cover story in the *Times Literary Supplement* on December 11, 2009.

Andrew J. Harvey, associate professor of English, teaches at Grove City College. A scholar of Renaissance and medieval

259

British literature who frequents the Blackfriars Playhouse in Staunton, Virginia, as well as the Folger Shakespeare Library, he is a convert to the Orthodox Church at peace with the beauty of theology and literature.

Jill Kriegel earned her Ph.D. in Comparative Studies from Florida Atlantic University. With emphases in nineteenth-century British literature and ancient Greek and early Christian philosophy, her dissertation explores Augustinian echoes in the novels of Charles Dickens. She has published articles in the *Saint Austin Review* (*StAR*) and *Logos: A Journal of Catholic Thought and Culture*. In addition, she is editor of the Ignatius Critical Edition of *Great Expectations* and the forthcoming edition of *Jane Eyre*. Jill teaches English at St. Joseph's Catholic School in Greenville, South Carolina.

Jonathan Marks is associate professor of politics at Ursinus College. He is the author of *Perfection and Disharmony in the Thought of Jean-Jacques Rousseau* (Cambridge and New York: Cambridge University Press, 2005).

Rebecca Munro teaches English at Belmont Abbey College, specializing in Shakespeare and the British Renaissance. She has contributed book reviews to Boston College's *Religion and the Arts* and presented papers on Shakespeare, and Renaissance and Medieval literature. At Belmont Abbey College, she is at the center of vibrant creative activity as advisor for the literary journal *Agora*, as well as the school's creative writing club, WIT Writers in Training. Activities that spring from both include four yearly on-campus celebrations of literary art and music, which she hosts with her editors.

Joseph Pearce is writer in residence and associate professor of literature at Ave Maria University in Florida. He is coeditor of the *Saint Austin Review* (www.staustinreview.com) and editor in chief of Sapientia Press. He is the author of two books on Shakespeare and has also written biographies and critical studies of J. R. R. Tolkien, C. S. Lewis, Oscar Wilde, G. K. Chesterton, and Alexander Solzhenitsyn.

Stephen Zelnick (Temple University) teaches "Shakespeare at the Movies" and has written on Daniel Defoe, Herman Melville, Joseph Conrad, and F. Scott Fitzgerald, as well as on curriculum design issues. He is cofounder of the Association for Core Texts and Courses, has directed Temple's Intellectual Heritage Program, and has served as vice provost for undergraduate studies. He consults on international curriculum projects.